OF SUMMITS AND SACRIFICE

T0324253

Of Summits and Sacrifice

AN ETHNOHISTORIC STUDY OF
INKA RELIGIOUS PRACTICES

Thomas Besom

UNIVERSITY OF TEXAS PRESS
Austin

Requests for permission to reproduce material from this work should
be sent to:
    Permissions
    University of Texas Press
    P.O. Box 7819
    Austin, TX 78713-7819
    www.utexas.edu/utpress/about/bpermission.html

♾ The paper used in this book meets the minimum requirements of
ANSI/NISO Z39.48-1992 (R1997) (Permanence of Paper).

LIBRARY OF CONGRESS CATALOGING-IN-PUBLICATION DATA
Besom, Thomas, 1960–
    Of summits and sacrifice : an ethnohistoric study of Inka religious
practices / by Thomas Besom. — 1st ed.
        p.   cm.
    Includes bibliographical references and index.
ISBN 978-0-292-72572-0
    1. Incas—Rites and ceremonies.   2. Incas—Antiquities.
3. Human sacrifice—Peru.   4. Mountains—Religious aspects.
5. Peru—Antiquities.   I. Title.
F3429.3.R58B47   2009
299.8′83230342—dc22   2008051918

For Kay and Don,
my parents,
who always encouraged my
interest in archaeology

CONTENTS

List of Illustrations ix

Acknowledgments xi

Prologue 1

ONE *Ethnohistory and the Inkas* 4

TWO Qhapaq Hucha *Sacrifice* 25

THREE *Other Types of Sacrifice* 44

FOUR *Mountain Worship* 64

FIVE *Mountain Offerings* 94

SIX *Reasons for Worshipping Mountains* 117

SEVEN *Material Correlates of Mountain Worship* 146

EIGHT *Conclusions* 157

Epilogue 164

Notes 167

Glossary of Andean Names and Terms 203

Reference List 209

Index 225

LIST OF ILLUSTRATIONS

MAP 1.1.   Continent of South America   5

MAP 1.2.   Inka Empire at the height of its power   6

MAP 1.3.   Inka Empire with the locations of sacrifices   10

FIGURE 1.1.   Inka emperor surrounded by members of various ethnic groups   7

FIGURE 1.2.   People of Kunti Suyu offering a child   9

FIGURE 2.1.   "Chosen women" spinning wool at an *aqlla wasi*   29

FIGURE 2.2.   *Khipu kamayuq* holding the knotted strings   31

FIGURE 2.3.   People of Qulla Suyu offering a llama   34

FIGURE 2.4.   Emperor celebrating Qhapaq Raymi   37

FIGURE 2.5.   Emperor helping to plow a sacred field   37

FIGURE 2.6.   Noble of Qulla Suyu   41

FIGURE 2.7.   Noble of Chinchay Suyu   41

FIGURE 2.8.   Inka official   41

FIGURE 3.1.   Noble of Qulla Suyu being tortured by the Inkas   52

FIGURE 3.2.   Inka soldier holding the head of a noble   53

FIGURE 4.1.   Thupa Yapanki consulting with Wana Kawri   71

FIGURE 4.2.   King and queen venerating Wana Kawri   75

FIGURE 4.3.   People of Anti Suyu offering a child   75

FIGURE 4.4A.   Side profile of a *waqa* on Mount Tantalluc   78

FIGURE 4.4B.   Front profile of a *waqa* on Mount Tantalluc   79

FIGURE 4.5.   Emperor using a sling to hurl projectiles   86

FIGURE 4.6.   People of Chinchay Suyu offering a child   90

FIGURE 5.1.   "Sorcerer" sacrificing a llama   97

FIGURE 5.2.   Emperor making a toast/offering to the Sun   107

FIGURE 5.3.   Young woman weaving on a backstrap loom   110

FIGURE 6.1.   Young woman irrigating the corn fields   124

FIGURE 6.2.   *Runas* moving a large stone   129

FIGURE 7.1.   Thupa Yapanki holding a *waman chanpi*   154

ACKNOWLEDGMENTS

First I would like to thank my family; the completion of this book is a testament to their support and encouragement through the years. I also am indebted to my friends and colleagues in the Department of Anthropology at Binghamton University, and to my housemates (past and present) at 3-½ Vincent Street; there is a direct correlation between my intellectual growth and our anthropological discussions over beer.

I am also grateful to the members of my Ph.D. committee—chairman William Isbell, Charles Cobb, Albert Dekin, Susan Ramírez, and Richard Trexler—for reading and commenting on my dissertation, on which this book is partially based. Their criticisms and suggestions have had a profound effect on the present work.

I would like to express my appreciation to the people in the Interlibrary Loan Office at Bartle Library on the BU campus. They located many obscure chronicles for me in institutions throughout the country; without their help, I could not have completed my research.

My work was funded by several sources. From the National Science Foundation, I received a Dissertation Improvement Grant. I was awarded a Mini-Grant by Binghamton University, a Putnam-Bedayn Research Grant by the American Alpine Club, and a Grant-in-Aid of Research by Sigma Xi. Binghamton University gave me a Dissertation Year Fellowship, which allowed me to complete much of the doctoral thesis.

Johan Reinhard and Elizabeth Benson, who served as readers for the University of Texas Press, made significant contributions to the book. Reinhard offered excellent suggestions for enhancing the quality of the scholarship, and Benson made valuable recommendations for tightening the prose.

I would like to acknowledge the generosity of Nina Versaggi and the archaeologists at the Public Archaeology Facility, Binghamton University, who let me use their computers to put the finishing touches on the manuscript. And I laud the work of Justin Miller, who helped to produce the maps and illustrations for the book.

Finally, I would like to thank Johan Reinhard for inspiring me to write about human sacrifice and mountain worship in the Andes.

OF SUMMITS AND SACRIFICE

PROLOGUE

Dedicated to Johan Reinhard

Exhausted, the young woman stopped and gasped in the rarified air. Once she had caught her breath, she turned away from the slope and toward the boundless space surrounding her. At this altitude, almost 6,700 m,[1] the sky above was the dark hue of lapis lazuli. Before her and stretching into the far distance, she could make out range after range of grey, brown, and yellowish mountains, completely devoid of vegetation. The highest points, capped with snow,[2] were so bright in the afternoon sun she had to squint when she looked at them. She had a headache from the intensity of the sunlight, was completely worn out from the strenuous ascent, nauseous from the lack of oxygen, dehydrated from the dry air, and cold. She had been cold for the last three days, the whole time that she and her entourage of priests and an imperial official had slowly been making their way up the peak. Now, with the wind picking up and the temperature dropping, she was starting to freeze. She drew her *lliklla* (shawl), which was greyish-brown with thin stripes of red, yellow, and blue,[3] tightly around her shoulders. Though it was thick and made from warm alpaca wool, it offered little protection against the bitter wind. As she stood shivering, a voice from just above her snapped her out of her stupor. It was one of the priests.

"We're almost there," he reassured her. "Once we reach camp, you can rest and warm up."

With this encouraging news, she turned back toward the slope and commenced her slow trudge upward.

The young woman, fourteen years old, was a subject of the Inka Empire. She had been born in a village near Lake Titi Qaqa. When she was only ten, a representative of the state called the *apu panaka,* who was visiting her native community, had seen her and been impressed by her beauty and grace. He had picked her to become an *aqlla*, a "chosen woman." Though considered a great honor to be so named, she had been sad when she was separated from her parents, whom she had not seen since, and taken to a provincial *aqlla wasi* (house of the chosen women). There she had lived for four years, being raised by the *mama-kuna*, the sacred "mothers." These women, who were highly respected and who remained chaste and cloistered throughout their lives, were dedicated to the service of the gods, in this case to Inti, the imperial Sun-god. The *mama-kuna* had patiently taught her to spin fine alpaca wool, weave exquisite textiles, cook, and make *chicha* (corn beer).

The young woman had recently been designated as a *qhapaq hucha* (sacrificial victim), another notable honor. She and her fellow *qhapaq huchas* for the year had been divided into four groups, one for each of the polity's four territorial divisions. She herself had been assigned to Qulla Suyu, the southeastern quarter. Then a *khipu kamayuq*—a state bureaucrat in charge of keeping records and accounts, who recorded information on knotted strings—had allocated her to a particular *waqa*—a sacred shrine or feature of the landscape. She was to be immolated on top of a high and holy pinnacle, located about 900 km to the southeast of Lake Titi Qaqa,[4] in a newly conquered desert region. The *khipu kamayuq* also had allotted her various ritual objects that would accompany her to the mountain-*waqa* and that would be offered to it along with her life. Among the objects were seven ceramic vessels, a wooden spoon, two wooden cups, six cloth bags, several elaborate textiles, and three female statuettes. One of the statuettes was fashioned from hammered gold. Another was made of silver, the third carved from Spondylus, spiny oyster shell.[5] All were dressed in miniature clothing and feather headdresses.[6]

The fourteen-year-old had left her homeland near Lake Titi Qaqa in early November, heading toward the southeast, accompanied by the imperial official, three priests, a number of laborers, some llama herders, and their beasts of burden, used to carry the offerings and supplies. The group had traveled overland in as straight a line as was practical, averaging little more than 20 km per day. Whenever possible, they had followed a royal road, but when it meandered, they were forced to strike out across the open countryside. At night they had sought shelter in a *tampu,* a way-station maintained by the state where they had been able to eat and sleep, or had set up camp under the stars. They had slowly made their way down the spine of the continent, and after about forty days had finally reached the Inka administrative center at Catarpe, near what is today San Pedro de Atacama in northern Chile.[7] There the young woman had taken part in a festival held in her honor. Lasting several days, it had included much drinking of corn beer, singing, and dancing. On the final leg of her journey, which had taken another ten days, she had gone from Catarpe across part of the driest desert on earth to the mountain-*waqa*.

At their camp near the base of the peak, the three priests had prepared themselves and the young woman for the sacrificial ceremony. They had continued their fasting, begun almost a month earlier, which meant abstinence from meat, *chicha, ají* (chile peppers), salt, and sexual relations. One of them had made her confess her sins to him. Then they had obliged her to take a ritual bath in a frigid mountain stream to purify herself; they had done the same. They had braided her long black hair into hundreds of tiny plaits[8] as a sign of her ethnic affiliation—being from the Lake Titi Qaqa area—and had given her new clothes and moccasins. They had painted her face red,[9] using a mixture of finely ground pigment and animal fat, and had presented her with a beautiful headdress consisting of a wool cap to which were attached white feathers.

Now, three days later, the fourteen-year-old was approaching their final camp, situated high on the peak;[10] she was glad to be reaching it, as she was freezing. She came up over a steep rise and ahead saw a low stone wall. She realized then that while she had been taking part in the various rites at the foot of the mountain, the laborers who had accompanied her had been working extremely hard up here. They had constructed a two-room hut of large rocks found in the vicinity. A sizable quantity of other building materials, including long wooden poles and mats made from tough *ichu* grass, had been transported to the top of the peak on the backs of the llamas. Employing the wooden poles as beams to span the walls of the stone hut, they had pulled a large mat over the poles to form a roof and then anchored it with stones. The remaining mats had been placed on the hut floor to serve as insulation. Finally, they had supplied the camp with firewood, various foods, vessels containing water and *chicha,* ceramic pots for cooking, plates for eating, and woolen textiles.[11]

By the time the young woman reached the hut, her ears, fingers, and toes were completely numb. She still felt sick due to the altitude, and because she was worried about the sacrificial ceremony that was to take place the next morning. She drank some water, about all she could keep in her stomach, grabbed an alpaca blanket, and curled up inside the structure. She tried to sleep as best she could.

One   ETHNOHISTORY AND
        THE INKAS

*After having experimented with several ways of relating . . . the
story of the Incas, who were Peru's natural rulers, it has seemed
. . . [that] nothing could be simpler or surer than to tell what I
many times had the opportunity of hearing as a child, from my
mother's lips, or from those of . . . our closest relatives.*
    *Every week, the members of her family . . . came to visit her.
On these occasions, the conversation turned almost invariably
to the origins of our [Inca] kings and to their majesty. It also
concerned the grandeur of their empire, their conquests and noble
deeds, their government in war and peace. (Garcilaso 1961: 42)*

In the middle of the fifteenth century, a small kingdom
in the highlands of southern Peru began to expand. Within one hundred years, it had become the largest state ever formed by an indigenous
people anywhere in the Americas. At the height of its power, the Inka
Empire stretched about 4,000 km from the Ancasmayo River that marks
the present border between Colombia and Ecuador[1] to the Mapocho River
in central Chile.[2] Its capital, Cuzco, was situated in the center (see Maps 1.1
and 1.2).[3]
    Inka expansion supposedly began during the reign of the ninth king,
Pacha Kuti, whose name means "cataclysm" or "he who transforms the
world." He subjugated various ethnic groups living near Cuzco, most
notably the Chanca. Pacha Kuti then turned his attention towards the
lower Urubamba Valley and Vilcapampa in the north, Vilcas and Soras in
the west, and the provinces of Aymara, Omasayo, Cotapampa, and Chilque
in the south. With these areas under his control, he defeated the Lupaca and
incorporated their lands on the southwestern shore of Lake Titi Qaqa into
the realm.[4]
    Between about 1463 and 1471, it appears that Pacha Kuti ruled the em-

South America

French Guiana
Guyana
Venezuela
Colombia
Surinam
Ecuador
Brazil
Peru
Bolivia
Paraguay
Chile
Atlantic
Ocean
Uruguay
approximate area enlarged in Maps 1.2, 1.3
Argentina
Pacific
Ocean
N

MAP 1.1.   *Continent of South America.*

pire with his son and chosen successor, Thupa Yapanki. During this period, Thupa defeated a number of peoples—including the Cañari, Quiteño, and Chimu—thereby adding northwestern Peru and a large part of Ecuador to the Inka state (see Figure 1.1). After his father's death in about 1471, Thupa Yapanki led his armies southward, where they subdued such diverse ethnic groups as the Quilca, Tampo, Moquehua, Locumba, Sama, Tarapaca,[5] Atacameño, Colla, Chango, Diaguita, Chiquillane, and Picunche;[6]

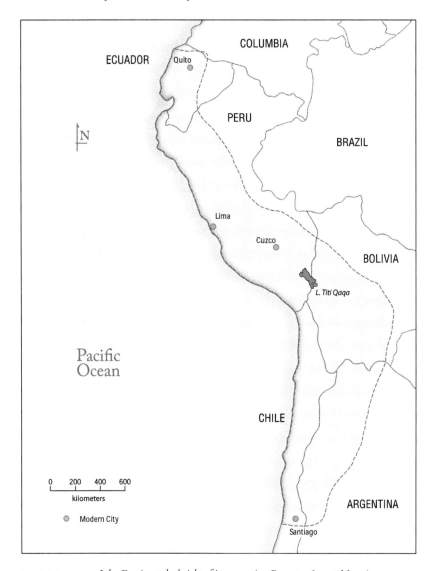

MAP 1.2.   *Inka Empire at the height of its power (see Rowe 1946: 205, Map 4).*

he annexed southern Peru, northern and central Chile, and northwestern Argentina.[7] Together these regions comprised Qulla Suyu, the southernmost of the four quarters into which the empire was divided.

Thupa Yapanki passed away in about 1493, and the *maskha paycha*—the red fringe worn by the king as a symbol of office—went to Wayna Qhapaq. He acquired new territories in northern Peru and Ecuador, and under his leadership, the state reached its greatest extent.[8] In 1532, Francisco Pizarro and an army of 260 Spanish mercenaries arrived in the country, initiating the Conquest of Peru.[9] At the same time that the foreign invaders were destroying the empire and transforming it into a colony, the so-called chroniclers, most of whom were Spanish, were recording information on the Inkas: their writings relate the "history" of this people, describe their beliefs and practices, and report on the administration of their state.

FIGURE 1.1.   *Inka emperor surrounded by members of various ethnic groups, who can be distinguished by their distinctive headgear (Guaman Poma 1980a: 336).*

Much research has been devoted to the emergence and expansion of archaic polities, including that of the Cuzqueños. A question less adequately addressed, but just as important, is how such a state survived after its formation. Kurtz thinks its continued existence was never assured. Rather, it had to be actively pursued and, to a large extent, depended on its leaders' ability to legitimate its authority,[10] usually through ritual.[11] I believe—based on a reading of the chronicles and the works of various Inka scholars—that after defeating the different ethnic groups at the southern extreme of the empire, the lords of Cuzco incorporated them into the polity using sacred rituals. The rites involved mountain veneration[12] and the sacrifice of *qhapaq huchas*,[13] specially chosen children and young women (see Figure 1.2).

Why these practices? I would suggest that both were important throughout the Andes. As the power of rituals partly derives from people's familiarity with them,[14] the Inkas specifically chose these two for manipulation.

Supporting the notion that mountain worship was very significant is a list, much abridged, from the late-sixteenth century source Albornoz of the empire's major *waqas* (holy sites, many of them peaks).[15] In Cayambe province, located in Ecuador, he says the people venerated three summits called Chimborazo, Chicchirazo, and Carorazo. In the region around the city of Quito, the principal *waqa* was a mountain named Piccinca (Pichincha).[16] Albornoz also tells us that the natives of Cajamarca, a province in the northern highlands of Peru, revered Apoparato, a volcano,[17] while the inhabitants of Tarma, an area in the central highlands, venerated a peak referred to as Guayoay Vilca.[18] Moving farther south, the indigenous people of Acari, a coastal province, had as one of their most sacred sites a summit known as Luhutare, which was composed of sand.[19] In the mountainous regions of southern Peru, the Collagua worshipped the peak Hambato (Ampato), while the inhabitants of Arequipa adored a volcano known as Putina (El Misti). Albornoz also notes that the native peoples in northern Chile revered numerous volcanoes and snow-capped summits.[20]

Human sacrifice was of considerable importance throughout the empire. According to Hernández Príncipe, a priest and extirpator who worked in the Huaylas province of northern Peru, members of an *ayllu* (kin group) in Recuay reported that they had contributed twelve people for immolation during the time of the Inkas. These victims, or *qhapaq huchas,* were distributed far and wide: four were sent to Quito; two to Lake Yahuarcocha, in the northern part of the realm; three to Cuzco; two to Lake Titi Qaqa, near the center of the state; and one to Chile.[21] Another kin group provided seven *qhapaq huchas,* two of which traveled to Quito, one to Cuzco, and two to Lake Titi Qaqa. The other two victims were sacrificed locally.[22]

FIGURE 1.2. *People of Kunti Suyu offering a child and guinea pig to the mountain-*waqa *Qhuru Puna (Guaman Poma 1980a: 246).*

Archaeological evidence supports the ethnohistoric data demonstrating the significance of mountain worship and human immolation. Between 1898 and 1999, the bodies of at least twenty-seven sacrificial victims were discovered on the slopes and summits of peaks in southern Peru, north-western Argentina, and the northern half of Chile (see Map 1.3). Johan Reinhard found six "mummies" on El Misti Volcano—three male, three female[23]—and the corpses of four people on Mount Ampato. In the latter case, three of the victims were probably female, one possibly male.[24] Four sets of remains were recovered from Pichu Pichu,[25] one from Sara Sara,[26] and one from Chachani;[27] all except one, the skeleton of a boy excavated on

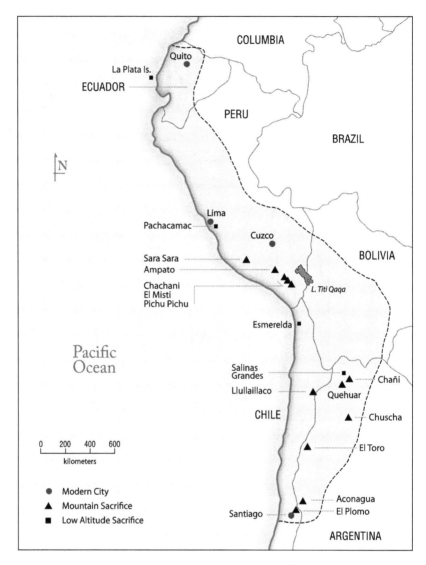

MAP 1.3.   *Inka Empire with the locations of important sacrifices (see Beorchia 1985: 416, map).*

Pichu Pichu, were likely female. These pinnacles are situated in the austral regions of Peru.

In northwestern Argentina, the cadavers of what were presumably young women came to light on Nevado Chuscha[28] and Quehuar,[29] the body of a youth was unearthed on the upper slopes of Cerro El Toro,[30] and the corpse of an infant of indeterminate sex was uncovered on Nevado Chañi.[31] The remains of three individuals, two females and an immature male, were excavated on Llullaillaco,[32] and the cadavers of boys were found on Aconcagua in west-central Argentina[33] and on El Plomo in central Chile.[34] Finally, a pair of mummies—one a young woman, the other a little girl—were recovered from Esmeralda, a hill on the north coast of Chile near the city of Iquique.[35]

As far as I know, during the past one hundred years no bodies have been discovered on the peaks of Ecuador, northern or central Peru, or western Bolivia.[36] Why not? It is especially puzzling given that Albornoz lists numerous peaks in the northern part of the Inka state that were considered sacred and that very likely received offerings of human lives. Reinhard provides one possible answer. He maintains that in the northern and central Andes the snow-line is considerably lower than in the southern Andes,[37] and the mountains tend to be more heavily glaciated. With more ice and snow, these peaks tend to be more technically demanding[38] than summits in southern Peru, northwestern Argentina, and northern Chile.[39] Thus, the lords of Cuzco— who had no crampons, ice axes, or other ice-climbing equipment—could not have even reached the high summits in the northern and central parts of the empire, let alone build structures or make sacrifices on them.[40]

There are other reasons why no immolation victims have been discovered in recent times on more northerly mountains. According to Reinhard, the Inkas most likely would have left offerings, including *qhapaq huchas,* for these peaks at sites below their permanent snow-lines. Such sites would have been relatively accessible to the Spanish priests and extirpators who waged systematic campaigns to wipe out all traces of the native religion.[41] In fact, there is ethnohistoric evidence of destruction of the corpse of a sacrificial victim buried alive on a mountain in northern Peru. The victim was a girl named Tanta Carhua, and Hernández Príncipe recorded his search for her final resting place:

> I went with much fear and distrust . . . and tired and fed up
> by the precariousness of the track, I lost my courage . . . but
> [finally] I recognized the site because of the sacrifices of llamas
> and the altars from where she was invoked. . . . We labored
> there for almost the entire day . . . and [in a shaft], made in
> the manner of a well, very well leveled out, . . . [we found]
> the *capacocha* [*qhapaq hucha*] seated, in the way of her pagan
> ancestors, with jewels in the shape of tiny pots and jugs and
> silver pins and silver charms.[42]

It is possible the Europeans discovered and destroyed not only the body of Tanta Carhua, but those of numerous other *qhapaq huchas* immolated in the northern and central parts of the polity. The few sets of remains that may have survived into modern times could also have been disturbed by treasure hunters, who have plundered archaeological sites throughout South America.[43]

ETHNOHISTORIC RESEARCH

Many questions surround the twenty-seven sets of remains found on sacred mountains of the former Inka Empire. How do we know they are examples of human sacrifice, and what were the most important characteristics of this practice? Was there more than one type of immolation, and can we determine the symbolism or purpose behind a particular immolation? Were all of the remains also connected with mountain worship? What are the major features of this practice, its material correlates, and how might we recognize a site where a peak was venerated? What was the relationship between this type of rite and human sacrifice? What might we discover in the archaeological record that would indicate why a specific summit was worshipped? Finally, how could the practices have been manipulated by the Cuzqueños to incorporate conquered peoples into the empire?

In the chapters that follow, I try to answer these questions, relying in part on sources of information independent of the archaeological data: the ethnohistoric works of a literate people who recorded the history and culture of the nonliterate Inka. The chronicles they produced provide a wealth of data on rituals from antiquity.

Why do I need two lines of evidence, and why must I — to the extent possible — keep them separate? To avoid making tautological arguments or using circular logic.[44] That is, I want to refrain from using (mis)interpretations of the archaeological data to gain a(n) (mis)understanding of ethnohistoric information, and applying this (mis)understanding to reinforce the original (mis)interpretation of archaeological materials. In such a case, I would risk simply confirming what I thought I knew (which could be wrong). A better procedure, and one that comprises part of the scientific method, is to employ an independent source of evidence to test my hypotheses. After first identifying and explaining patterns in the ethnohistoric data, I can then look for similar patterns in the archaeological record to confirm their existence and to shed new light on the record.

The Andean chronicles constitute the independent line of evidence required for my research. They were penned by a disparate group of people under a variety of circumstances. While most of the authors were Hispanic, a few were of mixed Spanish-indigenous descent. Some were administrators, judges, and scribes who were writing for the Spanish Crown; others were priests and high officials of the Catholic Church. Still others were soldiers-of-fortune who recorded their experiences for posterity.[45] The so-called "native chroniclers" belonged to elite Andean families that had been deprived of their power under colonial rule, and one goal of their writing was to demonstrate that their history was on a par with that of Europeans.[46] Several writers traveled extensively in the Andes, recording information on provincial customs and local beliefs; other chroniclers stayed in Cuzco, conducting interviews with the relatives of former Inka kings. A few individuals set pen to paper around the time of the Conquest, while others wrote their accounts after Peru had been under Spanish domination for over a century.[47]

Just as the authors of the chronicles were a diverse lot, so were the texts they created. A number of works are long narratives describing the history and culture of the Cuzqueños. The purpose of many of them is to legitimate, for the benefit of readers in Spain, the subjugation of Andean peoples.[48] Numerous civil records relate to administrative and judicial matters, among them the *visitas,* official censuses taken in indigenous communities to determine how much the inhabitants owed the Crown in taxes.[49] These reports are important to contemporary scholars interested in religion because they include questions about tribute, some of which supported state rituals, given to the Inkas before the Europeans arrived.[50] The civil documents also include testimony from lawsuits: "Justicia 413" deals with a land dispute between two ethnic groups, the Canta and Chaclla. The latter used a *qhapaq hucha* ceremony involving the conveyance of sacrificial blood as a way to usurp Canta territory.[51]

Not only are there civil records pertaining to colonial bureaucracy, but ecclesiastical documents having to do with the missionizing efforts of the Catholic Church. Among the religious records are treatises by priests, including Albornoz and Arriaga, who actively took part in the campaign to extirpate all vestiges of "idolatry" in Peru. Field reports by Hernández Príncipe, Calancha, and other members of the clergy provide information about local cults, including people's recollections of what these cults were like before the Conquest.[52] Proceedings from ecclesiastical suits relating to the Church's effort to stamp out Andean religion are another important source of information. As part of this brutal campaign, connected with the

Inquisition, individuals were charged with practicing idolatry and hauled before tribunals made up of ecclesiastical authorities. During their trials, the accused were allowed to speak, as were the accusers and witnesses. All their statements were included in the proceedings. Such documents—an example of which is the testimony of Hacas Poma—are great sources of data on native religion, including sacrifice and mountain worship, and on resistance to Catholic conversion.[53]

Although the Spanish chronicles contain valuable information, we have to be very critical in evaluating, and deciding whether to accept, the data they provide. Their authors could only make sense of the Andean world through the lenses provided by their European culture. As a group, the chroniclers had certain prejudices, fundamental beliefs about the workings of the universe, assumptions about the relationship between humanity and society, and basic ideas about social hierarchy, justice, and history—cultural baggage that influenced how they perceived the Inkas.[54] Each writer, as an individual, also had his own unique background: education, personal experiences, motivations, goals, and biases. These more specific features of his persona also would have affected how he saw the Andean world. Furthermore, the chroniclers did not exist and write in a cultural vacuum, but were part of the colonization process.[55] Consequently, their works are not simple records of Inka history and society, but reinterpretations of the Andean past that reflect the introduction of new political, social, economic, and religious institutions.[56]

This brings us to a fundamental question: How do we assess the reliability of a particular source? One method involves scrutinizing the author's life, looking for clues about how he approached his subject matter. In other words, we can examine the general and more specific characteristics of his persona in relation to his work. How might his prejudices have affected his understanding of Inka society? How would his vocation—say, as a Jesuit priest—color his perceptions of Andean religion? How might the data on indigenous culture have been manipulated to achieve personal goals?

IMPORTANT ETHNOHISTORIC SOURCES

One important and fairly reliable chronicler, whose work I cite frequently, is Pedro Cieza de León.[57] A soldier-of-fortune, Cieza arrived in the New World around 1535, shortly after the Conquest. During the next fifteen years, he witnessed the start of the transformation of the Inka

Empire into a Spanish colony.[58] He was intelligent and had keen powers of observation, qualities that served him well as he traveled around the Andes collecting information. In each region through which he passed, Cieza questioned the local inhabitants about their history and social institutions, even interviewing a descendent of Emperor Wayna Qhapaq in Cuzco in 1550. Everything he learned was meticulously recorded in his journals,[59] along with data from other authors, including Domingo de Santo Tomás and Pedro de la Gasca. Cieza's work stands out among the early chronicles because of his methodical and analytical approach, and because he benefited from the more in-depth and sophisticated exchange of ideas that took place in his day between Andean peoples and Europeans. Such exchanges could occur only after the Spanish had systematically studied the indigenous languages, and the conquerors and vanquished had lived together for almost a generation.[60] A final note about Cieza: because he shared with the Dominicans the belief that conversions to Christianity had to be voluntary, he was motivated to learn about local customs to show the native folk the error of their ways and to make them understand the "true" path to salvation.[61]

Another prominent and authoritative author, especially on matters relating to Inka theology, is Juan Polo de Ondegardo.[62] During the 1550s he served in Cuzco as the *corregidor,* a judicial and administrative official who represented the Spanish Crown. In this capacity he launched an exhaustive investigation of Andean beliefs, rituals, and shrines, and came to grasp the fundamental principles underlying native religion. Between 1561 and 1571 he wrote a series of reports, some of which deal with autochthonous theology, that were extensively copied by later authors, including Acosta and Cobo. Like Cieza, Polo was bright and diligent, and traveled widely in Peru. He also was well educated.[63] These features of his life and personality shine through in his work. Polo's rationale for studying the sacred practices of the Andes was different from that of Cieza, as he dismissed the idea that conversion had to be voluntary. Rather, he held that the indigenous people would only embrace Christianity and remain with the Church if coerced—and if the objects of their idolatry were demolished. Realizing that the Spanish could not eliminate all traces of native religion unless they understood it, Polo made careful inquiry into the subject as part of his anti-idolatry campaign.[64]

One of the best ethnohistoric works dealing with Inka culture in general—and with Andean religious practices in particular, including human sacrifice and mountain worship—was penned by Father Bernabé Cobo.[65] The quality of his writings can partially be explained by considering aspects

of his life and characteristics of his persona. First, he was given an excep-
tional education by the Jesuits, who taught him the importance of consci-
entious scholarship.[66] He also spent more than forty years in Peru, during
which he journeyed far and wide, working as a missionary and extirpator of
idolatry, and gaining considerable knowledge of the native peoples' sacred
rituals and beliefs.[67] He benefited from having access to the manuscripts
of many earlier scholars: Acosta, Arriaga, Cieza, Garcilaso, Pedro Pizarro,
Molina, Sarmiento, and Polo.[68] An intelligent and acute observer of human
behavior, Cobo had an eye for minute detail.[69] His motives for conducting
research on Inka theology were similar to Polo's in that he completely re-
jected the notion of Las Casas and Garcilaso that the prehispanic religion
of Peru had held partial truths and had been "preparatory" to the arrival
of Christianity. Instead, he firmly believed, as did many of his contempo-
raries, that the indigenous people had been the victims of a double decep-
tion: because of fallacious reasoning, they had allowed themselves to be
duped by the Cuzqueños, who claimed descent from the Sun, and to be
misled by demons. Cobo used his studies of Andean doctrine to demonstrate the faults in autochthonous people's thinking and the errors of their
ways.[70]

A significant indigenous chronicler is Felipe Guaman Poma de Ayala,
who wrote a thousand-page letter to the king of Spain containing a tremendous amount of information. It is, unfortunately, confused and contradictory as well. The chronicle is profusely illustrated with detailed pen-
and-ink drawings that, according to Silverblatt, are generally more reliable
than the text. The work is most convincing when it deals with Andean
religion.[71] In terms of background, Guaman Poma was from a noble family
that resided in the Ayacucho area. Because he was a native of Peru, some
scholars have idealized him and credited him with giving us an unbiased
look at pre-Columbian culture.[72] He lived and wrote in a colonial context,
however, so his perceptions of the prehispanic era were undoubtedly influenced by the social conditions and institutions of his time. Be that as it may,
he does provide an autochthonous model for interpreting Andean society
during the Inka period. Hence, Guaman Poma's chronicle, though it must
be read with care, is a unique and valuable source of data.[73]

Part of Guaman Poma's rationale for penning his manuscript was to
draw attention to the deplorable conditions in colonial Peru, including the
Europeans' mistreatment of indigenous people. The rhetorical method he
uses is to compare and contrast life under the Inkas with daily existence
after the arrival of the Spanish. Another motive for writing the manu-

script relates to Catholicism: having served as Albornoz's assistant during the latter's anti-idolatry campaign, he wanted future extirpators to employ the information provided to crack down on Andean religion. Thus, he hoped to strengthen the Catholic Church and to help native people accept the "true" faith. He did not, however, want Europeans to use his work as a pretext for further exploitation of the conquered natives.[74]

Of great value to researchers studying the sacred beliefs and practices of the Cuzqueños is the Huarochirí manuscript. This significant and fascinating document is the only work known in which a pre-Conquest set of myths is recorded in the original language, Quechua. It consists of a compilation of stories, all of which were part of an ancient religious tradition, recounted by an anonymous group of Andean natives. In addition to portraying the activities of superhuman beings (including the mountain-god Parya Qaqa) as they fight, mate, wander the countryside, interact with people, and receive sacrifices, the manuscript provides the rationale for various political, social, topographical, and cosmological relationships in the province of Huarochirí, located on the central coast of Peru, before the Spanish.[75]

As with Guaman Poma's work, contemporary scholars have tended to read the Huarochirí manuscript uncritically and to accept the notion that it presents a "pristine" view of prehispanic society,[76] but this document, too, is the product of colonialism. It is closely associated with Father Francisco de Avila—a Jesuit priest who labored to stamp out the last traces of Andean cults in Peru (hereafter, I will cite the Huarochirí manuscript as "Avila 1991")—although it is not known exactly what role he played in recording the myths.[77] The indigenous people whose testimony is preserved in the work had spent their entire lives under Spanish domination. Their recollections of the sacred legends had to be influenced by their interactions with colonial authorities, who had persecuted them for their beliefs and forced them to convert to Catholicism. Also, the act of transcribing their words only could have taken place after the Conquest, since the Inkas had no system of writing, and the Huarochirí stories were originally part of an oral tradition. One indication of the extent to which the text was influenced by European culture is that its overall structure parallels that of the Bible.[78]

What motivated Avila to support the composition of the Huarochirí manuscript? Salomon believes he intended to use the information in his attack on idolatry. Interestingly, the work seems to have been written, in part, independently of Avila and of Spanish misconceptions about Andean sacred beliefs, thus providing the most authentic expression of pre-Conquest religion that we have.[79] In particular, it reflects certain broad cultural concepts found in Inka cults that are alien to European theology.[80]

PROBLEMS WITH THE USE OF ETHNOHISTORIC SOURCES

Cieza, Polo, Cobo, Guaman Poma, and the Huarochirí manuscript are important and generally reliable sources. This does not mean that all the information they provide is of equal quality. Consider what Cobo says about giants. He tells us there is considerable evidence that these beings used to live in Peru and may have occupied much of America, but probably died out hundreds of years before the rise of the Inkas.[81] How do we evaluate such statements? Is it just a matter of determining whether they are true or false? Or do we need to figure out how Cobo reached these conclusions? What makes this author so remarkable, and fairly unique among the chroniclers, is that he provides the data on which his interpretations are based. In this case, he reports that enormous bones were discovered by Spaniards in Ecuador, Peru, Bolivia, and Argentina. His descriptions of the skeletal materials and the geological contexts from which they came are detailed enough to leave no doubt that what the Europeans found were the semifossilized remains of extinct megafauna. Cobo, however, could not interpret the bones in terms of modern paleontology; he had to use conceptual categories from seventeenth-century Spanish culture, one of which was "giants," who appear in Greek and Roman mythology (Polyphemus), the Bible (Goliath), and European folklore (Gog and Magog).

Returning to the original question, how do we assess the validity of Cobo's inferences? Given the discovery of the skeletal materials, and the fact that the existence of giants was taken for granted in seventeenth-century Europe, it seems logical for Cobo to conclude they lived in South America.[82] Nonetheless, most contemporary scholars would dismiss his interpretations. But, it is not just that he was wrong: once you disentangle his "facts" (what Cobo saw and heard from reliable people) from his cultural baggage (his belief in giants), you are left with virtually nothing. This can be a fundamental problem with many ethnohistoric sources in the Andes: although they can tell you about life in colonial Peru and the cultural background of their authors, they may contain very little hard data on the prehispanic era, or on the Inkas.

Although some Andean chronicles are considered good sources of information, others are regarded as unreliable because they contain distortions, inconsistencies, and misinformation. According to Randall, ethnohistorians frequently try to resolve the contradictions in a work by saying the author was lying, confused, or prejudiced; then they brand the work as suspect and disregard its data. A better approach, if a chronicler is found to be biased, would be to use caution in assessing the information, and not just assume all of it is wrong and throw it out.[83] Take the case of Garcilaso de la Vega, whose descriptions of sacred beliefs and practices in the Andes are largely fanciful.[84] The problems with his commentaries stem from the fact that his mother was a niece of Wayna Qhapaq,[85] and he was proud of his indigenous heritage. Consequently, he tried to prove to his Spanish readers that Inka culture was worthy of study, and that the differences between Christianity and Andean theology were not as profound as earlier authors had claimed,[86] to which end he played up certain features of native religion while deemphasizing other aspects.[87] Neither the particulars of his life, however, nor the questionable veracity of his manuscript can always help us to evaluate the truth of specific pieces of data. For instance, what are we to make of his statement that the inhabitants of Cac-Yauiri province venerated and made sacrifices to a hill with the shape of a sugarloaf?[88] The information seems reasonable.

Scholars trying to assess the veracity of a chronicler's work based on the details of his life face another problem: they are likely to discover contradictions that cannot be easily resolved and make it difficult to determine the quality of his data. Take the case of the Augustinian priests. One would expect them to be unreliable regarding Inka religion because of their biased and intolerant beliefs; on the other hand, while waging their campaign to wipe out all traces of Andean idolatry, they probably learned a great deal on the subject.[89]

Ethnohistorians looking at the prejudices of certain writers, and/or trying to explain conflicting information from different sources, sometimes create contradictions of their own. Many researchers think that early authors such as Cieza are more trustworthy because they interviewed people who lived under Inka rule. A late chronicler like Cobo, however, would have had several advantages over his predecessors, including what Randall calls the "perspective of time" and the availability of numerous works from which to obtain data.[90]

Ethnohistorians are not the only researchers who can be critiqued for how they deal with the chronicles. Randall says that archaeologists are worse because they sift through sixteenth- and seventeenth-century documents, picking out information that supports their interpretations of excavated materials while ignoring everything else.[91]

A STRUCTURALIST APPROACH TO ETHNOHISTORY

A better way to make use of ethnohistoric literature is through the structuralist approach advocated by Urton. Paraphrasing Zuidema, he notes that all written documents in the Andes were composed after the Spanish arrived, which means that every one of them, including the Huarochirí manuscript, bears some European influence. There are no completely autochthonous texts dealing with the structure, organization, and/or history of the Inka Empire. Because we lack the means to evaluate the historical accuracy of the chronicles, at least from an indigenous perspective, we cannot use them to create a reliable history of the Inkas. According to Urton, rather than reading the ethnohistoric sources "literally," we should interpret them "structurally"—meaning we should view them as purposeful representations, or misrepresentations, of prehispanic society and history. We need to be aware that in writing their texts, the Spanish chroniclers were influenced by a range of factors: the political, social, and ritual structures that existed in their own times and during the pre-Conquest era; the motivations and social contexts of the indigenous informants from whom they obtained their information; and their own backgrounds and agendas.[92]

How do we do research from a structural or "mytho-historical" perspective? Urton compares his methodology with that of scholars who favor a more literal approach. The latter tend to interpret differences between competing documents as discrepancies; for them, carrying out an ethnohistoric study involves resolving these discrepancies and deciding which source is more valid. Urton believes we should attempt to understand how and why various chroniclers—who may have used different informants or different types of informants—may have reached different conclusions about Inka society and history. Such a methodology is creative, allowing us to come up with a number of "approximations" of the Andean past, each of which reflects the unique viewpoint of an individual or group with its own motivations, biases, and ideas that induced it to represent Inka culture in a particular way.[93]

YET ANOTHER APPROACH

Some approaches to ethnohistoric research tell us a great deal about colonial society in Peru. Others shed light on how the chroniclers manipulated the past for their own ends or how they were compelled to produce a particular version of history. These approaches are not as useful for studying the Inkas themselves, and have even less utility for determining whether a specific bit of information relating to the Late Horizon is true. Given that much of our understanding of human sacrifice and mountain worship comes from pieces of data scattered through the chronicles, how can their veracity be evaluated?

There is a method that is employed, to a greater or lesser extent, by all researchers, although they are rarely explicit about it. Sometimes they use it unconsciously. It works as follows: as we read the publications of other scholars and engage in our own research, we build up a corpus of knowledge. This corpus can consist of information from many different types of sources, including archaeological, ethnohistoric, historic, ethnographic, iconographic, linguistic, physical, ethnobotanical, astronomical, agricultural, hydrological, and so on. From our body of knowledge, each of us constructs her/his own complex model. Every time we come across a new bit of data whose verity we want to test, we see how well it fits with our model. If we find the piece of information to be acceptable—that is, if it does not contradict any already held "facts," and is in harmony with our generalized perceptions—we can add it to our ever-growing corpus. It thus becomes part of the standard by which the veracity of other data will be tested in the future. If it goes against a previously adopted "fact," researchers have two options. They can modify their model so the new piece of information fits, and accept it. Or, what is more likely, they can reject it and consign it to a category such as "erroneous beliefs and misconceptions."

This method allows us to decontextualize a bit of data and to evaluate it on its own merits, rather than based on the strengths and weaknesses of the author in whose work it appears. The approach can be employed to refute Cobo's notion, though he is a reliable source, that giants lived in Peru. We reject it because it runs counter to twenty-first-century thinking, which does not permit us to put giants in the category "real beings." The methodology also lets us accept Garcilaso's statement that the inhabitants of Cac-Yauiri worshipped a hill, even if the chronicler is unreliable. But despite these uses, the approach is rife with problems. If a scholar uses it at a subconscious level, or is not explicit about how he employs it, then other researchers will not be able to tell how he assesses the veracity of his data, making it difficult for them to evaluate his work. Another shortcoming is that each person's corpus of knowledge is distinct, being based on a unique combination of sources, emphasizing certain aspects of a topic while downplaying others, and differing in terms of the quality of information comprising it. Thus to some degree, each scholar employs a different standard by which he measures the verity of new ethnohistoric data.

MY APPROACH TO ETHNOHISTORY

In my investigation of human sacrifice and mountain veneration, I have combined several approaches. On a general level, I examined all the ethnohistoric texts I could find, written by as many authors as possible, and extracted pertinent information on the two topics; at this stage, I accepted every bit of data. I then systematically organized the data set to look for patterns. When I found patterns that run counter to my accepted "facts" about the Inkas, or that contradict one another, I tried to account for them. They can often be explained in terms of the lives of the chroniclers. For example, suppose two groups of writers say things that are diametrically opposed. In such a case, I can determine which characteristics the members of each faction shared—such as biases, fundamental beliefs, educations, personal experiences, and motivations—and then try to figure out how the similarities in their personae might have led them to view Inka culture in the same way. I also can look at the variation between the two groups to ascertain if differences in their cultural backgrounds may have induced them to see Andean society in distinct ways. If several chroniclers present exactly the same data on mountain worship and/or human immolation, I can find out if the later authors were plagiarizing the works of earlier ones. It is also possible they were reporting on beliefs and practices that were well established and widespread in the Andes.

To be more specific about my ethnohistoric research, I took information obtained from the chronicles pertaining to human sacrifice and mountain veneration and reduced it to generalized descriptions of the practices. Through a reading of numerous authors—among them Cieza, Polo, Hernández Príncipe, and Cobo—I determined the types of immolations that were carried out during the Late Horizon and ascertained the major features of each type, its material correlates, and the reasons behind it. By consulting a different set of sources—including Albornoz, Avila, Guaman Poma, and Cobo—I have attempted to understand the relationship between Andean peoples and high peaks. I examined the kinds of offerings that were left for summits, the range of ceremonies that were devoted to them, and the motives behind these ceremonies. I also learned how to recognize a site in the archaeological record where such a rite took place.

I would like to reiterate that in working with, and discussing, the ethnohistoric data, I try to keep it separate from archaeological information. As stated earlier, by maintaining independent lines of evidence, I am attempting to avoid tautologies when it comes to interpreting archaeological data. Unfortunately, it is beyond the scope of the present work to actually compare and contrast the two types of evidence—a task that will have to wait for my next volume.

OUTLINE OF RESEARCH

In Chapter 2, I present data from the chronicles relating to *qhapaq hucha* immolation—the ritual slaying of young women and children by the lords of Cuzco. I talk about the victims themselves and discuss how they were gathered in the imperial capital, feasted, and redistributed to the provinces. I relate how they were put to death, and suggest reasons for their sacrifices. From the mass of descriptive information, I derive material correlates for the practice that represent a model for predicting what the remains from a *qhapaq hucha* immolation would look like in the archaeological record.

Chapter 3 deals with four other types of sacrificial victims found in the Inka Empire. They include *runas,* or male "citizens" of the state; the servants and/or relatives of a deceased ruler; captive warriors; and "substitute" victims. I present all relevant data recovered from the ethnohistoric documents: each type of victim, the manner in which he or she was dispatched, the distinctive features of the sacrifice, and the purpose(s) it may have served. I synthesize the facts from the chronicles and come up with material correlates for the four varieties of immolation.

Chapter 4 concerns mountain worship. I discuss the different ways Andean peoples conceived of high peaks—for example, as deities—and the diverse forms that mountain-gods were believed to take. I describe sacred sites associated with summits, cyclic and periodic rituals carried out for them, and miscellaneous practices connected with them.

Chapter 5 deals with the bewildering variety of items offered to peaks during the Inka period, including human lives, llamas, guinea pigs, metal items, shells, textiles, coca leaves, corn and corn products, feathers, and food. This section also covers nonmaterial contributions made to high pinnacles.

In Chapter 6, I examine the chroniclers' explanations for why Andean groups revered summits. The lords of Cuzco may have co-opted and manipulated mountain worship to create limits and boundaries, to tie conquered peoples to the state, and to reinforce imperial authority.

Chapter 7 is concerned with the material correlates of mountain veneration, distilled from the ethnohistoric data. I determine how to recognize sites where mountain-gods were venerated in antiquity, and discuss what artifacts might be found in the archaeological record that would give us a hint as to why a summit was revered.

In Chapter 8, I summarize the major points from each chapter, then consider some of the implications of this work for future studies in the Andes, particularly by archaeologists trying to interpret human remains and artifacts discovered on pinnacles in southern Peru, northwestern Argentina, and northern Chile.

THE SPELLING OF QUECHUA TERMS

In my work I use a number of words from Quechua, the language of the Inkas. Each of these words can be, and historically may have been, spelled in many ways; the term "Inka," for example, can be written "Inca" or even "Inga." One reason for the variation in orthography is that there is no one-to-one correspondence between the letters of the Spanish alphabet and sounds in Quechua. There are also regional differences in how the language is pronounced. For consistency's sake, I use a phonemic alphabet to write Quechua terms and names. Urioste discusses this alphabet—the symbols that comprise it and the sounds they represent—in his notes at the beginning of Guaman Poma's chronicle.[94] He also gives the phonemic spellings for many common and/or important nouns found in *La nueva corónica,* which I have adopted.[95] I make three exceptions to this general rule of writing Quechua words phonemically. When it comes to place-names, for the most part I employ the traditional Spanish orthography since many of these spellings have been around for a long time and are well established. The second exception relates to the names of indigenous chroniclers; I write them as they did, since their works are cataloged in libraries under the original spellings. Thus, we have "Guaman Poma" rather than "Waman Puma." Finally, when I quote a passage from a particular author, I preserve his orthography of Quechua.[96]

Two

QHAPAQ HUCHA SACRIFICE

> *The [qhapaq huchas, sacrificial victims] entered by the main*
> *square, and the Inca was already seated there on his golden*
> *throne; and in order were the statues of the Sun, Lightning-*
> *Thunder, and the embalmed Incas who were [attended by] their*
> *priests. They [the victims] marched around the principal square*
> *twice, worshipping the statues and the Inka, who with a joyful*
> *countenance greeted them; and when they approached him, [the*
> *Inca] spoke with secret words to the Sun, saying . . . "Receive*
> *these chosen ones for your service." (Silverblatt 1987:97)*

> *When this festival was over, they took the* capacochas *[qhapaq*
> huchas*] who were to remain in Cuzco to the* huaca *[sacred*
> *site] of Huanacauri or to the house of the Sun, and putting her*
> *[a particular victim] to sleep, they lowered her into a cistern*
> *without water, and . . . walled her in alive. (Hernández 1923: 61)*

Much of the information on the important practice of
human sacrifice in the Inka Empire comes from the Spanish and indigenous chroniclers of the sixteenth through eighteenth centuries. According
to some sources, a particularly notable type of immolation involved the
qhapaq huchas (often written *capacocha* or *capac hucha*). These children and
young women were specially chosen by imperial officials to be ritually slain
at religious shrines and other holy sites.[1] Although many of the chroniclers
discuss sacrificial rites involving women and youngsters (see Table 2.1), not
all of these works can be considered primary data sources because later
writers copied liberally from earlier ones without citing them.

Two chroniclers deny that the Inkas practiced human immolation, Garcilaso and Valera;[2] Garcilaso's descriptions of Inka religion, however, are
considered by some to be unreliable.[3] Not only were his commentaries

TABLE 2.1. CHRONICLERS WHO DISCUSS *QHAPAQ HUCHA* SACRIFICE

Chronicler	Original Publication Date (or Year When Written)	Date of Reprint	Pages Dealing with Qhapaq Hucha *Sacrifice*
Acosta	1590	1962	
		1880	304, 332, 344, 412–413
Albornoz	1583?	1967	26, 35
Alcayá	late 16th century?	1914?	161–162
Anónimo	17th century?	1904	227
Arriaga	1621	1968	88
		1920	
Avila	1598	1991	43/sec. 3, 67/sec. 99, 112/ sec. 280
Bello Galloso	1582	1897	189/sec. 14
Betanzos	1557	1996	46, 77–78, 132, 137, 162
		1987	51, 84, 142, 147, 177
		1968	247, 284
Cabello de Balboa	1586	1920	31
Calancha	1638	1931	61
Calancha and Torres	1657	1972	153/sec. 1, 155/sec. 4, 156/ sec. 5, 159/sec. 7, 168/ sec. 2, 173–176/secs. 6 and 8
Carabajal	1586	1965	207/sec. 14, 218–219
		1881	149/sec. 14, 167
Cieza de León	1553	1967	88, 93, 95–98, 215
		1959	150, 151, 180
Cobo	1653	1990	8, 27, 54, 57–60, 64, 65, 67–73, 77–82, 99, 111–112, 117, 151, 156, 170
		1979	143–144, 169, 235–238
Dávila Brizeño	1586	1881	72, 75
Díez de San Miguel	1567	1964	39, 92
García	1607	1981	98, 181
Guaman Poma de Ayala	1615	1980a	203, 221, 233, 236, 239, 240–247
		1978	63, 68, 71
Guerra y Céspedes	1582	1881	85/sec. 14
Gutiérrez de Santa Clara	1548	1905	438, 490
Hernández Príncipe	1622	1923	27–30, 32, 34, 41, 46, 52, 53, 60–63
Herrera	1610	1730	91, 92, 93

TABLE 2.1. (CONTINUED)

Chronicler	Original Publication Date (or Year When Written)	Date of Reprint	Pages Dealing with Qhapaq Hucha Sacrifice
Jesuíta Anónimo	1613	1918	186–188, 196
Jesuíta Anónimo	1600	1944	99
Las Casas	1550	1967	237–238
Matienzo	1567	1967	9
Molina of Cuzco	1575?	1943	
		1873	54–59
Montesinos	1644	1920	37, 43, 65
Murúa	1590	1964	11/fol. 188v, 16/fol. 191v, 99/fol. 252v, 104–105/fol. 256, 106/fol. 257, 109/fol. 258v, 113/fol. 261v, 120/ fol. 267, 137/fols. 280– 280v, 216/fol. 338v; 1946: 123, 265–267, 281, 286, 291, 295, 342
Noboa	1658	1986	169–170/fol. 26v, 248/fol. 117
Oliva	1598	1895	34
Pachacuti Yamqui	1613	1873	79, 85, 101
Paz Maldonado	late 16th century?	1897	150
Polo de Ondegardo	1571	1917	4–5, 8, 10, 12, 19–20, 22– 23, 24–30, 34–40
	1554	1916a	6–7, 26, 37, 40, 193/ sec. 8
	1571	1916b	92–94
	1567	1916c	193/sec. 8
	1567	1873	166–167
Ramos Gavilán	1621	1976	22, 23–27, 56, 61, 62, 65–66, 88
Rocha	1681	1891	8–9
Román y Zamora	1575	1897	225, 226
Ruiz de Navamuel	1570s?	1904	181
Santillán	1563	1968	392/sec. 27
Sarmiento de Gamboa	1572	1942	
		1907	56, 102, 122, 123, 126
Toledo	1573	1904	178
Velasco	1789	1978	67
Xerez	1534	1985	90
Zárate	1556	1968	51

written in Spain, about forty years after he left Peru,[4] but as the son of an Inka "princess,"[5] Garcilaso was sympathetic to his maternal kin and thus tried to prove to the Spanish that the Inkas had civilized the peoples they conquered, partly by prohibiting them from carrying out sacrifices.[6] Valera also had an Indian—and possibly Inka—mother.[7] He too seems to have been proud of his Andean heritage, and in his writings, he attacks Polo de Ondegardo for claiming the Inkas put children to death.[8] Because of these authors' biases, I discount their statements about immolation.

THE SACRIFICIAL VICTIMS

According to Cobo, a trustworthy source, the *qhapaq huchas* included boys and girls who were initially chosen when no older than ten, although they could be as young as four.[9] Selected for their good looks,[10] they could have no blemishes on their bodies—not even a freckle or spot.[11] A story is told of a beautiful young woman from Copacabana who was to be dispatched by the Inkas on an island in Lake Titi Qaqa. Before the ceremony began, the officiating priests examined her body to make sure it had no imperfections. Not finding any, they proceeded. Midway through the ritual, a priest noticed a tiny mole under her breast, whereupon he sent her away in shame, saying that if they had offered her, it would have angered the gods.[12] This account is interesting not only for the information it contains, but because it illustrates how common plagiarism was among the Andean chroniclers: Cobo and Calancha probably copied it from Ramos.

Another prerequisite to becoming a *qhapaq hucha* was virginity.[13] Cobo says that parents were often glad to see their daughters seduced at an early age because it meant the girls could not be taken away for immolation.[14]

Several authors state that the sacrificial victims were the children of *kurakas* (provincial nobles).[15]

Molina of Cuzco mentions that the institution of the *qhapaq hucha* was created by King Pacha Kuti.[16] Victims were considered to be tribute,[17] and were collected from villages and towns throughout the empire. They were sent to Cuzco, the capital, along with other forms of tribute, including fine cloth, flocks of llamas, gold and silver.[18] This means that an infant taken from the area around Quito in Ecuador, at the northern extreme of the state, would have had to travel over 1,600 km to reach Cuzco, located near the center.

Cobo tells us the process by which females became *qhapaq huchas* was different from that of males. Boys were selected and promptly sent to the

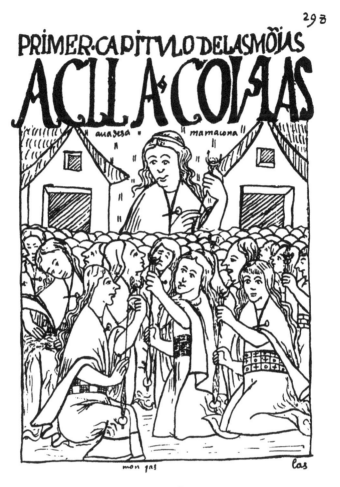

FIGURE 2.1.   *"Chosen women" spinning wool at an* aqlla wasi *(Guaman Poma 1980a: 273).*

capital.[19] Girls, who made up the bulk of the victims,[20] first became *aqllas,* "chosen women." They were picked for this honor by an imperial official called the *apu panaka,* who traveled the regions under his jurisdiction looking for maidens with pretty faces or good dispositions. When he found such girls, he took them to a provincial *aqlla wasi,* "house of the chosen women" (see Figure 2.1). There they were raised by *mama-kuna.* According to Cobo, the *mama-kuna* were like European nuns in that they had to remain chaste and cloistered throughout their lives, and were dedicated to the service of the gods. These women taught the chosen girls to spin wool and cotton, weave fine textiles, prepare food, and make *chicha* (corn beer). When the young virgins reached their early to mid teens, they were divided into three groups, each with a different purpose. Some became *mama-kuna* to replace those who had died, while the most beautiful ones were sent to the emperor, who made them his servants and concubines or distributed them to nobles whom he wished to honor. Many, however, were taken to Cuzco to be immolated during the year.[21]

THE FEASTING AND REDISTRIBUTION OF VICTIMS

Regardless of their origins, the *qhapaq huchas* were received in the capital with much celebration. Hernández describes their arrival for the festival of Inti Raymi, held in June. He says the specially selected infants and young women led a procession consisting of the principal *waqas* (often written *huaca* or *guaca,* less often as *uaca;* in this case, the word refers to idols), the *kurakas* (provincial rulers), and the commoners from their respective lands. Upon entering the city, this large procession was met by the local populace. The *qhapaq huchas* were taken to the Awqay Pata, the main square, where the emperor was seated on his golden stool[22] near the images of the major gods: Wira Qucha, the Creator; Inti, the Sun; Illapa, Thunder-Lightning; and Mama Killa, Mother Moon.[23] Lined up beside the sacred images were the mummies of past kings and the priests who attended them. The victims twice marched around Awqay Pata while paying homage to the Inka, his gods, and his ancestors. The emperor greeted them, made an offering of special *chicha* to the Sun, and rubbed powder (or corn beer dregs) over his body to share in the Sun's divinity. Then a prominent officiant slaughtered a white llama and mixed its blood with corn meal to make a dough that was distributed to the Inka and his counselors. Rituals honoring the *qhapaq huchas* continued for days and involved much feasting and drinking.[24]

At the end of a festival such as Inti Raymi, the Inkas dispatched as many as five hundred children and young women around Cuzco.[25] Many of the immolations were carried out at the Quri Kancha, the so-called Temple of the Sun, and at Wana Kawri, a hill with a stone on top that was significant in Inka mythology.[26] According to Betanzos, some youngsters met their deaths in pairs, a boy with a girl.[27]

A large percentage of *qhapaq huchas* were redistributed to the provinces for sacrifice. Molina says the victims were divided into four groups, one for

FIGURE 2.2.   Khipu kamayuq *holding the knotted strings on which he records information*
                (Guaman Poma 1980a: 332).

each of the empire's territorial quarters: Qulla Suyu, Chinchay Suyu, Anti
Suyu, and Kunti Suyu. They also were assigned to individual *waqas*—sacred
idols, shrines, and places—within the quarters. *Khipu kamayuqs*—officials
in charge of keeping records and accounts, who registered information on
knotted strings (see Figure 2.2)—took stock of the goods and animals that
were to accompany the infants and youths on their journeys. The goods
included gold and silver figurines representing people and llamas; fine cloth
of wool and cotton;[28] *chicha* made from special ears of black, white, and
yellow corn; brightly hued feathers; bags of coca leaves; *mullu* (Spondy-

lus shell); vessels made from precious metals and sometimes executed in miniature; different colored ears of maize;[29] and diminutive clothing.[30] Among the animals to be offered up with the *qhapaq huchas* were llamas and *quwis* (guinea pigs).[31] Certain items given to victims before their sacrifice were gender-specific. Young women received pins of precious metals, spoons, plates, bowls, cups, and other vessels made from gold, silver, wood, and ceramics.[32] Males—though not necessarily the boys chosen as *qhapaq huchas*—were given headbands, medallions, and *q'ipis* (bundles used to carry goods on the back like a knapsack).[33]

The *khipu kamayuqs* divided the materials and animals between the *waqas,* keeping a record of the portion being sent to each.[34] They had to be careful in their allotments because specific *waqas* could receive only certain types of goods; for example, a sacred spring might be offered children and shells, but not feathers or cloth.[35]

When the ceremonies in Cuzco had ended, and all the *qhapaq huchas* had been allocated to important provincial *waqas,* the victims left the imperial city with their entourages. Each group made its separate way, proceeding not along the royal roads but in as straight a line as possible between the capital and the sacred shrine or place, traversing hills, passes, valleys, and streams. The *qhapaq huchas* old enough to walk did so; the ones who could not were carried by their mothers or placed on the backs of others.[36] A few chroniclers state that children were taken to the *waqas* in litters.[37]

Besides a *qhapaq hucha* and his or her kin, the sacrificial procession included an imperial official of noble blood and several priests. According to Murúa, the priests had to remain stony faced, could not look around or speak, and at regular intervals had to stop to pray for the health and well-being of the emperor.[38] Also among the group were provincial people whose duty it was to carry the goods destined for the *waqa.*[39] The legal document known as "Justicia 413" gives the impression that only the natives of a particular region could carry offerings through that region; therefore, when the local bearers reached the boundary with another province, they had to transfer the goods to the neighboring people.[40] The document mentions that these bearers sometimes carried small gourds or pots containing the blood of immolated llamas, and that if they spilled a single drop, they were immediately killed and buried.[41] The final member of the procession had the job of leading a chorus of shouts from the group. These cries were directed at the Creator and were pleas for the health and prosperity of the Inka.[42]

If dusk caught the *qhapaq hucha* and his/her entourage on their journey, they stopped, no matter where they were. They would then dispatch llamas and scatter the blood among hills and rocks, which were considered holy. Some of the blood would be put in small gourds and pots. If there was a peak they wanted to honor with an offering, but which was too difficult to climb, they took a blood-filled pot and hurled it with a sling as far up the slope as possible, where it would smash to pieces, dispersing its contents.[43]

So esteemed were sacrificial victims that when they were met by another traveler on the trail, the latter would prostrate himself on the ground, not daring to look up until the procession had passed. When a sacred child or young woman walked through a village, the inhabitants stayed in their houses out of respect.[44]

The *waqas* to which the *qhapaq huchas* journeyed for immolation included a wide range of sacred places, buildings, and objects. Many prominent *waqas* were high peaks and hills (see Figure 2.3).[45] Other natural features that received offerings of people were springs,[46] lakes,[47] caves,[48] rocks,[49] ravines,[50] flat spaces,[51] islands,[52] the confluences of rivers,[53] and trees.[54] Some significant *waqas* were parts of the landscape that had been modified by humans, such as cultivated fields,[55] or man-made structures such as the palaces of emperors,[56] tombs,[57] temples, houses,[58] and plazas.[59] Among the objects that received sacrifices were numerous idols and statues, some painted, others carved.[60] They were made from a variety of materials including precious metals, wood, clay, and stone, and could represent humans, animals, fish, birds, vegetables, and so on.[61] A few of the more unusual things to be honored with human immolations were a pillar and a dead fox.[62]

Some *qhapaq huchas* did not have to travel far to reach their final destinations. Cobo and Polo list many holy shrines and places near Cuzco that were offered children; the victims would have arrived at these *waqas* within hours or days of departing from the capital.[63] Other *qhapaq huchas* had to walk thousands of kilometers. Hernández mentions that children from the province of Huaylas were immolated in Quito, close to the empire's northern border; at Lake Titi Qaqa, near the center; and in Chile, at the southern end of the state.[64] It may have been weeks, if not months, before these victims made it to their respective *waqas*.

A few *qhapaq huchas* returned to their homelands to be dispatched. Hernández tells of a girl named Tanta Carhua who went to Cuzco to take part in sacrificial rites. But the Inka, to show his respect for the child's father, sent her back to her native province so she could be put to death there.[65]

FIGURE 2.3.   *People of Qulla Suyu offering a llama and basket of coca leaves to the mountain-*waqa *Willka Nuta (Guaman Poma 1980a: 244).*

THE SACRIFICIAL RITES

The *qhapaq huchas* were received at their destinations by officials called *waqa kamayuqs.*[66] After they were honored with festivals patterned after those held in the capital,[67] the victims took part in a series of rites that varied depending on the purpose served by their deaths.[68] On the day of their sacrifices, they were dressed in fine clothing, that of the women often brightly colored and decorated with feathers.[69] Sometimes the victims' faces were smeared yellow or painted red with a substance such as bixin,[70] a dye derived from the seeds of the annatto tree, which was meant to honor the Sun.[71] They were given food so they would go to the gods satiated and happy,[72] made to drink corn beer until intoxicated,[73] and occasionally offered coca leaves to chew.[74] Just before meeting their ends, various customs were observed, such as playing drums, flutes, and trumpets made from large shells;[75] singing solemn songs;[76] and leading the victims two or three times around the *waqas*.[77] The actual immolations were performed by priests who had prepared themselves by fasting,[78] which meant abstinence from meat, *chicha, ají,* salt, and sexual relations.[79]

Death came to the victims in different ways: some were suffocated;[80] others were strangled,[81] at times with cords;[82] some received blows to the head[83] or neck,[84] while others were drowned.[85] The chroniclers state that chosen women and children also had their beating hearts cut out and their throats slit.[86] In a ritual called *piraq,* the victim's blood was used to draw a thick line across the face of an idol, from ear to ear and passing over the bridge of the nose.[87] The blood might also be spattered on a *waqa* or smeared all over it.[88]

Many victims were buried alive.[89] After a deep, flat-bottomed shaft had been dug using only pointed sticks—no metal tools[90]—the *qhapaq hucha* was lowered into it and seated in an upright position.[91] Then the appropriate offerings were placed around him or her, and the shaft was sealed.[92]

Sacrificial victims were deified after their deaths and honored at yearly festivals.[93] Following Tanta Carhua's immolation, the youngest of her seven brothers was designated as a priest to perpetuate her cult and would answer questions put to the *qhapaq hucha* with a high-pitched voice. His position was passed down to his descendants or to those of another brother.[94]

REASONS FOR SACRIFICE

The ethnohistoric sources offer a variety of explanations for why the Inkas immolated children and young women. One significant motive was placating the gods,[95] chief among which were Wira Qucha,[96] Inti,[97] Illapa,[98] Mama Killa,[99] Pacha Mama (Mother Earth),[100] and Mama Qucha (Mother Sea).[101] Offerings of *qhapaq huchas* were made to propitiate significant *waqas:* sacred idols, shrines, buildings, places, and features of the landscape.[102] Some *waqas*—such as the site of Pacha Kamaq,[103] where the universe was said to have been created,[104] and Lake Titi Qaqa[105]—were known throughout the Andes. Others—including Wana Kawri,[106] the hill near Cuzco with the hallowed stone on top, and the mummies of past kings[107]—were important primarily to the Cuzqueños. On the provincial level, prominent *waqas*—many of them snow-capped mountains[108] and stones[109]—also were appeased with human sacrifices.

Certain *waqas*—Pacha Kamaq, Wana Kawri, Willka Nuta, Aconcagua, and Qhuru Puna—were well-known oracles. Whenever the Inkas sought their advice on weighty matters, they ritually slew people.[110] Cobo says that when the lords of Cuzco needed information critical to the well-being of the state, such as whether a province was going to rebel, they would use a special type of divination accompanied by the sacrifice of infants.[111] The chronicler Murúa relates how when Thupa Yapanki became gravely ill, the queen had a notable "sorcerer" consult his idols and oracles to see if the emperor would die—a consultation that included the immolation of children.[112] As mentioned earlier, Hernández notes that after young people were put to death as *qhapaq huchas,* they were deified, and their advice was sought by their communities on local matters.[113]

According to various chroniclers, infants and young women were immolated during critical periods in the life of the Sapa Inka (emperor). Sacrificial rites were held when he first received the royal fringe that served as a symbol of office[114] and while he was on the throne to guarantee a peaceful reign.[115] *Qhapaq huchas* were sacrificed whenever the Sapa Inka became sick to ensure his recovery[116] and his continued good health.[117] Ethnohistoric sources also inform us that immolations were performed when the emperor attended to important business,[118] went to war,[119] married,[120] had a son and possible successor by his principal wife,[121] and died.[122]

Cobo describes two types of *qhapaq hucha* sacrifices in the empire: those that took place on a cyclical basis, and those associated with one-of-a-kind events.[123] Examples of the former include immolations made for the yearly festivals of Inti Raymi,[124] held in June,[125] and Qhapaq Raymi,[126] celebrated in December (see Figure 2.4).[127] Each festival may have involved the ritual slaying of five hundred children.[128] The latter type of sacrifice took place in times of great necessity: when there was famine, mass death, pestilence, war, or a natural disaster.[129] Immolations might be carried out to avoid such calamities, too.[130] Some children and/or young women were dispatched following earthquakes[131] and eclipses, both solar and lunar.[132]

The institution of the *qhapaq hucha* was linked to fertility[133] and agriculture.[134] Herrera tells us that boys and girls were put to death before planting began and after the harvest.[135] Cobo says such sacrifices were carried out to ensure an abundance of food.[136] Both Cobo and Polo state that infants were immolated at a *waqa* called Sausero, a *chakra* (cultivated field) located out-

FIGURE 2.4.   *Emperor celebrating the festival of Qhapaq Raymi (Guaman Poma 1980a: 232).*

FIGURE 2.5.   *Emperor helping to plow a sacred field (Guaman Poma 1980a: 224).*

side Cuzco, whenever the emperor went there to plow (see Figure 2.5).[137] Polo discusses another rite celebrating the shelling of the maize that took place on a venerated hill called Mantocalla and involved ritualized drinking, the burning of ears of corn carved from wood, and the slaying of youngsters.[138]

Qhapaq hucha sacrifice was also connected with water, which was essential to agriculture.[139] According to Ulloa, the Inkas offered victims—though he does not specifically state they were infants or young women—to five peaks that were covered with snow during winter. In the spring, water from the melting snow fed the rivers that were tapped to irrigate fields.[140] Murúa mentions that when there was little rain in the Andes, it was customary to immolate children for the benefit of the *waqas,* high peaks, and/or thunder-god.[141] Polo maintains that at a prominent spring named Corcopuquio, in the Cuzco area, boys and girls were put to death in special rites.[142] As Hernández relates in telling the story of Tanta Carhua, there was an implicit link between the *qhapaq hucha* and water. Before the child's sacrifice, her father, Caque Poma, brought together the people of Aixa to build an irrigation canal. After it was completed, Poma Caque celebrated by sending his daughter to the imperial capital as a *qhapaq hucha*. When Tanta Carhua was sent by the emperor back to her native land, she was buried alive on top of a mountain overlooking the canal.[143]

Although water was vital for farming, an overabundance of rain or ice could destroy plants, and Herrera says that infants were slain during years of bad weather, presumably because the crops were threatened.[144] Murúa makes a similar statement, noting that when the earth was barren due to excessive rainfall, ice, or hail, boys and girls were sacrificed.[145] Youngsters were also immolated to honor the thunder-god, who controlled a wide range of atmospheric phenomena, including hail.[146]

The institution of the *qhapaq hucha* was associated not only with agriculture, but with other aspects of the Inka economy as well. Labor was critical to the polity, and the Inkas may have sacrificed children and young women to augment human fertility and thus increase the size of the labor pool. During immolations made to Wira Qucha, the Cuzqueños prayed for the people to multiply.[147] Betanzos and García (the latter citing the former) describe the ritual burial of two infants, a boy and a girl, along with a set of vessels and utensils such as a married couple might have.[148] Such a rite may have been intended to increase fecundity. Sacrifices were carried out for the general health of the people too.[149]

The sacrifice of children and young women was sometimes connected with specialized production. Hernández relates the case of a group of *mitmaq-kuna* (settlers) transplanted by the Inkas from their native land to the province of Huaylas, where they manufactured ceramics. The two *qhapaq huchas* that the settlers received from the state were offered to some deep pits along with *sañu mama* (good-quality clay). They made these offerings to prevent their clay sources from drying up and to ensure success in pottery production.[150]

The ritual slaying of boys and girls also marked the conclusion of significant projects. Cieza describes a ceremony in Vilcas dedicating a newly built temple to the Sun. This rite was presided over by Wayna Qhapaq, who donated gold and silver to the temple, assigned *mama-kuna* and priests to work there, ordered that provisions be sent there, and had *qhapaq huchas* immolated.[151]

Human sacrifice was tied to the Inka social structure and political organization as well.[152] According to Calancha, parents could raise their status in a community and enhance their prestige by offering an infant for ritual slaughter.[153] Hernández mentions that two local descent groups dispatched a pair of children to cement their alliance.[154] He also claims the political power of a *kuraka* was based on the immolation of a *qhapaq hucha,* citing the case of Caque Poma, discussed earlier.[155]

The sacrificial rite was concerned with boundaries: while making their long journeys, many specially chosen boys, girls, and young women radiated outward from Cuzco, the center of the state, to the territorial limits of Inka control.[156] Hence, they defined the borders of the empire at that point in time. The institution of the *qhapaq hucha* was associated with regional boundaries too. "Justicia 413" suggests that the only people who could carry offerings through a province were the natives, which means that every time a frontier was reached between two adjoining regions, the sacred goods had to be transferred from the members of one ethnic group to those of another.[157] As the procession made its way across the landscape, the sequential meeting of peoples at their respective borders would have established the territorial relationships between ethnic groups within the state.[158]

Qhapaq hucha rituals could, on the other hand, be manipulated to change boundaries. "Justicia 413" discusses a case in which the Chaclla transported sacrificial offerings beyond the stones marking the border between their lands and those of the Canta, thereby laying claim to Canta territory.[159]

The institution of human immolation created a sacred network. This network was similar to the *siq'e* system in the Cuzco area, which consisted of 41 *siq'es* (lines) that radiated out from the Quri Kancha, the Temple of the Sun, and along which there were at least 328 *waqas*.[160] The state-wide system existed on a grand scale: as the chosen women and children walked from the capital to the individual *waqas* to meet their deaths, they followed straight lines[161] that were sometimes hundreds,[162] if not thousands, of kilometers long, tracing the symbolic links between the heart of the empire and its extremities.[163]

Each *qhapaq hucha* sacrifice that took place in a province could have created a local hierarchy of sacred shrines and a local system of sight-lines.[164] Take the case of Tanta Carhua, who was offered to the Sun on a high peak in Aixa. She was subsequently deified and worshipped by provincial folk who could not easily reach the site of her interment from the surrounding hills;[165] consequently, a ring of secondary shrines was created around the primary *waqa,* her burial place. Between each secondary shrine and the primary one was a direct line of sight, which was a feature of Cuzco's *siq'e* system.[166] An intriguing thing about this local network of *waqas* is that it had at its apex, and its focal point, a shrine that partially honored Inti, the patron god of the polity. Since Tanta Carhua's tomb was a node on the state-wide system of symbolic lines, the provincial system would have been integrated into the imperial one.

The *qhapaq huchas* made clear the unequal relationship between Cuzco, the hub of the empire's political and religious power, and the regional centers. Victims were taken from the provinces as tribute[167] and then redistributed to them as gifts made through the "generosity" of the state. Many *qhapaq huchas* were dispatched to venerate the Sun, which was not only the principal Inka god, but also the emblem of the conquering polity.[168] To make sure this message of imperial dominance and generosity was not lost on local peoples, the Inkas had them participate in the sacrificial processions[169] and worship the victims after their immolations.[170]

MATERIAL CORRELATES OF
QHAPAQ HUCHA SACRIFICE

What features of *qhapaq hucha* sacrifice as described by the chroniclers would enable us to recognize victims if we were to come across their remains in the archaeological record? First, age. Males would be between four and ten. Females would tend to be older, between about ten and fifteen. It is possible that an *aqlla* could be even more mature; Guaman Poma tells us that the principal age-grade of the "chosen women" consisted of females in their early twenties, some of whom undoubtedly were immolated.[171]

A significant material correlate of *qhapaq hucha* sacrifice is the victim's clothing and accoutrements. Boys were often put to death in alien lands but would probably have been dressed in their native clothes.[172] Their attire would very likely contrast with the garments of the people in whose territory the immolation took place and with those of the Inkas. Consider the hypothetical case of a boy from Qulla Suyu, the southeastern quarter of the empire, who was the son of a *kuraka* (see Figure 2.6). He would wear a knee-length *unku* (tunic), a mantle, moccasins, and a hat shaped like a truncated cone. He might sport a wide bracelet on one arm and a pendant shaped like a sideways "H" hanging under his chin.[173] If he were ritually slaughtered in Chinchay Suyu, the northwestern quarter, his clothing would differ from that of a male discovered in a local burial. Assuming the local male was from the provincial nobility (see Figure 2.7), he probably would be dressed in an *unku*, a mantle, sandals, and a wide, feathered collar. On one arm he might have a bracelet, and around his head a band called a *llawt'u,* fixed to the front of which would be an insignia shaped

ELCATORZECAPITAN
MALLCO:CASTILLA
PARI

collasuyo

mall co

EL.DO ZE CAPITAN
CAPACAPOGVAMAN
CHAVA

chinchaysuyo

capac

FIGURE 2.6.   *Noble of Qulla Suyu with a tunic, mantle, moccasins, distinct hat, bracelet, and H-shaped pendant (Guaman Poma 1980a: 148).*

FIGURE 2.7.   *Noble of Chinchay Suyu wearing a tunic, sandals, headband with distinct insignia, bracelet, and feathered collar (Guaman Poma 1980a: 144).*

ALGVAZILMAIOR
CHACNAICAMAIOC
LVRINCVZCO

al guazil mayor   cha pay

FIGURE 2.8.   *Inka official wearing a tunic with the q'asana pattern, mantle, sandals, headband with distinct insignia, and earplugs (Guaman Poma 1980a: 316).*

like an upside-down horseshoe and a feather.[174] Clothing could also mark
an imperial official (see Figure 2.8), who most likely would wear an *unku*
with a typical Inka motif such as a checkerboard[175] or *q'asana* pattern.[176]
He also would sport a mantle, sandals, a *llawt'u,* and large earplugs.[177] Not
only would there be a difference between the costumes of a victim and
the natives, but between their hairstyles. The young boy from Qulla Suyu
would have long hair that fell onto his shoulders and partway down his
back.[178] In Chinchay Suyu, males kept their hair about shoulder-length,[179]
while the Cuzqueños cut theirs very short.[180]

Aqllas immolated as *qhapaq huchas* would also be distinguished by their
clothing and hairstyle (see Figure 2.1). As these specially chosen girls and
young women were cut off from their home provinces and became, in
effect, the property of the state,[181] they no longer dressed in their native
garments. Instead, their attire resembled that of the elite women of Cuzco:
an *aqsu* (ankle-length "dress") that was fastened at each shoulder by a *tupu*
(large pin) and bound at the waist by a sash, a *lliklla* (long mantle) that was
secured by a third pin, and sandals.[182] The main colors in their clothing may
have been white, red, yellow, and dark blue.[183] *Aqllas* had long hair that was
parted down the middle, and hung loosely down their backs.[184]

Another way to recognize a *qhapaq hucha* sacrifice in the archaeological
record would be through the goods that were left with a victim. According
to the chroniclers, offerings could include anthropomorphic and zoomorphic figurines of gold and silver, fine cloth, feathers, bags of coca leaves,
Spondylus shell, various types of vessels (including miniature ones), and
food. *Aqllas* were buried with spoons, plates, bowls, and cups made from
gold, silver, wood, and ceramics. Sometimes llamas and guinea pigs were
immolated and interred with victims.

If we wanted to prove that the remains were that of a *qhapaq hucha,* we
would have to demonstrate that the person was intentionally slain. If the
victim had been strangled by hand, we might find that the hyoid bone or
thyroid cartilage is fractured.[185] A person strangled by a cord may have a
broken hyoid or, more commonly, a fragmented thyroid; also, the use of a
ligature sometimes leaves a mark, which can vary from prominent to barely
visible.[186] A child or young woman killed by a blow to the head could have
any of four types of skull fractures: linear, diastatic, depressed, or stellate.[187]
Assuming that the remains are well preserved, it would be easy to tell if a
victim's throat was cut or heart removed. Victims buried alive would probably have no visible marks or wounds.

Additional correlates of *qhapaq hucha* sacrifice include how and where a
victim is interred. Some children and young women were entombed alive

at the bottoms of deep shafts, while others were placed in pits subsequent to their deaths. Most were buried alone, though occasionally a pair of infants, a boy and a girl, were immolated together. The victim was usually placed in a seated position and surrounded by offerings. Interments took place at important sites and shrines, including on the tops of high peaks, near sacred stones, and in front of cult images.

Other miscellaneous features of the *qhapaq huchas* might help us identify them, but we could only check for many of these features if the recovered remains were unusually well preserved. One such trait would be the victim's physical perfection: children and post-adolescent females who were ritually slain could have no blemishes, moles, warts, or spots on their bodies. We do not know how rigorously this rule was enforced, however, especially in times of emergency, such as during a severe drought or epidemic, when the Inkas might sacrifice numerous people. Ethnohistoric sources tell us that victims were often given *chicha* to drink and, less frequently, coca leaves to chew right before their immolation; if the liver of this person were well preserved, we might be able to test it for the metabolites of alcohol and cocaine. The chroniclers state that *qhapaq huchas* were feasted first in Cuzco and then in a provincial capital, which likewise may have involved the consumption of corn beer and coca. If these substances were ingested at least ten days before the victim's death, we might be able to detect traces of BZE, a metabolite of cocaine, or coca-ethylene, a cocaine/alcohol metabolite, in the hair.[188] On the face of an infant or young woman we might find yellow pigment and/or red bixin. And if we were to examine the contents of the victim's stomach, we might discover the remains of the last meal.

Archaeological evidence might also help to determine why a sacrifice was made. A *qhapaq hucha* ritually slain as part of a festival celebrating the corn harvest might be interred with special ears of corn. A victim put to death to end a drought might be left with Spondylus shells, considered to be the "daughters" of the sea and therefore appropriate offerings for water.[189] An immolation tied to fertility might include a pair of children or some anthropomorphic statuettes. Lastly, a boy, girl, or post-adolescent female whose ritual dispatch was related to the exploitation of a resource, such as gold, might be buried near the resource—in this case, at the entrance to a mine.

Three

OTHER TYPES OF
       SACRIFICE

The Inkas practiced not only *qhapaq hucha* sacrifice, but at
least four other types of human immolation. According to the ethnohistoric sources, they put *runas* (male "citizens") to death, ritually slew captive
warriors, carried out *necropampa* sacrifices, which consisted of burying victims with a deceased ruler, and performed "substitute immolations." The
latter involved offering the life of one person so another individual who
was very sick might live.

RUNA SACRIFICE

The *runas*—low-status, able-bodied men aged between
twenty-five and fifty—comprised the backbone of Inka society. They
headed households, paid taxes in the form of *mit'a* labor, and served in the
Inka army.[1] Although apparently not as common as *qhapaq huchas* sacrifice,
runas were sometimes dispatched by the state in sacred ceremonies. For a
list of chroniclers who discuss this practice, see Table 3.1.

The chroniclers provide little information on how the *runas* became sacrificial victims. Gutiérrez describes a rite from the territory of the Collao
involving several men who volunteered for the honor of being ceremonially put to death.[2] Díez says that communities in the province of Chucuito
had to give men to the Inkas as tribute, and they were then offered to the
waqas.[3] An anonymous Jesuit maintains that these male victims, like the
specially chosen children and young women, could have no blemishes or
moles on their bodies.[4] Las Casas, whose words are echoed by Román y
Zamora, states that they had to be virtuous, virgins, and free from the stains
of sin.[5] These last requirements sound too Catholic, though; it may be a
contradiction to say that a *runa* had to be a virgin, since Andean peoples did
not reckon their ages in years, but assigned an individual to an age-grade

TABLE 3.1. CHRONICLERS WHO DISCUSS *RUNA* SACRIFICE

Chronicler	Original Publication Date (or Year When Written)	Date of Reprint	Pages Dealing with Runa Sacrifice
Albornoz	1583?	1967	35
Anónimo	17th century?	1904	227
Avila	1598	1991	70/sec. 110
Calancha & Torres	1657	1972	155/sec. 4
Cieza de León	1553	1985	88, 222
		1967	93, 95–99, 215
		1959	150–151, 180
Díez de San Miguel	1567	1964	85, 92, 106
Gutiérrez de Santa Clara	1548	1905	490–493
Jesuíta Anónimo	1613	1918	187, 188, 192, 196
Las Casas	1550	1967	237–238
Murúa	1590	1964	113/fol. 261v
		1946	281, 370, 371
Oliva	1598	1895	136
Oviedo y Valdez	1535–1557	1959	101
Pachacuti Yamqui	1613	1873	104
Polo de Ondegardo	1567	1916c	193/sec. 8
Rocha	1681	1891	8, 24–25
Román y Zamora	1575	1897	226
Ulloa Mogollón	1586	1885	44–45/sec. 14
Xerez	1534	1985	90
Zárate	1556	1968	51

based on social position, marital status, and generation. To be categorized as a *runa,* a male may have had to be married,[6] in which case he would not be "free from sin."

Before being ritually dispatched, *runas* were treated in the same manner as *qhapaq huchas,* which is to say they were dressed in fine clothing, of wool[7] or white cotton.[8] They were given sandals, headbands, and all kinds of gold adornments, among them bracelets, rings, earspools, and necklaces.[9] They were made drunk on *chicha.*[10] Preceding their deaths, various rites were held: the delivery of earnest speeches by priests, the singing of solemn songs, chanting, dancing, and the playing of drums and various other musical instruments, including trumpets fashioned from large shells.[11] As with the *qhapaq huchas,* the actual sacrifice of the *runas* was carried out by priests,[12] who had prepared for the ceremony by fasting, which involved abstaining from sex and from eating chiles and salt.[13]

The men were killed in different ways. Some supposedly had their beating hearts removed,[14] though this method sounds more Aztec than Inka, while others were strangled,[15] hit on the head with a club,[16] or decapitated.[17] Live burial, a common means of putting children to death, does not seem to have been used with the *runas*. Once a male victim was dead, his blood might be smeared across the face of an idol[18] or sprinkled onto a sacred stone, temple, or holy site.[19] Victims were often interred near the *waqa,* along with offerings such as precious metals, splendid clothing, vessels made from gold and silver, corn beer, and food.[20]

The ethnohistoric sources report that adult males were often sacrificed to significant Inka gods. Las Casas asserts that every new moon, four or five victims, including *runas,* were put to death to honor Wira Qucha.[21] Oviedo y Valdez claims that the beating hearts of men were cut from their chests and offered to Inti.[22] Polo maintains,[23] and his words are repeated verbatim by Murúa,[24] that immolations of adult males were made to the thundergod, while Cieza implies that the Cuzqueños ritually slew *runas* at the Quri Kancha, a temple devoted to their most important deities.[25]

According to the chroniclers, male victims were dispatched in rites meant to venerate mountain *waqas,* both around the capital and in the provinces. Cieza gives a detailed description of the killing of men on Wana Kawri, a sacred peak near Cuzco. He says that the victims were decked out in finery, given *chicha* to drink, serenaded with somber songs, strangled, and buried at a sacred site on the peak.[26] Pachacuti Yamqui tells us about three hundred *runas* from Upatari who reached the capital laden with gold. Their arrival coincided with an extreme cold spell, so Thupa Yapanki—fearing the crops would be destroyed—had the *runas* taken to a sacred mountain called Pachatusun, where they were ceremonially killed and interred with the gold.[27] Ulloa notes that the principal *waqas* in the province of the Collaguas and Cavanas were five snow-capped summits called Collaguata, Suquilpa, Apoquico, Omascota, and Gualcagualca (Hualca Hualca). Each received sacrifices of adult males.[28] Albornoz provides an inventory of hallowed pinnacles throughout the Inka Empire,[29] the most significant of which were honored with immolations of men.[30] Cieza states that in Kunti Suyu, the southwestern quarter, there was a temple on a revered and snow-covered peak known as Qhuru Puna (Coropuna). Sometimes *runas* were ritually put to death there.[31]

Adult males were slain for the benefit of other types of *waqas,*[32] too, including Lake Titi Qaqa. On a small island in the middle of the sacred lake, the Inkas built a shrine where they killed men in special ceremonies. In the province of the Carangas there was another body of water that was greatly venerated (perhaps Lake Poopó?) and that received sacrifices of *runas*.[33] Male victims were also immolated to honor idols,[34] stones,[35] and structures.[36] Albornoz lists an assortment of *waqas* in the Inka state—many of which were important enough to be offered the lives of men—that include trees,[37] caves,[38] fountains,[39] islands,[40] a plot of land,[41] altars,[42] a pillar,[43] a star,[44] and a dead fox.[45] Cieza notes that after being sacrificed, victims were semideified like Catholic saints.[46]

Various chroniclers discuss a connection between the immolation of *runas* and agriculture. Zárate describes a yearly festival held by the Indians of the sierra that involved putting adult males to death during the harvest of the maize.[47] As mentioned earlier, the natives of the Arequipa area sacrificed men to five snow-covered peaks that provided meltwater for irrigating the fields.[48] According to Albornoz, certain summits and volcanoes were considered especially worthy of veneration: ones which were snow-capped, which "looked toward the sea" (the ultimate source of all liquid on earth), or which gave rise to rivers that watered tracts of land. To honor such peaks, the Inkas slew *runas*.[49] Polo maintains that this type of victim was usually killed to pay homage to Thunder,[50] a god associated not only with the rain that was essential for agriculture, but also with hail and ice, which could devastate crops. And there is Pachacuti's story, mentioned above, about the three hundred males who were ritually dispatched on Mount Pachatusun to end a cold spell threatening crops.[51]

According to several ethnohistoric sources, the immolation of men was related to health in the Inka state. Polo tells us,[52] and again his words are echoed by Murúa,[53] that such victims were sacrificed whenever pestilence or other disasters swept the land, causing many people to die. Calancha and Torres report that *runas* were offered up whenever the king became sick, and likewise when he expired.[54]

The killing of men in special ceremonies was also linked to oracles. Zárate discusses the yearly maize festival in the sierra during which the local people dispatched either a human or a llama. The heart and entrails of the llama were removed and examined for signs that the coming year would be good or bad;[55] the text is unclear if this was done with the human victim as well. Cieza says that the lords of Cuzco sacrificed *runas* to three *waqas* with oracular functions: Wana Kawri, Aconcagua, and Qhuru Puna. The first was the hill near the capital with a stone on top where the "devil" was supposed to speak,[56] the second a temple affiliated with the province of Hatun Cana,[57] and the last the high mountain with a shrine on its slopes where continuous prophesies were given.[58]

In one case, adult males appear to have been put to death in a dedication ceremony. Cieza mentions that Wayna Qhapaq traveled from Cuzco to Vilcas, where he celebrated the completion of a solar temple by having men immolated.[59]

A *runa* might also be dispatched to serve as an intermediary between his people and the gods. Gutiérrez describes a Collao rite in which an adult male volunteered to be killed, whereupon he was decked out in fine clothing and gold adornments, and then hit in the back of the neck with a club. In death he became an "ambassador," sent to deliver a message to a deceased and deified king.[60]

Runa immolations, like those of the *qhapaq huchas,* can be divided into two types: those that took place on a cyclical basis, and those connected with singular events. Cyclical events included the annual maize festival detailed by Zárate[61] and the celebrations that Albornoz asserts were carried out by the Inkas to honor prominent *waqas.*[62] Rites connected with the dispatching of *runas* because of pestilence, widespread death,[63] or the ill health of the king[64] fall into the second category. Additional ceremonies relating to one-of-a-kind events include the slaying of the three hundred men on Pachatusun[65] and the immolation of men as part of the dedication of a sun temple.[66]

MATERIAL CORRELATES OF
RUNA SACRIFICE

The essential attributes of *runa* sacrifice as described by the chroniclers can be used to determine if a particular set of archaeological materials is from a *runa* immolation. A victim of this type would be male, between about twenty-five and fifty, with a body sound and free of blemishes. The cause of death should be discernible: he may have been strangled, in which case his hyoid bone or thyroid cartilage might be fractured,[67] or he could have been hit on the head with a club, which would have left a linear, diastatic, depressed, or stellate skull fracture.[68] If his throat was cut, or heart removed, there should be little problem identifying the wounds, assuming the body is sufficiently intact. A man intoxicated with *chicha* before his death might have traces of metabolized alcohol in his liver, assuming the organ is extremely well preserved, which is unlikely.

TABLE 3.2. CHRONICLERS WHO DISCUSS CAPTURED WARRIOR SACRIFICE

Chronicler	Original Publication Date (or Year When Written)	Date of Reprint	Pages Dealing with Warrior Sacrifice
Alcayá	late 16th century?	1914?	156
Avila	1598	1991	120/sec. 321
Betanzos	1557	1996	87–90
Cabello de Balboa	1586	1920	35
Cieza de León	1553	1985	222
Cobo	1653	1979	143, 154
Gutiérrez de Santa Clara	1548	1905	438
Murúa	1590	1962	61/fol. 34–34v

Cultural traits of a *runa* sacrificial victim would include fine clothing of wool or cotton. He might wear sandals, a *llawt'u* (headband), and such adornments as a bracelet, rings, and necklace made of gold, silver, and copper. He most likely would be buried near a *waqa:* on top of or within sight of a hill or mountain, close to a temple or shrine, in front of a stone or altar, in a holy cave, or on an island. He would be interred with an assortment of high-status goods, including precious metals, splendid clothing, and vessels of various materials, some of which might contain food remains or corn beer residue.

It would be difficult to determine from archaeological remains why an immolation took place. An adult male ritually slain during a maize festival might be entombed with dried ears of corn, or a man dispatched to bring rain might be buried with Spondylus shell, which was commonly associated with water. Generally speaking, however, it would be hard to ascertain why a sacrifice had been made, especially in the case of a *runa* sacrifice connected with a singular event.

WARRIOR SACRIFICE

Another type of immolation that probably was not uncommon among the Inkas involved warriors captured in battle. (For a list of sources that discuss this practice, see Table 3.2.) Only a few Andean chroniclers discuss the practice. Cobo reports that during the reign of Thupa Yapanki, the inhabitants of Collao province rebelled. The king put down this insurrection and returned to Cuzco, where he celebrated by having numerous prisoners killed to honor Inti, the Sun-god.[69] The same author maintains that after Wayna Qhapaq crushed revolts by the Mojo, Chiriguano, and other ethnic groups, he commanded that the captives from his military campaigns be taken to a temple at Lake Titi Qaqa and dispatched in Inti's name.[70] Murúa relates that Thupa Yapanki conquered many peoples and provinces in Chile, whereupon he marched home with great riches and large numbers of prisoners. In the capital, the most important *kurakas* were separated from the rest of the captives and offered to the Sun.[71] Cabello de Balboa claims that Pacha Kuti started the practice of ritually slaying soldiers taken in battle. Subsequent to subjugating the Collao, this emperor returned to Cuzco with Collao Cápac, leader of the defeated group, who was put to death to thank Inti for granting the Inkas victory.[72] Gutiérrez says that the lords of Cuzco venerated *waqas* by making daily immolations to them of slaves captured in war.[73]

In the Huarochirí manuscript, there is a description of a provincial rite involving the slaying of an enemy warrior. When the inhabitants of a village in Huarochirí took a man prisoner in battle, they proffered him food and drink, and put him to death in a special ceremony. Then they flayed his face and made it into a mask. Called a *huayo,* this mask was brought out for a festival, carried around in a litter, given offerings, hung together with maize and potatoes, and worn by a dancer in the main plaza.[74] Cieza notes that during fights between neighboring groups, individuals were inevitably captured by their enemies. The prisoners were taken to temples or *waqas* and made drunk on corn beer before being dispatched by priests who cut off their heads with stone or copper knives.[75]

The ethnohistoric sources provide few details about warrior sacrifice, and the data they do furnish is inadequate for deriving material correlates. How do we make up for this lack of information? By considering several related Inka practices. First, there was the mistreatment of prisoners before they were killed, and the desecration of their weapons and insignia. Second, certain punishments were meted out by the emperor to the soldiers and *kurakas* of rebellious provinces; because these punishments often resulted in death, and included a ritual component, they might be called sacrifices. Third, there was the mutilation of warriors' corpses.

Betanzos, who discusses the degradation of captives, asserts that after the Inka defeat of the Sora, King Pacha Kuti ordered their lords to be dressed in long tunics that reached to their feet, and to which were sewn red *borlas.* It may have been humiliating to wear these tunics because the length was suggestive of women's garments, and the presence of the red *borla,* a wool fringe that served as a royal emblem, probably symbolized their conquest by the Cuzqueños. Adding to their debasement, they had to splash *chicha* on themselves and pour maize flour on their heads.[76] The emperor commanded that the rulers of other subjugated peoples be similarly treated, and he had the clothing, military insignia, and weapons of his prisoners gathered together so he could tread on them.[77] Sarmiento maintains that Pacha Kuti walked on the captives themselves, who had been thrown to the ground; while being abused, they had to remain silent and could not raise their eyes.[78]

The Inkas had brutal means for castigating rebellious leaders and their soldiers, such as pulling their eyes out (see Figure 3.1). Some of these ritualized killings could almost be considered immolations. Alcayá reports that the Chiriguano once invaded the territory of another ethnic group, which retaliated by attacking the Chiriguano, taking two hundred prisoners. The captives were marched to the imperial capital so the king could decide what to do with them. He ordered that all of them be taken to the tops of snow-capped peaks, stripped, bound hand and foot, and made to spend the night; of course, they froze to death.[79] Betanzos states that after the conquest of the Sora and other peoples who lived southeast of Cuzco, Pacha Kuti had the nobles thrown into jail with hungry jaguars. During the three days that the lords were confined, they most likely were eaten.[80] Betanzos mentions that several *kurakas* captured by Wayna Qhapaq near Quito were put in a prison with jaguars, pumas, bears, and snakes.[81] He also discusses an incident involving Pacha Kuti and some mutinous captains. The king defeated them in battle and took them prisoner, whereupon he had them hung, their heads cut off and stuck on posts, their bodies burned, and their ashes scattered from hills.[82] Garcilaso reports that the inhabitants of Puna rebelled against Wayna Qhapaq and killed a number of Inka nobles through treachery. To castigate this group, the emperor captured several thousand warriors and had them executed: they were drowned, hung, beaten with their own weapons, or had their skulls pierced with picks and lances.[83]

Once the Cuzqueños had dispatched an enemy soldier, they treated his body with contempt, often mutilating it and fashioning war trophies from it. Cieza claims that after Pacha Kuti vanquished the Chanca, he commanded that a large house be built at the site of the battle. There were kept the remains of the dead Chanca, whose corpses had been flayed, their skins stuffed with ashes and straw. In some cases, their bellies had been fashioned into drums, and their hands positioned so it looked like they were playing the instruments; in other instances, flutes had been placed in their mouths.[84] Cobo maintains that after Thupa Yapanki squelched an uprising

FIGURE 3.1.   *Noble of Qulla Suyu being tortured by the Inkas (Guaman Poma 1980a: 124).*

by the Sora, he had their two principal lords killed, their heads chopped off and put on pikes, and their bodies skinned. Their hides became the heads of drums.[85] According to Guaman Poma, the Inkas not only fashioned drums from the skin of their enemies, but drinking vessels from their skulls, flutes from their long bones, and necklaces from their teeth.[86] Several of this chronicler's drawings show Inka warriors holding trophy heads (see Figure 3.2).[87] Cobo says that soldiers wore strings of human teeth, extracted from the mouths of men they killed in battle, around their necks.[88]

Mangling the corpse of a foe was not the only way to degrade him.

FIGURE 3.2.   *Inka soldier holding the head of a noble from Qulla Suyu (Guaman Poma 1980a: 130).*

Betanzos tells us that following one large military engagement, Pacha Kuti forbade anyone from burying the bodies of the vanquished so they would be eaten by foxes and birds, and so their bones would be visible on the battlefield, serving as permanent reminders of the fate of Inka enemies.[89]

Mutilating a warrior's corpse did not always imply dishonoring him, though. In the case described by Avila, the villagers from Huarochirí venerated the mask they made from a prisoner's face, carrying it in a litter for two days, and giving it offerings of food and drink.[90]

The ethnohistoric sources provide few explanations for why the lords of Cuzco and other Andean groups immolated warriors. Several authors—among them Cobo,[91] Murúa,[92] and Cabello[93]—note that the Inkas ritually slew enemy soldiers to pay homage to the Sun. Such offerings probably were meant to thank Inti, the patron god of the conquering state, for giving his children victory in their military campaigns. Warriors may also have been put to death to celebrate masculine courage. In the story from Huarochirí, as a villager danced while wearing the flayed face of his enemy, he would say, "This is our valor!"[94] Another possible reason for dispatching prisoners relates to fertility. Avila mentions that the mask would be hung along with maize and potatoes, and that offerings would be left for it, presumably so it would share its "vital powers"[95] and increase the fecundity of the crops.

Material Correlates of Warrior Immolation

We can derive some material correlates for warrior sacrifice from the data contained in the chronicles. The imperial army was made up mostly of *runas* fulfilling their labor obligations to the state. As these individuals were the ones most likely to be captured in battle and dispatched in special rites, the vast majority of victims should be able-bodied males between twenty-five and fifty,[96] as with *runa* immolation. Warrior sacrifice, however, differs in the treatment of victims. Whereas a man would be buried in fine garments and with great riches in a *runa* sacrifice, a captive warrior would probably be interred with little or no clothing and few, if any, goods. Captive soldiers are said to have been stripped bare, and a warrior slain by his foes would rarely be entombed with his weapons or insignia, for to have done so would have been to show him respect. Instead, most prisoners were humiliated and demeaned, and their personal belongings were often gathered together, tread on by the emperor as a symbol of conquest, and stored in a special building. A sacrificed captive would only be buried with military accoutrements if they had been purposely broken.

In terms of burial, the body of a *runa* who was ritually dispatched was handled differently from the corpse of an immolated warrior. The former was respectfully interred in a carefully dug grave, the latter haphazardly dumped in a shallow pit or left unburied, in which case there could be gnaw marks on the bones made by rodents, foxes, and other animals. If the soldier's body had lain around for a while and conditions were dry, there also could be maggots and beetle larvae preserved in the thoracic cavity and soft tissue.[97]

Victims of a *runa* sacrifice were slain quickly and painlessly: they were often given corn beer to drink and/or coca leaves to chew so they would be intoxicated when they met their ends. Warriors, in contrast, went to their deaths sober and in pain, often from being tortured. I would not expect to find the metabolites of alcohol and/or cocaine in the liver, assuming it were well preserved, of a soldier. There might be different kinds of wounds visible in the soft tissue of such a victim made by stabbing, smashing, chopping, and/or slashing weapons, and marks left on the bones. The body of a warrior might also have been bound hand and foot.

The body of a *runa* chosen for sacrifice by his own people was supposed to be perfect; it would not have been mutilated. The corpse of a soldier killed by his enemies might be badly disfigured, even cut to pieces. Sometimes the head may have been chopped off for a trophy, in which case there would be one or more cervical vertebra missing from the body because they would be articulated with the skull. Extensive damage to the face might be evident if the teeth had been knocked out so they could be strung into a necklace. Also, an arm or leg might be mangled from the removal of a long bone for fashioning a flute. If the head or corpse was flayed to make a mask or drum, there might be cut marks on the underlying bones.

It would be difficult to determine why a particular captive was sacrificed based solely on materials from the archaeological record. If he had been offered to the Sun, his remains might be discovered near a temple or shrine dedicated to Inti. On the other hand, if his ritual slaughter was connected with fertility, he may have been interred with dried potatoes, maize, or other cultigens. His flayed face, assuming it was made into a mask, may be found with various agricultural products. A warrior dispatched as part of a celebration of masculine valor may have been extensively mutilated; people might also have tried to appropriate his courage by fashioning trophies from parts of his body, which would have been worn or displayed on special occasions.

NECROPAMPA

The fourth type of immolation, called *necropampa,* involved the sacrifice of the wives, children, and servants of a deceased lord or king, and their subsequent burial with him. A number of ethnohistoric sources discuss this practice and its connection with the Inkas (see Table 3.3).[98] Betanzos maintains that when Pacha Kuti expired, his wives, sons, daughters, and retainers were asked if they wanted to follow him into the next

TABLE 3.3. CHRONICLERS WHO DISCUSS *NECROPAMPA* SACRIFICE

Chronicler	Original Publication Date (or Year When Written)	Date of Reprint	Pages Dealing with Necropampa Sacrifice
Acosta	1590	1880	313–314, 344, 433
Anónimo	1573	1897a	93–94/sec. 167
Atienza	1572	1931	155
Bello Galloso	1582	1897	193/sec. 14
Betanzos	1557	1996	131–132, 162
		1987	141–142, 177
Cieza de León	1553	1985	222, 223, 230, 262–264, 266–268, 309, 310, 357–358
		1959	110, 274–276, 308–310, 311–312
Cobo	1653	1979	161
Herrera	1610	1730	92
Matienzo	1567	1967	9, 128, 129
Montesinos	1644	1920	65
Murúa	1590	1964	99/fol. 252
		1962	35, 104
		1946	76, 245
Oviedo y Valdez	1535–1557	1959	101
Pachacuti Yamqui	1613	1873	100, 104
Pizarro	1571	1921	226
Polo de Ondegardo	1571	1916b	92
Ramos Gavilán	1621	1976	72
Toledo	1580	1989	414/sec. 5
Zárate	1556	1968	52

world. The high-status people who said yes were dressed in fine clothing and adorned with gold and silver jewelry, while lower-status individuals received items appropriate to their position in the emperor's household. The victims took part in a great celebration that included singing, dancing, eating, and drinking *chicha*. Once intoxicated, they were strangled and interred with their lord. Women went to the grave holding small jars of corn beer, bags of coca leaves, and pots containing toasted and cooked maize; they were surrounded by plates, bowls, jars, and tumblers of gold and silver. Men were placed in the tomb according to the work they did for the king during their lives.[99] The chronicler Pachacuti gives additional information on the rituals relating to the death of King Pacha Kuti; he says the monarch was buried with many of his pages and old captains so they could continue to help him in the afterlife.[100]

Betanzos and Pachacuti also discuss the interment of Thupa Yapanki. According to Betanzos, when the emperor expired, he was honored in the same way as his predecessor, meaning he was entombed with numerous people whose final wish was to go with him to the other world. Some were so impatient to join him that they strangled themselves—the men with rope, the women with their *chumpi* (belts).[101] Pachacuti states that Thupa Yapanki was buried not only with his most beloved wives, but with attendants and administrative officials, all of whose services he would need.[102] Thupa was succeeded by Wayna Qhapaq. With this monarch's demise, Cobo tells us, more than a thousand individuals were killed and interred with him, many offering themselves of their own free will, content to die for him.[103] Among the victims were women he had loved, retainers, and bureaucrats who had worked for him; their sacrifices were preceded by funerary rites that included eating, drinking, singing, and dancing.[104] Atawalpa, Wayna Qhapaq's son, was executed by the Spanish conquistadors in 1533. According to Pizarro, the Inkas then hung one of his sisters, several Indian women, and a number of his soldiers so the victims could follow him to the afterlife.[105]

As documented by numerous ethnohistoric sources, *necropampa* sacrifice was practiced by various provincial groups during the Late Horizon and early colonial period. Cieza provides a description of the sepulture of a lord from the Puerto Viejo area in Ecuador, and asserts that on the day of his burial, the local folk gathered to cry, sing, drink, and dance to the sound of drums and other instruments. Then they lowered the deceased into a deep pit along with jewels, food, vessels containing *chicha,* and two or three beautiful women he had loved. Live children were sometimes entombed with such a *kuraka.*[106]

Zárate talks about a typical funeral held for a local ruler that does not appear to have been very different from the one detailed by Cieza. The ceremony involved dressing the lord in his finest garments and placing him in a vault, seated on his *duho* (a low stool that symbolized his high status). Around him were placed gold and silver vessels. Two or three of his favorite wives were ritually slain; to avoid conflict between them as to who should have this honor, the *kuraka* usually decided before he died. Along with the women, some of his officers and boys who had worked as attendants were killed and interred with him. The reason given for these immolations is that when the local ruler returned to life, he would expect to be served and would want the companionship of loved ones.[107]

The ethnohistoric sources mention few motives behind *necropampa* sacrifice. The most common explanation for why folks were put to death and buried with a king or lord was so they could assist him and keep him company.[108] Bello Galloso discusses the practice as it existed in the region around Cuenca, Ecuador. He implies that if a *kuraka* were to wake in the other world and find that he lacked some necessity—such as food, drink, or attendants to wait on him—he would become angry and punish his own people. Therefore, they considered it vital to send children and other individuals with him to the grave.[109] Cieza maintains that the interment of a ruler with live victims brought prestige.[110]

Betanzos hints at a connection between *necropampa* sacrifice and social hierarchy. There are periods in the historical trajectories of monarchies that are unstable, one of which begins with the death of a ruler and ends with the consolidation of power by his/her successor. During such a transition of authority, the new leader needs an institution or practice that can be relied upon to reaffirm the existing social order, with the new leader at its apex.[111] The funerary rites for a deceased emperor probably fulfilled this function in the Inka state. According to Betanzos, the monarch was buried not only with his principal wives, but with a few of his children, servants, and officers, each wearing the clothing and accoutrements considered appropriate to their gender, status, and office in the household. At least some people were placed in the tomb according to the jobs they had held; the door-keeper was positioned near the entrance.[112] Thus, the imperial social system was reproduced in the grave, though in simplified form. The hierarchical system could have been made explicit to the living populace, and been reinforced in their minds, through their participation in the public ceremonies by which the king and his companions were laid to rest.

Material Correlates of Necropampa Sacrifice

The data from the chronicles can be used to formulate material correlates for *necropampa* sacrifice. A victim of this type of rite would be located in a tomb along with the tomb's principal occupant: a high-status individual who often, though not always, would be male, and who would tend to be fairly old. The victim could be male—as in the case of a son, retainer, or officer—or female—such as a wife, daughter, or servant. Unlike the victims of other forms of sacrifice, these individuals would be from varied age-grades: young, elderly, or anything in between. Regarding the manner in which *necropampa* sacrifice victims met their end, several ethnohistoric sources mention strangulation and hanging,[113] which can fracture the victim's hyoid bone or thyroid cartilage. Four works discuss live interment, which would leave no mark on the body.[114] With respect to the number of people whose remains might be found as part of a single burial, it could range anywhere from one—not including the corpse of the deceased lord—to more than a thousand, although the last figure, quoted in connection with Wayna Qhapaq, is probably an exaggeration.

Because victims put to death in *necropampa* rituals were treated with reverence, I would expect their bodies to have been carefully laid in a sepulture. Generally, they should be well dressed, wear a variety of adornments, and be surrounded by grave goods. Looking closely at a specific burial, we should see clear differences between individuals with respect to the quality, quantity, and diversity of materials associated with them; their clothing, jewelry, and other possessions should vary depending on their status, gender, and occupation. The higher the status, the better the quality, and the greater the quantity and diversity, of items left with her or him. A woman of high birth who was the principal wife of a lord might wear a mantle and an ankle-length dress bound at the waist by a sash, all of fine alpaca wool. The main hues in her outfit might be white, red, and yellow, and she would likely be wearing a necklace and bracelets made of gold and silver. Surrounding her might be plates, bowls, jars, and tumblers, likewise of precious metals. A female of lower status might have the same basic outfit as her noble counterpart, but one made from rougher and naturally colored llama wool. She might have a necklace or bracelet, though of silver or copper, and any bowls and jars at her side would probably be wood or ceramic. Both women might hold jars of corn beer and pots containing cooked food. Male victims might also have been laid in the grave with their specialized tools or placed in an appropriate part of the tomb. This differential treatment of people in *necropampa* sacrifice contrasts with the other three types of immolation—*qhapaq hucha, runa,* and warrior—where the respective victims were treated in a similar manner.

According to the chronicles, before individuals were ritually killed and interred with their lord, they were feasted, which included eating, drinking *chicha,* and possibly chewing coca. Consequently, I would expect to discover the remains of the victim's last meal in her/his stomach and perhaps metabolites of alcohol and/or cocaine in the liver, though this organ deteriorates quickly. If the person drank and chewed at least ten days before

TABLE 3.4. MAJOR FEATURES OF THE DIFFERENT TYPES OF SACRIFICE DISCUSSED BY THE CHRONICLERS

	Types of Sacrifice			
Features of Sacrifice	Necropampa *(Burial with Deceased Ruler)*	Runa *(Able-Bodied "Citizen")*	*War Captive*	Qhapaq Hucha *(Specially Chosen Child or Woman)*
Number of Victims	one (for local noble) – thousands (in emperor's case)	one–several	one–several	one, pair
Sexes of victims	Subtype A: female (daughter, concubine, wife) Subtype B: male (son, servant, official)	male	male	Subtype A: male or female (child) Subtype B: female (aqlla-kuna, one of the "chosen women")
Age(s) of Victim(s)	A and B: child–older adult	post-adolescent youth to middle-aged adult	post-adolescent youth to middle-aged adult	A: 4–10 years old (child) B: 10 years old to young adult
Cause(s) of Death	suffocation, strangulation, burial alive	strangulation	severe bodily trauma: result of blows, torture, dismemberment, decapitation	strangulation, burial alive, throat cut, blow to head
Position(s) of Body(ies)	extended, fetal	extended, fetal	splayed, haphazardly dumped	fetal

Adornments Worn	social status of individual	generally, best clothing and adornments owned by victim	(loincloth), *unku* (tunic), cloak, sandals adornments: *llaut'u* (headband), bracelet of precious metal	group B: clothing and adornments of noble woman: *aqsu* (dress) bound at waist by sash; *lliklla* (mantle) fastened at chest by *tupu* (pin) main colors of clothing: red, yellow, white
Associated Artifacts	A: gold and silver vessels, bags of coca leaves, remains of food items B: material items indicating occupation and social status of victim	gold and silver vessels, *qipi* (knapsack)	none–few	A and B: human and animal figurines of gold, silver, copper; Spondylus shell; coca leaves; feathers; textiles B: spoons, bowls, plates
Special Features	A and B: victim buried with high-status, relatively old male or female	burial carried out at site of *uaqa* (religious shrine or sacred place) According to Las Casas, such sacrifices were rare.	victim not formally interred; may have been dumped in pit victim not usually buried with uniform or weapons victim's hands or feet may be bound	A: sometimes a pair of children buried together, male with female A and B: burial sometimes carried out at site of *uaqa* Sacrifice often took place in what was to child a foreign province; child's clothing should differ from that of local people. According to Guaman Poma, such sacrifices were relatively common.

TABLE 3.5. CHRONICLERS WHO DISCUSS SUBSTITUTE SACRIFICE

Chronicler	Original Publication Date (or Year When Written)	Date of Reprint	Pages Dealing with Substitute Sacrifice
Acosta	1590	1880	344
Calancha and Torres	1657	1972	155/sec. 4
Cobo	1653	1990	112–113
Herrera	1610	1730	92
Montesinos	1644	1920	37
Murúa	1590	1964	120/fol. 267
Ramos Gavilán	1621	1976	73

her/his immolation, there might be a metabolite of alcohol and cocaine fixed into her/his hair shafts. For a comparison of the basic features of *qhapaq hucha, runa,* warrior, and *necropampa* sacrifice, see Table 3.4.

SUBSTITUTE SACRIFICE

The fifth type of immolation, which seems to have been less important than the other four, has been termed "substitute sacrifice." (For a list of sources that discuss this practice, see Table 3.5.) The practice involved offering the life of one person to a deity to pacify it so it would not take the life of another individual. The Andean chroniclers provide little information on this kind of immolation, perhaps because it mostly took place at the household level rather than at the more visible community, provincial, or imperial levels.

Acosta provides one description of substitute sacrifice (and his words are repeated by Cobo and Ramos), saying that when an Indian got very sick, he would consult a diviner or priest. If told he was going to die, then the man, regardless of his social status, would ritually slay his son to honor Wira Qucha or Inti. He would ask the god to accept the vitality of his child in place of his own, thus hoping to escape death.[115] Herrera reports that when a *kuraka's* health was failing, he sometimes would offer his son to a *waqa,* invoking the idol and imploring it to spare him.[116] At the imperial level, the Inka practice of dispatching *qhapaq huchas* when the king was ailing may have been a form of substitute immolation (see the discussion in Chapter 2). Calancha and Torres report that men also were sacrificed when the emperor was sick,[117] which is not surprising since he was considered the "father" of his people.[118]

The ethnohistoric sources tell us nothing about how substitute victims were slain, nor anything about the ceremonies that preceded and succeeded their deaths. No details are offered about where a victim was interred, or about the grave goods left with him. This paucity of information makes it difficult to derive material correlates for the practice. Nevertheless, it appears that victims were usually male, between the ages of four and twelve. If the victim was a child of a *runa* and his immolation took place at the household level, his body may be buried close to a habitation structure, perhaps under the floor. If he was the son of a *kuraka* and his life was offered to a *waqa,* his remains would likely be entombed nearby. A victim's corpse would have been treated with respect and carefully laid to rest, perhaps with grave goods. The quality of the clothing and adornments—and the quality and quantity of other items buried with the victim—would tend to reflect his social status.

Four   MOUNTAIN WORSHIP

*They [the Indians of Peru] worshiped . . . hills which were
different in shape or substance from those nearby, being formed
of earth or sand, where the rest were rocky, or vice versa. Also
included was the snow-capped mountain range and any other
sierra or high peak which had snow on it, boulders or large rocks,
cliffs . . . as well as the high places and hilltops called* apachitas.
(Cobo 1990: 45)

As I state at the outset, I believe—based on the ethnohistoric sources and the work of Andean scholars—that the Inkas manipulated
two types of ritual to unify the southern part of the empire. The first was
human sacrifice, which we have examined in detail. The second type of rite
was mountain worship, the subject of this chapter.[1] Mountain veneration
was very important and widespread in the Andes. As with immolation, a
great deal of data was recorded on the practice by the chroniclers of the
sixteenth through eighteenth centuries, who are listed in Table 4.1.

Not all chroniclers are primary and independent sources; later writers
copied extensively from earlier ones, usually without citing them. Cobo's
list of sacred shrines in the Cuzco area is taken verbatim from Polo.[2] Likewise, Murúa's description of *apachitas* is taken almost word for word from
Polo.[3]

When I started investigating mountain worship, I thought the research
would be simple and straightforward. The more ethnohistoric documents I
read, however, the more I realized how wrong I was, for they discuss a bewildering variety of beliefs and practices connected with high peaks. Some
of this variation probably relates to regional differences, change through
time, and the individual authors' biases. I suspect, though, that much of
the variation reported by the chroniclers relates to the sheer complexity of
Andean religion.

THE NATURE OF MOUNTAINS AS
REPRESENTED IN THE CHRONICLES

Two authors, Arriaga and Avila, assert that Andean peoples venerated summits as gods.[4] Two others take the opposite viewpoint: Valera says emphatically that the natives of Peru did not regard mountains as deities, nor as living beings. Rather, certain peaks—those that stood out from the rest because of their heights or other distinctive features—were respected and used as places of worship. Such summits were said to be the creations of Illa Tiksi, whom Valera equates with the eternal god of Christianity.[5] Valera's position is echoed by Garcilaso.[6] Why is there such a discrepancy between the assertions of Arriaga and Avila, and those of Valera and Garcilaso? The first pair were Jesuits who took part in the brutal campaign to wipe out the indigenous religion of the Andes.[7] By portraying native beliefs and practices as pagan—that is, by claiming the Peruvians worshipped summits as gods—they were trying to justify their ruthless campaign.[8] Valera and Garcilaso, the sons of indigenous women, were sympathetic to the autochthonous people[9] and wanted to show the Spanish that Andean religion was similar to Christianity; they deny that high mountains were considered deities.[10]

Many authors say that peaks and hills were venerated as *waqas,*[11] the term for anything imbued with sacred power. In their respective works, and sometimes in different parts of the same work, mountain-*waqas* are conceived of in various ways, including (1) as the physical manifestations of living and divine beings; (2) as the fossilized remains of mythical heroes; (3) as the residences of deities or the places they occupy; (4) as oracles;[12] and (5) as *paqarikus,* the "places of origin" of specific ethnic groups.[13]

Mountain-Waqas *as the Manifestations of Living and Divine Beings*

Paz Maldonado, writing in the late sixteenth century, gives examples of high summits thought of as living and divine beings. In the region around Quito, the indigenous folk believed that two volcanoes—Chimborazo and Tunguragua—were, respectively, male and female, husband and wife. Not only did the peaks communicate, they visited one another and had sex.[14] Ulloa lists the five mountain-*waqas* near Arequipa thought to behave in an anthropomorphic way; they periodically got angry and had to be placated with offerings, including human sacrifices.[15] Avila and Dávila Brizeño recount a myth in which the two main charac-

TABLE 4.1. CHRONICLERS WHO DISCUSS MOUNTAIN WORSHIP

Chronicler	Original Publication Date (or Year When Written)	Date of Reprint	Pages Dealing with Mountain Worship
Acosta	1590	1880	308
Agustinos	1557	1918	35
Albornoz	1583?	1967	20–21, 26–35
Anónimo	late 16th century	1897b	132
Arriaga	1621	1968	23–24, 165/sec. 1
Avedaño	1617	1904	380
Avila	1598	1991	43/sec. 3; 67/sec. 99; 72/secs. 119–121; 74–76/secs. 135–140; 93/ sec. 209; 94/sec. 213; 112/sec. 281; 122/sec. 329; 128/sec. 357
		1904	388
Ayala	1614	1976	275, 278–280, 282–283
Bello Galloso	1582	1897	172/sec. 14, 173–174/ sec. 16, 179/sec. 14, 184/sec. 14, 189/sec. 14, 193/sec. 14
Betanzos	1557	1996	44
		1987	49–50
		1968	245
Bibar	1558	1966	138
Cabeza de Vaca	1586	1885	71/sec. 14
Cobo	1653	1990	45, 54, 58, 60, 61, 65–67, 72, 73, 75, 77, 79, 81–83
Fornee	1586	1885	217/sec. 14
Garcilaso de la Vega	1609	1991	171–172
		1961	91–92
Guaman Poma de Ayala	1615	1980a	253
		1978	76
Guerra y Céspedes	1582	1881	85/sec. 14
Herrera	1610	1730	91, 93
Jesuíta Anónimo	1613	1918	183, 189, 190
Mercado de Peñalosa	1586	1885	57

TABLE 4.1. (CONTINUED)

Chronicler	Original Publication Date (or Year When Written)	Date of Reprint	Pages Dealing with Mountain Worship
Molina of Cuzco	1575?	1873	4–5, 8–9, 17–18, 55–57, 59
Monzón	1586	1881a	172/sec. 14
		1881b	188/sec. 14
Murúa	1590	1964	110/fol. 260, 112–113/ fols. 261–261v
		1946	271–272, 281–284, 289, 398
Noboa	1658	1986	248/fol. 117
Pachacuti Yamqui	1613	1873	96, 104
Paz Maldonado	late 16th century?	1897	150–152
Polo de Ondegardo	1571	1917	4, 8, 9, 10–12, 15, 20–22, 28, 29, 33, 34, 36, 38–42
	1554	1916a	43, 193/sec. 8
	1571	1916b	114
	1567	1916c	189–191/secs. 1, 9–12, 193/sec. 8, 194/sec. 1, 198/sec. 5
	1567	1873	155
Ramos Gavilán	1621	1976	68
Rocha	1681	1891	8
Sarmiento de Gamboa	1572	1907	212
Torres	1657	1974	95
Ulloa Mogollón	1586	1885	40–41/sec. 1, 44–45/ sec. 14
Valera	1590	1968	157
Velasco	1789	1978	61–62

ters—Parya Qaqa (usually written "Paria Caca"), a snow-capped peak, and Wallullu (often written "Huallallo," "Guallallo," or "Uallullo"), a volcano— are portrayed as supermen.[16] In this story, Parya Qaqa battles Wallullu and throws water and hail at him until he extinguishes the latter's fire and defeats him.

*Mountain-*Waqas *as the Fossilized Remains
of Mythical Heroes*

Another legend from Avila takes place in central Peru and
explains how various features of the natural landscape formed; these features are described as the petrified remains of monsters and a mythical
hero. The tale involves Parya Qaqa chasing Wallullu, who tries to destroy
his pursuer by sending a giant two-headed snake and a huge parrot with
open wings against him. Parya Qaqa strikes the snake with a golden staff
and breaks off one of the parrot's wings, turning both to stone. Defeated,
Wallullu flees to the lowlands. To make sure the volcano-deity never returns, Parya Qaqa leaves a brother, Paria Carco, to keep watch at a pass
overlooking the tropical region of Antis, and he becomes a snow-capped
peak and *waqa.*[17]

*Mountain-*Waqas *as the Residences of Deities*

In a third myth related by Avila, a mountain (though not
necessarily a *waqa*) is depicted as the residence of a supernatural being:

> Parya Qaqa and his [four] brothers entered this crag and made
> it their home, saying, "Here I [a single god with five manifes-
> tations] shall dwell."[18]

An earlier passage states that Parya Qaqa "established his dwelling on the
heights."[19] We are told that Wallullu resides at a place called "Upper Paria
Caca," which is a mountain and *waqa.*[20] Also, Wallullu is said to enter a
summit known as Caqui Yoca and to hide there.[21]

*Mountain-*Waqas *as Oracles*

Velasco discusses the oracular nature of the volcano Coto-
paxi, located in the northern part of the Inka state. He tells us the peak was
highly esteemed by the Peruvians because one of its eruptions foretold the
fall of the empire at the hands of foreign invaders.[22] An anonymous source,
writing in the 1570s, talks about the inhabitants of Chapi, a village near
Quito. Before going on a trip, these folks would climb to the top of a high
hill, leave an offering, and ask what the future held for them. They particularly wanted to know if they would die while on the road.[23] Matienzo
does not see the mountains themselves as augurs, but says it was common

for *waqas* with oracular functions to be situated on peaks.[24] Cieza[25] reports on Qhuru Puna, one of the most venerated summits in Kunti Suyu,[26] and mentions there was a *waqa* on its slopes that served as an oracle. Betanzos states that in Guamachuco province, there was an idol located on a lofty peak. Many people—including Atawalpa, who would later become emperor—made sacrifices to the idol and put questions to it about the future. Its prophecies were made known by an old man.[27]

Mountain-Waqas *as* Paqarikus

Numerous ethnic groups worshipped peaks as *paqarikus,*[28] which can be loosely translated as "places of dawn/birth."[29] Molina of Cuzco recounts a creation myth that explains the relationship between high summits and human origins. In the beginning, Wira Qucha fashioned the progenitors of each nation from clay, painting these figures with the clothing they were to wear and giving them hair of the proper length. Then the god brought the statues to life. He ordered them to go underground, follow subterranean passages, and emerge at specific points on the earth's surface. Many of the ancestors appeared from mountains and hills, which became their *waqas.*[30] Ulloa tells us that the Collagua, who dwelt in the Arequipa area, believed they originated from the volcano Collaguata; the Cavana, who lived nearby, thought their ancestors came from Mount Gualcagualca.[31] According to Albornoz, the members of an ethnic group in Parinacocha considered Sara Sara to be their *paqariku,* while the inhabitants of Tomebamba regarded Guasaynan as their place of dawn.[32] Paz Maldonado discusses another people who resided near Tomebamba; he says they revered Chimborazo Volcano for the role it played in their origin myth.[33] It has been reported that the Indians of Guamachuco traced their lineage to a mountain called Guacat,[34] and that the residents of Urcos believed they came from the peak Ausangate.[35]

There is another type of origin story that relates to lofty summits considered to be *waqas.* The legends comprising this category typically concern a man who is saved from a primordial flood by a peak and goes on to become the progenitor of an ethnic group and to establish a cult devoted to the mountain.[36] In the version told by the Cañari of southern Ecuador, two brothers take refuge from a deluge on a hill called Huaca Yñan. As the waters surrounding the hill get deeper, it grows higher, so the men remain dry. When the flood subsides, the brothers mate with a parrot that has taken female form, thus becoming the ancestors of the Cañari, and begin to worship Huaca Yñan.[37]

In a variant of this myth from the Huarochirí area, a man is warned by his llama that the ocean will soon overflow, inundating the world. The man grabs food for five days and hurries with his llama to the top of Mount Villca Coto, where he finds various animals: pumas, foxes, guanacos, and condors. Immediately, the ocean starts to rise. Five days later, the waters subside, by which time everyone on earth has drowned except the man, who begins to multiply and repopulate the region.[38] A similar story was recorded in Ancasmarca province, close to Cuzco. It involves a herder whose llamas become depressed and stop eating during the day, and who spend their nights staring up at the sky. When the man asks them why they are so distracted, they point to a group of stars overhead and tell him the celestial bodies are discussing the earth's destruction by an enormous flood. Upon hearing this news, the herder calls together his six children and urges them to gather all their food and livestock, whereupon they make their way to the top of Ancasmarca Hill. As the floodwaters rise, so does Ancasmarca, and as the waters recede, so does the peak; the man and his children are saved and go on to people the land.[39] Albornoz says that the inhabitants of Tomebamba believed their progenitor was rescued from a deluge by a mountain-*waqa* known as Puna.[40]

The different conceptions of mountain-*waqas* were not mutually exclusive. Consider the case of Wana Kawri. Cieza notes that this hill near the capital was one of the most revered places in the empire, second only to the Quri Kanchi, the Temple of the Sun.[41] He says its sacredness could partially be attributed to the vital role it played in the origin myth of the Inkas, and partly to its function as an oracle. Sarmiento recounts a Cuzqueño legend illustrating this point. It begins with the appearance of eight siblings—four brothers (Manqu Qhapaq, Ayar Awka, Ayar Kachi, and Ayar Uchu) and four sisters (Mama Uqllu, Mama Waqa, Mama Ipakura, and Mama Rawa)—from their *paqariku,* which was called Qhapaq T'uqu ("royal window"). They immediately set out in search of fertile lands to conquer and people to subjugate. After various adventures, they climb to the summit of Wana Kawri, where they have a tremendous view of the Cuzco Valley with a rainbow arching over it. They take the rainbow to be an omen that they should settle there. Then Ayar Uchu, the youngest brother, begins to turn into a *waqa* of stone (as a fossilized hero, he is called Wana Kawri). Realizing what is happening, he makes his siblings promise that before they celebrate a festival or carry out a major ritual, they will

FIGURE 4.1.   *Thupa Yapanki consulting with Wana Kawri and other* waqas *on the past and future (Guaman Poma 1980a: 235).*

venerate him. He also foretells the day when the Inkas will be great lords, inaugurating Wana Kawri as an augur.[42]

To corroborate the notion that Wana Kawri was associated with divination, we return to the chronicler Cieza. He maintains that there was an oracle on the hill where the Devil spoke to the Cuzqueños.[43] One of Guaman Poma's drawings (see Figure 4.1) shows Thupa Yapanki consulting a group of *waqas,* including Wana Kawri, on the past and future of the world.[44]

THE FORMS THAT MOUNTAIN-DEITIES TAKE

In the ethnohistoric literature, mountain-*waqas* are represented in a number of ways. Villca Coto, according to Avila, is a peak located between the towns of Huanri and Surco, while Parya Qaqa is said to be a snow-capped summit, as is his brother Paria Carco.[45] Some mountain-deities have the attributes of active volcanoes.[46] Pachacuti Yamqui recounts a story in which a *waqa* called Cancuay sends forth fire.[47] In the Huarochirí manuscript, Wallullu flames up "in the form of a giant fire reaching almost to the heavens,"[48] Parya Qaqa has breath like bluish smoke,[49] and his son, Maca Uisa, is depicted with bright greenish-blue vapor issuing from his mouth.[50]

Mountain-*waqas* could appear as humans too. One myth portrays Parya Qaqa as a "full-grown person" who goes to a village called Huaqui and sits down at a banquet with the locals.[51] In other legends, he turns into five brothers whose names are Parya Qaqa, Churapa, Puncho, Paria Carco, and Sullca Yllapa.[52] This "unfolding" of a single deity into various distinct beings, each with its own character and powers, is not unique to the Huarochirí myth-cycle. Based on his analysis of ethnohistoric documents, Demarest argues that the Inka god Inti could be similarly unfolded into four celestial deities.[53]

A mountain-*waqa* could also assume the guise of an animal; Parya Qaqa takes the form of five eggs on a high peak, from which hatch five falcons that fly away.[54]

Mountain-deities were associated with meteorological phenomena[55] and sometimes took on the attributes of storm-gods. Parya Qaqa appears on the summit of Condor Coto as five *runto*,[56] a word that translates both as "eggs" and "hailstones."[57] When this mythical character gets angry at the people in the village of Huauqui Usa, he bombards them with red and yellow hail.[58] In Dávila's narration of his encounter with Wallullu,[59] Parya Qaqa uses hailstones as weapons.

At various points in the Huarochirí myth-cycle, Parya Qaqa is connected with cloudbursts and uncontrolled water.[60] He punishes the inhabitants of Huauqui Usa not only by pelting them with hail, but by inundating them with rain; the rain becomes a flood that rushes down a mountain slope, creating mudslides that carry the people away.[61] In Avila's account of Parya Qaqa's battle with Wallullu, the former deity becomes five brothers who produce a red and yellow downpour that comes from five directions;[62] in Dávila's variant of the story, Parya Qaqa is alone and fights with torrents of water.[63] There is another Parya Qaqa legend in which the god is associated with precipitation: while visiting San Damián, he gets angry because nobody will offer him a drink and destroys the hamlet with red and yellow rain or with a red downpour, depending on the version.[64]

Maca Uisa, like his father Parya Qaqa, is linked with cloudbursts and the unchecked flow of water. He once helped the Inka put down a revolt by going to the top of a hill and making it rain so hard that the rebels were swept away.[65] A final *waqa* from the Huarochirí manuscript that is connected with unregulated water is Collquiri, who appears on a mountain overlooking the hamlet of Yampilla and falls in love with a young woman living there.[66] He vows to marry her, but first he must dig a hole from a spring to the hamlet's fields; upon completion of this task, so much water rushes through the hole, it threatens to destroy the crops.[67]

Other meteorological phenomena identified with mountain-*waqas* include wind, fog, snow, and lightning. There are several instances where Parya Qaqa makes the wind blow, including when he is dwelling on Mount Condor Coto in the form of five eggs,[68] and when he is offended by the Colli because they will not invite him to drink. In the second example, he sends the Colli flying head over heels with a fierce gale.[69] A brief passage in the Huarochirí manuscript links Parya Qaqa to fog: before this *waqa* wipes out the inhabitants of San Damián, he produces a small cloud of fog that appears from a high peak.[70] Other episodes in the myth-cycle connect Parya Qaqa with snow. In one story, he is identified as a snow-capped summit,[71] while in another, he gives a "snow garment" to his son, Huatya Curi, who proceeds to dance in it, dazzling and blinding a group of spectators.[72] Paria Carco, one of Parya Qaqa's brothers and a mountain-deity in his own right, is likewise said to wear a mantle of white.[73] Cases of lightning use by *waqas* include the confrontations between Parya Qaqa and Wallullu, where the former blasts the latter with bolts.[74] Also, when Parya Qaqa eradicates the inhabitants of San Damián, he flashes lightning at them,[75] and when Maca Uisa destroys the Sapa Inka's enemies, he hurls bolts at them.[76]

SACRED MOUNTAINS, VENERATED STONES, AND IDOLS

Both Polo and Cobo, the second having plagiarized the work of the first, give detailed descriptions of the *siq'e* system around Cuzco.[77] As I explain in Chapter 2, this system consisted of 41 *siq'es* (sight-lines) that radiated out from the Quri Kancha, and that were from a dozen to several dozen kilometers long.[78] Arranged along the lines were approximately 328 *waqas*, of which 45, or about 14 percent, were mountains and hills. In Chinchay Suyu, the northwestern quarter of the Cuzco Valley (and of the empire as a whole), the fifth sacred site on the first *siq'e* was a hill called Sonconancay.[79] In the southwestern quarter, Kunti Suyu, the second *waqa* on the ninth line was the large hill Micayurco.[80] Molina lists several hallowed summits in the region surrounding the capital, including Achpiran, Succanca, Omoto Yanacauri, Ccapac Uilca, Queros Huanacauri, Rontoca, Collapata, Cuti, Suntu, Cacha Uiracocha, Yacalla Huaca, Rurama, Urcos Uiracocha, and Sulcanca.[81]

In the provinces, many prominent *waqas*—perhaps a higher percentage than in the Cuzco area—are said to be peaks and hills. Acosta states that in Nazca, situated on Peru's south coast, the people regarded a hill of sand to be their most revered site.[82] According to an anonymous Jesuit, the members of two ethnic groups, the Huacho and Yauyo, worshipped such mountains as Parya Qaqa, Tembraico, and Cunia Villca.[83] Ayala mentions that in the province of Chinchay Cocha, the populace had as its main *waqa* a rounded summit called Raco,[84] while in southern Ecuador, the Cañari venerated high peak Huaca Yñan.[85]

Albornoz inventories mountain-*waqas* throughout the Inka Empire.[86] For the Arequipa area, he lists Sara Sara, Sulimana, Qhuru Puna, Ampato, and the volcano Putina[87] (El Misti) as being important.[88] Guaman Poma discusses the principal *waqas* in each quarter of the state, at least 57 percent of which are high peaks. In Chinchay Suyu, they are Zupa Raura, Parya Qaqa, Wallullu, Ayza Bilca, Carua Razo, and Razu Bilca; for Qulla Suyu, he mentions Ausan Cata and Willka Nuta; among the mountains in Anti Suyu are Saua Ciray and Pitu Ciray; and for Kunti Suyu, he names Qhuru Puna and Putina.[89] Additional chroniclers who talk about the worship of particular summits in the provinces include Agustinos, Avila, Bello, Monzón, Paz, and Ulloa.[90]

Let us return to our discussion of the *siq'e* system of the Cuzco Valley. According to Cobo and Polo, many peaks and hills incorporated into the local network of lines had sacred idols and venerated stones, the latter known as *wanqas,* on their pinnacles. The seventh *waqa* of the sixth *siq'e* in Anti Suyu was a knoll called Curauacaja, on top of which was the preserved body of a puma.[91] In Qulla Suyu, the third sacred site on the first line was a round hill bearing the name Churucana that had three *wanqas* on its summit.[92] The ninth *waqa* of the sixth *siq'e* in Chinchay Suyu was the hill Quiangalla, on which were two pillars.[93]

Albornoz documents mountain-*waqas* in the provinces with stones or

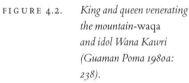

FIGURE 4.2.   King and queen venerating
the mountain-waqa
and idol Wana Kawri
(Guaman Poma 1980a:
238).

FIGURE 4.3.   People of Anti Suyu
offering a child to the
mountains Saua Ciray
and Pitu Ciray, which
have idols on them. The
creature on the left is an
otorongo, or jaguar
(Guaman Poma 1980a:
242).

idols on their crests. One peak, in this case with a *wanqa* on it, was Sara Sara,
located near Arequipa in southern Peru. Another summit was Mollotoro.
A principal *waqa* of the Cañari, it had numerous idols on it, placed there by
order of Thupa Yapanki. A hillock referred to as Andazana, situated in the
province of Quito, had a small stone on top.[94]

The detailed illustrations of Guaman Poma show a number of mountain-
waqas with idols on them. In two pictures—one titled "Capítvlo de los
ídolos" (see Figure 4.1), the other "De los ídolos Ingas" (see Figure 4.2)—
Wana Kawri is portrayed as having an anthropomorphic effigy on its pinnacle. An additional drawing, "Idolos i vacas de los Andi svios" (see Figure
4.3), depicts Saua Ciray and Pitu Ciray with statues on their crests, while
"Idolos i vacas de los Conde svios" (see Figure 1.2) shows Qhuru Puna with
a figure on top.[95]

Some hills and peaks considered *waqas* had stones or idols on their summits; in some cases, the stone or statue that was located on a mountain was itself the *waqa*. Think about Cuzco's *siq'e* system. Cobo and Polo tell us that in Anti Suyu, the ninth sacred shrine on the second line bore the name Cascasayba and consisted of a group of stones on Quisco Hill.[96] In Chinchay Suyu, at the sixth hallowed spot on the ninth *siq'e* stood a large *wanqa*, Apu Yauira, situated on a hill known as Piccho.[97] And in Qulla Suyu, the third *waqa* on the eighth line was a stone pillar on a knoll referred to as Mudca.[98]

The same pattern was found in the provinces. Albornoz reports that the members of an ethnic group known as the Palta venerated the *waqa* Acacana, which consisted of several stones on a summit.[99] In the province of Guaylas, the inhabitants' most revered object was Matarau, a *wanqa* on Mataras Hill, and in the region of Carua Conchuco, one of the principal *waqas* was a stone called Caruachuco that sat atop the hill Coana.[100]

It is unclear from the ethnohistoric sources what difference there was, if any, between a mountain-*waqa* with a stone on its summit and a *wanqa* on a peak. I suspect that if a rock was important enough to be mentioned in reference to a sacred peak, it was probably considered sacred as well. Does it necessarily follow that a mountain would be venerated because it had a stone on its pinnacle that was considered a *waqa*?

Perhaps the confusion can be cleared up by the chronicler Arriaga. He tells us that in the Andes, people worshipped not only the *waqa* itself, but—assuming the *waqa* was an object—the spot where it was found and the locale where it was placed. Such sites were called *samana*. All loci from which the object was invoked were considered to be hallowed and were referred to as *kayan*.[101]

Arriaga's information suggests that in each case—a mountain-*waqa* with a stone on top, and a *wanqa* on a summit—the rock and peak would both be venerated. Indeed, the ethnohistoric literature describes instances where both the hill and the idol on its slopes are said to be *waqas*. The most famous example is Wana Kawri. According to Cobo, the name "Wana Kawri" referred to the high hill situated two and a half leagues, or about 12 km,[102] from Cuzco along the royal road to Qulla Suyu, and also to a *wanqa* atop the peak. This sacred stone—described as being "of moderate size, without representational shape, and somewhat tapering"[103]—was thought to be the fossilized form of Ayar Uchu, the youngest brother of Manqu Qhapaq, mythological founder of the Inka Empire.[104] Together, the hill and rock were considered to be among the most prominent *waqas* in the empire.

DIVERSITY OF *WAQAS* ON MOUNTAINS

The chroniclers discuss a variety of objects that were revered on summits, some of which were noted above: *wanqas,* the puma's body, a pair of pillars, and anthropomorphic idols. There are many more. The Augustinian priests mention two hallowed items that were left on a hill near the settlement of Guamachuco by Wayna Qhapaq. These items, called *magacti,* were pitchers of water.[105] According to Molina, the Indians of Maras worshipped Raurana, a pair of stone falcons set on an altar on a lofty pinnacle,[106] while Ramos states that the Yunguyo, who lived by the shores of Lake Titi Qaqa, had an idol referred to as Copacati that was situated at the top of a hill. Copacati is said to have been a horrible figure, carved in stone, with snakes curling around it.[107] Albornoz tells us that at the site of Pacha Kamaq, one of the holiest spots in the empire, there was a gold figurine representing a fox that had been placed on a low peak.[108] Hernández says that the people from the village of Chaupis had two principal idols, Huaman Cusma and Rao Cusma, the first of which was of stone and shaped like a bird, the second a round crystal. They were venerated on a summit.[109] Monzón reports that the Rucana would go to high mountains to worship statuettes that represented llamas and were made of stone or clay.[110]

The ethnohistoric sources also enumerate many sacred edifices on peaks and hills. Cobo and Polo note that in the northeastern quarter of the Cuzco Valley, the fourth hallowed shrine on the third line was a temple referred to as Chuquimarca. Devoted to the worship of the Sun, it sat on Mantocalla Hill.[111] Likewise in Chinchay Suyu, the fifth *waqa* on the fourth *siq'e* was called Guamancancha, was situated on a knoll, and consisted of an enclosure with two *buhíos* (huts with thatched roofs) inside.[112] In the provinces, Albornoz documents the case of a house on Gallase's summit that was worshipped by the Chachapoya Indians and bore the name Guixicoc.[113] Fuente states that there was an *adoratorio* (shrine) on the pinnacle of Mount Potosí in Bolivia where the Comarcano left offerings, and Cieza says there was an important temple on Qhuru Puna.[114] Velasco reports that two mountains in Ecuador, Cayambe and Ashuay, had buildings on them devoted to the Sun.[115] Paz discusses Chimborazo, the volcano near Quito, below whose snow line were revered edifices where the local people gathered for rituals.[116]

Besides buildings, there were other kinds of sacred structures on and around peaks. Cobo and Polo mention a terrace bearing the name Rauaypampa that was built into the slope of Chinchincalla, a hill near the Inka

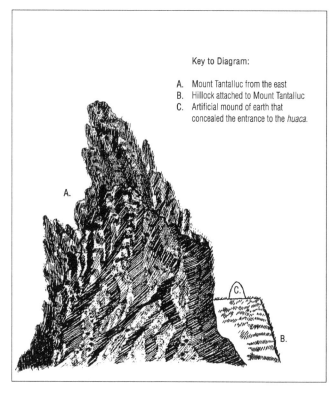

Key to Diagram:

A. Mount Tantalluc from the east
B. Hillock attached to Mount Tantalluc
C. Artificial mound of earth that
    concealed the entrance to the *huaca.*

A.

C.

B.

FIGURE 4.4A.   *Side profile of a* waqa *on Mount Tantalluc in the province of Caxamarca, discovered and excavated in 1765 (Martínez Compañón 1991: lámina LXXXV, p. 9).*

capital; it was adored because the emperor occasionally lodged there.[117] According to Velasco, near the solar temple on Mount Ashuay were a pair of venerated baths that were square and made of stone. Carved into them were figures—one representing a puma, the other a lizard—from which flowed warm water.[118] Martínez Compañón has two drawings (Figures 4.4a and 4.4b) of a hallowed structure with the outward appearance of a conically shaped mound located on a level spot at the base of Mount Tantalluc in the province of Caxamarca.[119]

A final type of *waqa* found on summits and in mountain passes is the *apachita.* Gonçález defines "apachita" as a mound of rocks representing a ritual carried out by travelers.[120] This gloss is echoed by Arriaga, Ayala, Murúa, Polo, Ramos, and Sarmiento.[121] Cobo and Acosta maintain the word refers not to the mass of stones, but to its locale: the pinnacle, pass, or high point on a road where a person would pick up a rock and add it to the growing pile.[122] To further complicate matters, Garcilaso claims the term *apachita* is a Spanish corruption of *apachecta*. He tells us the Quechua word has little to do with physical things (i.e., a gap between mountains or stones); rather, it alludes to the act of a traveler making an offering to a deity in thanks for giving him the strength and stamina to ascend a hill.[123]

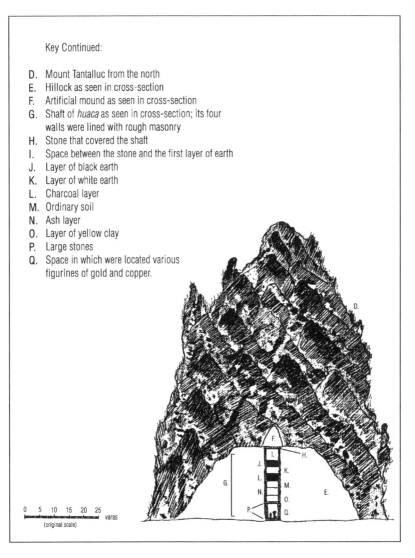

Key Continued:

D. Mount Tantalluc from the north
E. Hillock as seen in cross-section
F. Artificial mound as seen in cross-section
G. Shaft of *huaca* as seen in cross-section; its four walls were lined with rough masonry
H. Stone that covered the shaft
I. Space between the stone and the first layer of earth
J. Layer of black earth
K. Layer of white earth
L. Charcoal layer
M. Ordinary soil
N. Ash layer
O. Layer of yellow clay
P. Large stones
Q. Space in which were located various figurines of gold and copper.

0 5 10 15 20 25
varas
(original scale)

FIGURE 4.4B.   *Front profile of a* waqa *on Mount Tantalluc (Martínez Compañón 1991: lámina LXXXV, p. 9).*

Of the three definitions of *apachita,* I think that Garcilaso's is the most suspect. His agenda was to prove to Europeans that Andean religion was not idolatrous, nor altogether different from Christianity. When discussing the topic of worship, he downplays the importance of the object being venerated, such as a *waqa,* and emphasizes either the act itself or what he sees as the ultimate focus of the adoration: in this case, Pacha Kamaq, a creator god.[124] Though suspect, there might be some truth to his gloss.

It is possible that Gonçález's interpretation of the word *apachita* is just as valid as that of Cobo and Acosta. As noted earlier, "waqa" could refer to both the thing being worshipped (e.g., a mound of rocks) and its location (e.g., a summit or pass).

According to Cobo and Polo, about 22 percent of the sacred sites near the Inka capital were closely identified with lofty pinnacles: they either were mountain-*waqas* or had revered stones, shrines, and temples situated on their slopes.[125] Of the venerated sites that Albornoz lists in the provinces, about 54 percent are related to summits.[126]

FIRST-HAND DESCRIPTIONS OF HALLOWED MOUNTAIN SITES

In the ethnohistoric literature there are first-hand accounts, most penned by Spanish priests, of the discoveries and desecrations of hallowed mountain sites. Arriaga incorporates several accounts by different authors into his work, including a long passage by the priest and visitor Alonso García Quadrado. Confusingly written, it describes how its author found a *waqa,* in the form of a hermaphroditic idol, on a hill near the town of Hilavi. Made of stone, it had the image of a man on one side, that of a woman on the other, and carved representations of large snakes and toads at the feet. It was 6 yards (5.5 m) high and had been set on a stone foundation—the top of which was covered with fine sheets of gold—so that the male half faced the rising sun, the female part the setting sun. In front of each image was a square altar of stone about a span and a half (approximately 30 cm)[127] high. García had the statue pulled down and destroyed.[128] Arriaga's book contains part of a letter written by Hernández Príncipe, the priest and licentiate who participated in the campaign to stamp out paganism in Peru. In the piece, he relates how he tried to climb a crag near the town of Chochas, guided by some local people. He made it halfway up before stopping. He instructed his companions to continue the ascent and to retrieve a *waqa* called Llaxavilca, which had an anthropomorphic torso, an inclined head, and two eyes, one larger than the other. It sat on a flat stone with a second idol and was surrounded by the bones of sacrificed llamas.[129] Arriaga reproduces another letter by Hernández in which he talks about a statue known as Quénac. Quénac was located on top of a hill, and had a face but no arms or legs. It had been buried to a depth of about a yard (90 cm), along with the remains of offerings, and a copper trumpet used to assemble the local folk for rituals. All these items were unearthed and demolished.[130]

In a remarkable document written by Hernández in 1621, he describes how he discovered the body of Tanta Carhua (see Chapter 2). Taking up his narrative, he tells how he walked a league (almost 5 km) from the town of Ocros to a sacred site on a mountain, where he came upon some altars. He also found the remains of llamas that had been immolated, and a well-like structure filled with dirt. He immediately set to work digging into the shaft. At a depth of 3 *estados* (over 5 m), he reached the corpse of the *qhapaq hucha,* curled up in a fetal position. Badly decomposed, she wore what had once been fine clothes, but which were falling apart, and she was surrounded by silver offerings, including little pots, jugs, *tupus* (pins), and other items.[131]

Yet another first-hand work was produced by Martínez Compañón.[132] It consists of the detailed drawings he made (see Figures 4.4A and 4.4B) of the *waqa* located at the foot of Tantalluc Hill in Caxamarca. According to his diagrams, a person standing at the venerated site would have seen nothing more than an artificial mound on a level space. When Martínez excavated the mound in 1765, however, he came upon a large flat stone, which he removed, only to discover a square shaft. Its walls were faced with stone masonry, and it had been filled almost to the top with dirt. Digging into the structure, he went through a series of distinct strata, among them black earth, white soil, charcoal, "common" earth, ash, and yellow clay. Below the clay layer was a second flat rock, under which he found a small chamber containing figurines of gold and copper, anthropomorphic and zoomorphic in form. At the bottom of one of Martínez's diagrams (Figure 4.4b) is a scale that indicates the shaft was 5 *varas* (about 4.3 m) wide and 24 *varas* (approximately 21 m) deep. These measurements seem wildly exaggerated. He also produced a regional map in which the distances are given incorrectly in *varas,*[133] a small unit of length, rather than in leagues, a large unit of distance; in his picture of the mountain-*waqa,* he probably makes the same mistake, which may mean that the unit of measure should be the *span* rather than the *vara.* In that case, the shaft would be 1.1 m wide and 5.5 m deep.

CYCLIC RITUALS THAT TOOK
PLACE ON MOUNTAINS

During the month of Aya Marq'ay Killa, which roughly corresponds with November,[134] the Inkas carried out a series of cyclic rites on mountains around the capital. These rituals were in preparation for the observance of Wara Chicuy, the ceremonies and trials by which adolescents from royal lineages attained the status of men.[135] Molina tells us that the designated youths would ascend Wana Kawri and offer a sacrifice on the summit to the sacred stone, asking its permission to be initiated the following month. They would then spend the night there before descending, commemorating the start of the journey made by their mythical ancestors from Wana Kawri to the valley of Cuzco. Each day of Aya Marq'ay Killa, three llamas were immolated on the hallowed pinnacle: one in the morning, one at noon, and one at night.[136]

A rite preceding Wara Chicuy also took place on a small hill and *waqa* called Chacaguanacauri. Cobo and Polo mention that adolescents to be initiated climbed it and gathered bunches of a special grass, which they attached to their lances.[137]

Wara Chicuy was a yearly celebration held by the Inkas during Qhapaq Raymi,[138] which most closely corresponds with December.[139] According to Molina, at sunrise on the tenth day of the month, youths in the process of becoming men walked to the top of Wana Kawri Hill,[140] where they stood before the *wanqa*. It had been dressed in fine clothing and adorned with feathers.[141] Priests handed the initiates tufts of wool from five sacrificed llamas, which they blew into the air, at the same time praying that the Creator, Sun, Thunder, and king be forever young, and that the latter be always prosperous. The adolescents were given *warak'as* (slings) and *ch'uspas* (cloth bags), both symbols of maturity, and admonished to be brave.[142]

Five days later, they made a morning ascent of Anahuarqui, a hill located about two leagues (almost 10 km) from Cuzco with a *waqa* on its summit that bore the same name. Each youth offered the idol a handful of wool. Meanwhile, priests connected with the cult of Anahuarqui immolated five llamas in the names of the Creator, Sun, Moon, and Thunder, and burned the flesh of the animals. The initiates were whipped on their arms and legs by relatives and urged to have valor and endurance, after which the entire congregation sang a solemn song called a *taki*. As the rituals continued, the adolescents lined up in front of the *waqa* and, at a signal given by a finely dressed official, ran as fast as they could down the hill to the spot where they had spent the previous night. This race was very dangerous; youths sometimes died in falls. Its purpose was to honor Anahuarqui, said to have run as swiftly as a puma during the primordial flood. At the end of the ordeal, the initiates were met by maidens holding small jars of *chicha* for them to drink.[143]

Several days later, the adolescents got up at dawn and climbed a third peak, Raurana, which had two stone falcons on top. The *waqa kamayuq*, officiating priest, slaughtered five llamas in honor of the Creator, Sun, and Moon. As before, the youths were flogged by relatives, admonished to be good warriors and to never retreat, and made to sing a special song. They also were given gifts symbolic of their newly acquired status: *waras* (breechcloths), gold earspools, special *unkus* (tunics), and feathered diadems.[144]

The chroniclers present conflicting information about the rituals connected with Wana Kawri, Anahuarqui, and Raurana. According to Cobo and Polo, the footrace began on Anahuarqui but ended at Rauaraya (Raurana), where the initiates who ran badly were punished.[145] Pachacuti asserts that the adolescents sprinted to Wana Kawri, the fastest receiving bright feathers—the slowest, black breeches.[146]

Cobo discusses two other peaks in the Cuzco area that were associated with Wara Chicuy: Sabaraura and Yauira. The youths undergoing puberty rites congregated on the former hill, where twelve young llamas were immolated, half of whose bodies were subsequently cremated, the other half buried. The initiates made individual offerings to the *waqa* and were whipped. Then they walked to Yauira, where the same sacrifices were carried out. They danced, were again beaten, and received special gifts, including loincloths, ear ornaments, diadems, helmets, and disks of gold and silver that were hung around their necks.[147]

Both Cobo and Polo mention a sacred custom observed by the Inkas on a hill called Quinoacalla.[148] This annual custom was affiliated with the celebration of Qhapaq Raymi, though not necessarily with the ceremonies and trials by which adolescents became men. Instead, it entailed resting.

Fernández claims that just as the Cuzqueños carried out initiation rituals on summits near the capital, so provincial people held similar rites on their local peaks.[149]

Cieza tells us about the periodic ceremony involving human sacrifice that took place on Wana Kawri but had nothing to do with Wara Chicuy (see Chapter 2). According to the chronicler, on special days the *waqa kamayuqs* would lead men and women before the *wanqa* representing Ayar Uchu. The males were dressed in fine wool clothing, with headbands, large medallions, bracelets, and sandals, all of gold, and the females wore colorful garments decorated with feathers and pins of gold. The priests made grave speeches and sang songs meant to convince the victims they should be happy because they were going to serve the *waqa,* after which the officiants compelled them to drink *chicha* from gold cups until they were intoxicated. As the ceremony progressed, the victims were strangled and buried near the *wanqa,* males with bundles on their backs and surrounded by gold vessels, females with spoons, bowls, and plates. These immolations were celebrated with festivals during which there was dancing and singing, and thereafter the victims were venerated as saints.[150]

Murúa and Molina describe cyclic rites observed throughout the empire that were connected with mountains, including the large *qhapaq hucha* processions. Such processions, which were bound for significant *waqas,* were made up of imperial officials, priests, and commoners who carried offerings. At certain points along the way, llamas were sacrificed and their blood sprinkled onto the flanks of lofty peaks and the summits of lower hills. If the mountains were too steep to climb, the sacred fluid was sealed in small, clay vessels that were propelled with slings as far up the slopes as possible, where they shattered, dispersing their contents.[151]

An anonymous Jesuit, writing around 1600, provides a detailed report concerning a local ritual that appears to have been periodic and closely linked with a peak. He says that on a specific day, the inhabitants of four Aymara villages would get together to climb this peak, but that the route was so difficult and the incline so great, some of the elderly only made it partway up before they had to stop. On top was a *waqa* called Pisi. It had been placed at the edge of a flat open space where the members of each village gathered to observe their own ceremonies and to honor the idol in their own way.

The Jesuit relates that during the festival of Pisi, the crest of the mountain was alive with the sound of drums, flutes, and human voices. One person would chant a line from a prayer, and a chorus would echo it. There also would be slow, steady movement as the villagers performed their solemn dances. Worshippers approaching the idol assumed an attitude of respect, which involved placing their left hands on their heads, stretching their right hands out in front of their faces with the palms facing the *waqa,* and making a kissing sound with their lips. Some people would prostrate themselves on the ground. Many participants made offerings to Pisi, the simplest of which were their own plucked eyebrows. Those who brought more important gifts—such as clothing, gold, *quwis* (guinea pigs), and livestock—had prepared themselves beforehand by shaving and painting their faces red. They would step toward a priest, who stood in the middle of the flat space by a large bonfire, and hand him the offerings. If given an animal, he slit its throat, sprinkled its blood over the idol, and burned its flesh in the fire.[152]

Velasco left a chronicle that is relatively late and that seems to be exaggerated, but is worth mentioning nonetheless. In this work he claims that the ancient Cañari, from the province of Cuenca, carried out a yearly ceremony on a peak known as Supayurco. The ritual took place just before the harvest and involved walking a hundred young children to a cave on the crag, placing them on a stone altar, and sacrificing them with a flint knife; their bodies were buried in the vicinity. Velasco says that when he visited the region in 1755, the practice persisted.[153]

According to the Huarochirí manuscript,[154] the Yunca, who lived in the river valleys near Peru's central coast, used to gather at Mount Parya Qaqa to worship. During their cyclic rites, they offered *tikti,* a food prepared from the thick residue of corn beer,[155] coca leaves, and other items to the summit. Then they returned to their respective villages, where they held festivals lasting about five days and involving much dancing.

Avila touches on a ritual that seems to have taken place regularly and was related to a pinnacle called Tambo Sica. As part of the rite, the Checa decorated their llamas with bells and ear tassels, and set off for the peak with the animals in tow. Along the way, they blew trumpets fashioned from conch shells. When they reached Tambo Sica, they broke up into individual households and venerated their respective *caullamas* (possibly statuettes resembling llamas), which were kept on the mountain.[156] Each *caullama* represented a deity responsible for the fertility of a household's livestock.[157]

SINGULAR AND INTERMITTENT CEREMONIES CARRIED OUT ON PEAKS

The author Pachacuti mentions the one-of-a-kind ritual performed during the reign of Thupa Yapanki that entailed immolating three hundred men from Anti Suyu on a summit.[158] Murúa describes a singular ceremony carried out by King Pacha Kuti in southern Peru. A large volcano—perhaps El Misti, also known as Putina—located three leagues (about 14.5 km) from Arequipa was erupting violently, sending flames high in the air, belching sulfur, catapulting rocks, and spewing out an enormous cloud of ash. So great was the force of the eruption, it destroyed the city and killed many people. Thus the king, who was determined to placate and quiet the volcano, had numerous llamas slaughtered in its honor. He

FIGURE 4.5.   *Emperor using a sling to hurl projectiles from his litter (Guaman Poma 1980a: 307).*

ordered his men to carry him in a litter as close to the peak as possible, whereupon he took a sling and hurled clay balls filled with sacrificial blood far up its slope (see Figure 4.5). When the balls found their mark, they broke, scattering their sacred contents.[159]

Oberem has published fragments of the wills of an Ecuadorian *cacique* and *cacica*—that is, "headman" and "headwoman"—who also were husband and wife. The documents deal with strange rites that took place on the tops of various hills. In the first piece, which is dated 1585 and was left by Don Sancho Hacho, the *cacique* declares that during the Inka era he was buried alive on a knoll called Pinipullo (an event that was part of the ceremony by which he married his sister). When he appeared from his interment, he was given control of all the land around him, as far as he could see. The second fragment is from the will of Doña Francisca Sinasigchi and is dated 1580. In it, she says the emperor had her entombed on a hill, and when she left the burial place, she received all territory visible from her lofty vantage point.[160]

The Augustinian priests discuss a mountain ritual performed intermittently. During times of drought, local "sorcerers" in Guamachuco were expected to fast for several days and climb a peak where two *waqas* were located. Known as *magacti,* these *waqas* consisted of sacred pitchers full of water that had been left by Wayna Qhapaq. The sorcerers would stay on the summit until it rained, venerating the pitchers, and suffering from cold and hunger.[161]

OTHER PRACTICES ASSOCIATED WITH MOUNTAINS

According to several chroniclers, hilltop ceremonies were sometimes carried out not for the mountain-deities, but for other gods. Cobo and Polo tell us that in the northwestern quarter of the Cuzco Valley, the eighth *waqa* on the fourth line was a sacred summit that bore the name Chuquipalta. Offerings were made there to three stones representing the Creator, Sun, and Thunder.[162] In the same section of the valley, the seventh hallowed site on the seventh *siq'e* was a round hill referred to as Churuncana, where rituals, including child sacrifice, were conducted to honor Wira Qucha.[163] In the southeastern quarter, the third *waqa* on the first line was a hillock called Churucana. On its pinnacle were three *wanqas,* in front of which various rites were observed so the Sun would not lose its strength.[164]

Molina provides examples of mountain ceremonies carried out near the capital that honored gods unrelated to the peaks. As part of the initiation of Inka youths, which as we have seen took place during Qhapaq Raymi, five llamas were slaughtered on Anahuarqui. The offerings were dedicated to the Creator, Sun, Moon, and Thunder. Several days later, another five llamas were put to death, and libations of corn beer poured onto the ground. These rites were performed on Raurana but were intended primarily for the benefit of the Creator, Sun, Moon, and Thunder, and only secondarily for the mountain-*waqa*.[165] On Chuquicancha, an esteemed crag in the northeastern quarter of the Cuzco Valley,[166] the Inkas buried the corpses of sacrificial victims. The lives of these victims were consecrated to the Creator, Sun, Moon, Thunder, and Earth.[167]

Rituals observed on summits in the provinces were sometimes meant to honor Inti. Noboa reports on such a ceremony in Cajatambo. He says the local populace, under orders from the Inka, ascended a hill known as Nabincoto. Once on top, they took two young boys—who were brothers and whose bodies had no physical defects—and entombed them alive in a large earthen jar along with silver vessels. They also slaughtered numerous llamas. The sacrifices were meant for the Sun, not for a mountain-spirit.[168] Tanta Carhua, the *qhapaq hucha*, was considered an offering to Inti rather than to a peak.[169] Velasco mentions that the two prominent summits in Ecuador, Cayambe and Ashuay, had temples on their slopes where ceremonies were carried out for the Sun.[170]

Not all events that took place on pinnacles were sacred. Consider Alcaya's story about the execution of the two hundred Chiriguano on the tops of snow-covered mountains.[171]

A rite glorifying a peak did not have to be observed on the peak itself, but could take place on a nearby hill or crag with a clear view of the object of veneration.[172] In the Huarochirí manuscript, it says that some groups in central Peru, including the Checa and Yunca, used to travel to Parya Qaqa to worship. Then they started going to another summit called Ynca Caya, from which they could see Parya Qaqa's snow-capped pinnacle, to carry out rituals in the latter's honor. One ritual involved a race. The participants would scramble up Ynca Caya's slope, driving their male llamas before them, and the first animal to reach the top was considered to be much loved by Parya Qaqa. This event took place during a period of worship known as Auquisna, which fell around Easter or Corpus Christi.[173]

According to Avila, at the high point of their ritual calendar, the Concha people adored Parya Qaqa from the crest of Mount Huaycho; the Suni Cancha also venerated this peak from another pinnacle, while the Chauca Ricma and the residents of such villages as Santa Ana and San Juan honored Parya Qaqa from a pinnacle known as Acu Sica. Before the arrival of the Spanish in Peru, the custom had been for these groups to make the journey to Parya Qaqa itself to worship.[174]

Hernández gives an example of a mountain-top shrine that was glorified by the local people from the surrounding hills: the tomb of Tanta Carhua.[175]

A ceremony associated with a hallowed mountain could take place in a city, village, valley, or almost anywhere. Cobo and Polo state that in the northwestern quarter of the Cuzco Valley was a sacred hill referred to as Quiangalla. Two pillars on the hill denoted the arrival of summer: the season began when an imperial official—standing at a specific point in or around the capital, and having an unobstructed view of the summit—saw the sun pass between the pillars.[176] Another venerated pinnacle near Cuzco was Sucanca. Like Quiangalla, Sucanca had two markers on it. When a priest in the city or on the valley floor witnessed the passage of the sun between them, it was time to plant the corn, and a festival was held. The festival involved making offerings to Inti of llamas, clothing, and camelid figurines of gold and silver.[177] I should emphasize that the daily observance of the changing relationship between the sun and a revered hill was considered a sacred rite.

Few chroniclers state explicitly that the Peruvian natives carried out mountain ceremonies in mundane places such as the hamlets where they lived or fields where they worked: when a ritual was performed on a high peak, the ethnohistoric sources took note of the fact; when it occurred in a less exotic setting, they usually did not mention it. An anonymous Jesuit informs us that the members of two ethnic groups, the Huacho and Yauyo, worshipped Auquichanca and Cuniavillca, which were summits believed to be related, the latter being the son of the former. Celebrations were held for them four times a year, including around Corpus Christi when the constellation Oncoy, the Pleiades, reappeared in the sky. During these festivals, the Huacho, Yauyo, and other peoples from as far away as Cuzco gathered to dance and observe solemn rites.[178] We are never told where the events took place, though it seems likely their settings would have been Huacho and/or Yauyo villages.

Guaman Poma's drawings show mountain rituals being observed in a city, possibly in a village, and in flat open spaces within sight of sacred peaks. His picture titled "De los ídolos Ingas" (see Figure 4.2) portrays the emperor venerating Wana Kawri from the capital with his *quya* (queen) and daughter. He has assumed a respectful posture: he is on his knees with hands raised in front of his chest, palms outward and facing the *waqa,* which is in the middle distance.[179] The illustration "Idolos i vacas de los Chinchai svivs" (see Figure 4.6) depicts a man from Chinchay Suyu worshipping Parya Qaqa. He is genuflecting and looking toward the mountain-*waqa,* which looms before him. In his hands he holds a sacrificial victim, while behind him a woman bears another gift for the pinnacle, and in front is a fire where the offerings may be burned. At the bottom of the drawing, the legend says that the scene takes place in Parya Qaqa,[180] which may refer to a village.[181] Another sketch, "Idolos i vacas de los Andi svios" (see Figure

FIGURE 4.6.   *People of Chinchay Suyu offering a child and plate of* sankhu *to the mountain-*waqa *Parya Qaqa (Guaman Poma 1980a: 240).*

4.3), shows a male from the northeastern quarter of the empire honoring two summits, Saua Ciray and Pitu Ciray. He too kneels, faces the *waqas,* and grasps an offering. In back of him, a second figure holds a sacrificial victim. The setting for the picture is a level space with a clear view of the peaks.[182] "Idolos i vacas de los Colla svios" (see Figure 2.3) depicts two men from Qulla Suyu with gifts for Willka Nuta, a venerated peak. Both figures focus their attention on the *waqa* and are probably genuflecting. As in the case of the previous sketch, the action takes place on a flat and open piece of land within sight of the mountain.[183] The illustration entitled "Idolos i vacas de los Conde svios" (see Figure 4.3) portrays two worshippers from the southwestern quarter kneeling before Qhuru Puna, each of whom looks toward the *waqa* and has an offering. The rite is spatially separated from the pinnacle.[184]

A mountain ceremony could be even further removed from the object of veneration: it could involve a representation of the sacred summit. Cobo and Polo assert that in the northeastern section of the Cuzco Valley was a stone called Maychaguanacauri that was much revered because it was shaped like Wana Kawri Hill. Rites were carried out for it, and all kinds of things sacrificed to it.[185] Ayala maintains that in Chinchaycocha province there was an isolated hill with two pinnacles, known respectively as Yanayacolca and Raco. Raco was said to be Yanayacolca's brother and a deity. Each year before sowing, the natives performed ceremonies before effigies of Raco located in the middle of their fields. The effigies would take the form of a *wanqa* (which stood about 1 *tercia,* or 28 cm high) or a *pitacocha* (a large bundle of straw that was bent in half and partially buried so that it resembled the peak). Offerings were made to these representations, the hill indirectly invoked for the fertility of the crops.[186] The Augustinian priests relate that the inhabitants of Guamachuco had two stone idols, Yanaguanca and Xulcaguanca, which symbolized hallowed summits. When these people were attacked by outsiders, they venerated their idols and asked for the strength to repel the invaders; at other times, they celebrated festivals for Yanaguanca and Xulcaguanca.[187]

Ulloa Mogollón left a record of a strange, yet intriguing form of mountain worship that involved transforming humans into representations of peaks. The Collagua, an ethnic group that dwelt near the city of Arequipa, believed their *paqariku* (place of origin) was a snow-capped volcano called Collaguata. It stood out from lesser pinnacles in the region. To honor it, they bound the malleable heads of their newborn children to make them tall, thin, and slightly tapering, in imitation of the peak's shape. Ulloa also reports that the residents of Cavana province, who like the Collagua lived close to Arequipa, thought they originated from the summit Gualcagualca, which they considered holy. As an expression of their devotion, they wrapped white cords tightly around the heads of their babies, circling the crowns numerous times. This procedure caused the skulls to flatten out on top and become very wide, mimicking the outline of Gualcagualca. The chronicler says it was easy to distinguish the Collagua from the Cavana because the shapes of their heads were so distinct.[188]

THE RELATIONSHIP BETWEEN PEOPLE
AND MOUNTAIN-*WAQAS*

The inhabitants of the Andes greatly honored lofty summits, carrying out a variety of rites on their behalf and leaving all kinds of offerings for them. The relationship was not entirely one-sided, though; people expected something in return for their "generosity"—including water, fertility, good weather, and so on—as required by the traditional Andean concept of reciprocity. If the mountain-deity did not live up to its obligations, its devotees could turn on it. As a case in point, mull over the following story from the Huarochirí manuscript. During the reign of Thupa Yapanki, revolts broke out in several provinces, whereupon the king mobilized his armies and sent them to vanquish the rebellious groups. To no avail, his men were slaughtered by the thousands. In desperation, Thupa called together the most important *waqas* of the realm, including Maca Uisa, Parya Qaqa's child. Once they were assembled, the emperor addressed them, asking for their help, and threatening them if they withheld it.[189]

> Why should I serve you and adorn you with my gold, with my silver, with basketfuls of my food, and drinks, with my llamas, and everything else I have? Now that you've heard the greatness of my grief, won't you come to my aid? If you refuse, you'll burn immediately![190]

In this instance, the king did not have to resort to violence to get what he wanted from the *waqas*.

In another incident, some Inkas all but waged war against an idol connected with a pinnacle. According to Betanzos, during the armed conflict between Atawalpa and Waskar, the former ordered that a sacrifice be made to a prominent *waqa* and oracle on a high peak in Guamachuco. He also commanded that a question about the future be put to it. The reply, which came from an old man who spoke for the idol, so enraged Atawalpa that he ordered his army to surround the mountain while he climbed to the top. There he took an axe and beheaded the stone statue and the old man. He had his men pile an enormous amount of firewood on the summit, burn it, collect the remains of the idol and bones of the old man, and grind them to dust. He scattered this dust to the wind.[191]

THE RELATIONSHIP BETWEEN THE
DEAD AND MOUNTAINS

Just as many ethnic groups believed they had originated from lofty pinnacles, so they thought they returned to these peaks at death. The people of Qulla Suyu believed that their deceased went directly to Qhuru Puna,[192] while the inhabitants of Huarochirí imagined that the departed went to Parya Qaqa.[193]

Guaman Poma tells us that the populace of Kunti Suyu sometimes buried their dead in the hills.[194] This practice seems to have been widespread and continued into the Colonial period; Polo, writing in the late sixteenth century, says it was common for the Indians to secretly dig up their dead from churchyards and cemeteries, and re-inter them in the mountains.[195] Murúa provides similar information, but adds that the departed were re-entombed with their forebears, by which he means the sacred mummies of their ancestors. This reunion took place in the hills and was an occasion for celebration involving ritual eating, drinking, and dancing.[196] The anonymous Jesuit asserts that while working in the provinces of the Huacho and Yauyo, he went climbing among some peaks, where he discovered several caves. In them were numerous mummies. They were squatting, wore their own clothing, and had their own food. The walls of the caves were spattered with the blood of sacrificed animals.[197]

Five   MOUNTAIN OFFERINGS

Diverse items were sacrificed to/on peaks in the Inka Empire, with the most significant and sacred offerings being human lives.[1]

HUMAN SACRIFICE

People were frequently immolated on summits around Cuzco. Cobo and Polo state that children were ritually slaughtered in honor of Mantocallas Hill, which was greatly venerated.[2] Guaman Poma reports that each year the Inkas put ten infants to death to pay homage to Wana Kawri,[3] while Cieza tells us that adults, both men and women, were slain on this summit in elaborate rituals.[4] Pachacuti recounts the story of the three hundred men from Upatari who were killed and buried on Mount Pachatusun,[5] located near the capital.[6]

Human beings were offered to summits not only in the vicinity of Cuzco, but in the provinces. Victims included men, women, and children.[7] Whereas Paz asserts that in the highlands of Ecuador, the inhabitants dispatched young women on the slopes of Chimborazo Volcano,[8] Ulloa says that in the region around Arequipa, the local folk sacrificed people to Collaguata, Suquilpa, Apoquico, Omascota, and Gualcagualca. They could only carry out the immolations, however, when ordered to by the king.[9] Guaman Poma states that in Chinchay Suyu, the natives consecrated the lives of five-year-old infants to the high pinnacle of Aysa Uilca.[10] And in the southeastern quarter, an ethnic group called the Poma Canche buried two adolescents, a boy and a girl of about twelve, to venerate the peak Canchi Circa.[11] Velasco talks about the Cañari's annual slaughter of a hundred children (which seems like an exaggeration) in a cave on Mount Supayurco.[12] In this instance, as in the case of Pachatusun, it is difficult to tell if the sacrifices were meant to honor the peak or some other god. In two stories from the Huarochirí manuscript, infants are offered to Wallullu.[13]

There are numerous examples from the area around the capital of people being sacrificed to *wanqas* and idols on hills. Cobo and Polo report that in the northeastern section of the Cuzco Valley, a *waqa* called Cascasayba, which consisted of stones placed on the hill Quisco, received immolations of children.[14] The authors tell us of a sacred site in Qulla Suyu on Cuipan, a peak. It featured five *wanqas,* in whose honor the Inkas put infants to death.[15] Cobo and Polo also assert that in the southwestern part of the valley was a large hill referred to as Anaguarque that had numerous idols on it that were likewise offered children.[16]

Many stones, idols, and temples on high summits in the provinces received human sacrifices. Herrera says that before the natives of Peru visited their religious shrines, which were often situated on mountains, they slaughtered infants,[17] while Cieza asserts that the Inkas had a temple on Qhuru Puna, where men and women were immolated.[18] The drawings of Guaman Poma show human lives being offered to *waqas* on peaks. In his illustration entitled "Idolos i vacas de los Andi svios" (see Figure 4.3), we see a kneeling figure holding a baby; this infant is to be ritually slain to the idols on the crests of Saua Ciray and Pitu Ciray.[19]

Representations of humans were also offered to/on mountains, both in the Cuzco Valley and in the provinces. Cobo and Polo maintain that there was a hill close to the capital called Chuquipalta on whose crest the Inkas made sacrifices of figurines made of gold and resembling boys and girls.[20] The same authors tell us that on Mantocallas Hill, in the Cuzco area, human effigies were burned. The images had been carved from firewood and dressed to look like men and women.[21] Another pinnacle in the region, known as Llulpacturo, received miniature children of gold and silver.[22] I should note that these summits were offered not only figurines representing people, but real human immolations, leading me to believe that the two practices were connected. Molina asserts that the Inkas distributed sacrificial materials to all major *waqas,* many of them hills and peaks in the provinces. The materials included gold and silver statuettes of men.[23] Albornoz furnishes similar information,[24] while Martínez provides the drawing (see Figure 4.4B) of the mountain-*waqa* in Caxamarca that consists of a deep shaft at the bottom of which is a chamber that contained at least one anthropomorphic idol of gold or copper.[25]

CAMELID SACRIFICE

Second only to human sacrifice in sacredness and importance was the immolation of camelids (llamas, alpacas, and guanacos). In
the chronicles, these animals are often referred to as "carneros/corderos de
la tierra," which translates as "sheep of the land [of the Andes]." Only males
could be killed, as females were needed for breeding.[26] All the beasts had to
be healthy; they could have no blemishes or deformities.[27] When sacrificing llamas, the Cuzqueños considered such things as the appropriate number of animals,[28] their colors and markings,[29] the quality of their wool,[30]
and their ages.[31] These factors varied depending on the god receiving the
offering, the gravity of the petition being made, the desired result of the
immolation, the type of ritual involved, and the festival during which it
took place.[32] According to Inka custom, brown llamas were suitable for
sacrifice to the Creator, but only as part of certain ceremonies, while white
alpacas with thick woolly fur were appropriate offerings for Inti during
other rites. Mottled animals occasionally were put to death to venerate
Thunder.[33]

A llama to be immolated was sometimes garlanded with flowers.[34] It
was led several times around the idol to which it was being dedicated[35]
and then handed over to a ritual specialist[36] who turned the beast's eyes
toward the *waqa,* said a prayer, and slit its throat.[37] If the rite took place in
Cuzco, the body might be divided into four quarters and—without losing
any blood—placed in a large fire. Each of the four pieces was completely
burned. Then the ashes were collected, the bones ground up, and the sacred
powder saved in a special storehouse.[38] In a drawing titled "Indios qve mata
el carnero" (see Figure 5.1), Guaman Poma illustrates another method of
sacrificing a llama. The picture shows a beast with its four legs bound
together and its head held down by a young man. A "sorcerer" kneeling
beside the animal has cut open its left side and reaches his right arm into
the chest cavity to pull out the heart, while nearby a young woman holds
a vessel to receive the organ.[39] Arriaga describes a similar rite. He says that
after such an immolation, the llama's blood was sprinkled on a *waqa* and its
flesh divided among the people present.[40]

In the ethnohistoric literature, there are many instances of camelids
being offered to mountains near the capital. Cobo and Polo report that on
Mantocallas Hill, animals were put to death and their bodies cremated,[41]
while the stones on the summit of Cariurco received sacrifices of spotted
llamas.[42] Molina asserts that throughout the month of Hauca (Guaman
Poma calls this period "Aymuray Killa"[43]), which started in the middle of

FIGURE 5.1. *"Sorcerer" sacrificing a llama by extracting its heart through a slit in its side (Guaman Poma 1980b: 826).*

May, the Inkas slaughtered beasts of burden on numerous peaks, including Succanca, Omoto Yanacauri, Ccapac Uilca, Queros Huanacauri, Rontoca, Cuti, Suntu, Cacha Uiracocha, Yacalla Huaca, Rurama, Urcos Uiracocha, and Sulcanca. On a particular morning, they would take a llama to the top of Wana Kawri, kill it, and burn it; that evening, they would lead another animal to the mountain Achpiran, where they believed the Sun set, and immolate it.[44]

As part of Wara Chicuy, the initiation rites held for royal adolescents in

December, the lords of Cuzco offered camelids on peaks around the capital. According to Molina, on the tenth day of the month priests slaughtered
five llamas on Wana Kawri.[45] Cobo says that young animals were used for
this ceremony, and that their deaths were slow: an officiant would grab a
camelid, slit open one of its veins, and lead it around the summit so it left a
trail of blood; when it finally collapsed, it was cremated on the spot.[46] Five
days later, five beasts were sacrificed on Anahuarqui Hill.[47] And several days
after that, five more were put to death, this time on Raurana.[48] Cobo also
asserts that during Wara Chicuy, twelve young llamas were slaughtered on
Sabaraura, and another twelve on Yauira; once the sacrifices on these peaks
were over, half the bodies were burned, the rest buried.[49]

Camelids were immolated to venerate pinnacles not only around Cuzco,
but in the provinces. Paz reports that some of the inhabitants of the Quito
area considered Chimborazo to be their place of origin; they honored it
by killing "sheep of the land" on its slopes.[50] Bello Galloso asserts that the
people of the Cuenca region revered volcanoes and hills, to which they
slaughtered beasts of burden,[51] while Monzón discusses a province in the
highlands of southern Peru. He tells us this land was occupied by two ethnic
groups, the Rucana and Sora, whose members sacrificed llamas to high
peaks before their conquest by the Inkas.[52] Ulloa says that the Collagua
had as their principal *waqas* the mountains Collaguata, Suquilpa, Apoquico,
Omascota, and Gualcagualca, which they venerated by ritually slaughter-
ing camelids.[53] Guaman Poma has a drawing called "Idolos i vacas de los
Colla svios" that portrays a man kneeling before Willka Nuta and holding
a black llama he is about to offer.[54] In the Huarochirí manuscript, there
is a passage where the Inka emperor decrees that thirty men should serve
Parya Qaqa. These men immolate a camelid belonging to the deity, in part
to show their devotion to him.[55] Dávila reports that while working in the
Huarochirí region in the late sixteenth century, he confiscated four hundred "sheep of the land" from the local inhabitants, who each month killed
animals on Parya Qaqa's behalf.[56]

Murúa talks about the movement of sacred offerings, including llamas,
from Cuzco to the provinces for special festivals. He says this distribution
of offerings was carried out by processions of people moving across the
landscape in straight lines. Each evening the individual groups stopped,
immolated animals, and sprinkled their blood among the hills.[57] The same
author recounts the story about Pacha Kuti, who tried to placate the erupting volcano by scattering blood from sacrificial "sheep" on its slopes.[58]

The ethnohistoric literature describes two instances of children being
immolated on summits as offerings to the Sun: the pair of brothers on

Nabincoto, and Tanta Carhua on the pinnacle in Aixa. Later, beasts of burden were slaughtered at the mountaintop sites too. What is not clear, though, is whether the secondary offerings of llamas were meant for the Sun, the deified youngsters, or the hills.[59]

During the Inka era, camelids were put to death to venerate idols and stones situated on peaks.[60] The anonymous Jesuit discusses the Aymara *waqa* Pisi, located on a mountain, during whose festival the people made offerings of "sheep" through a priest. The religious officiant accepted the animals, cut their throats, sprinkled their blood on the idol, and cremated their remains.[61] According to Monzón, the Rucana kept representations of camelids made of stone and clay on high summits. These figurines received immolations of llamas.[62] Noboa asserts that in the region of Cajatambo, near the old villages of Quirca and Yanaqui, were twin knolls that stood side by side, on whose crests were *wanqas*. The stones were covered with blood from sacrificed camelids; at the foot of each one were the burned bones of the animals.[63] Albornoz provides a list of provincial *waqas* on pinnacles that were given "sheep" for ritual slaughter.[64]

Statuettes of llamas were offered to/on summits around Cuzco and in the provinces. Cobo and Polo report that near the capital was a peak called Sucanca that received not only immolations of real camelids, but gifts of miniature animals executed in silver and gold.[65] Molina and Albornoz tell us the Inkas sent a variety of sacrificial materials, including little beasts of burden of gold and silver, to the most important *waqas* of the realm, a large percentage of which were hills and lofty pinnacles.[66] Martínez's picture of the mountain shrine in Caxamarca shows a structure containing what appears to be a llama statuette of gold or copper.[67]

GUINEA PIG SACRIFICE

A common offering in the Andes was the *quwi,* or guinea pig,[68] often referred to in the chronicles as a "conejo" (rabbit). Arriaga tells us that people killed them by turning them on their backs and using a thumbnail to slice open their bodies right down the middle.[69]

Quwis were sacrificed to peaks and idols on summits.[70] Ulloa says that groups living in the Arequipa area immolated these animals as part of rituals relating to the mountains Collaguata, Suquilpa, Apoquico, Omascota, and Gualcagualca.[71] Monzón reports that the inhabitants of Guamanga venerated local hills by, among other things, slaying guinea pigs.[72] The chronicler also discusses the Rucana, who kept statuettes in shrines on high pinnacles; to honor the figurines, they dispatched the rodents, burned their bodies, and buried the ashes near the shrines.[73] Guaman Poma states that in Chinchay Suyu, the Yauyo offered "conejos" to Parya Qaqa's image,[74] while in Anti Suyu, the natives showed their reverence for the mountain-top *waqas* Saua Ciray and Pitu Ciray by killing "white rabbits."[75] In Guaman Poma's drawing entitled "Idolos i vacas de los Conde svios" (see Figure 1.2), a kneeling man holds a *quwi,* which he is about to sacrifice to the idol on Qhuru Puna's summit.[76] The Anonymous Jesuit says that an Aymara priest standing before Pisi would take rodents in hand, cut them open, sprinkle their blood on the *waqa,* and cremate their bodies.[77] Noboa, referring to the two *wanqas* on adjoining hills in Cajatambo, reports that at the base of each stone were the remains of guinea pigs immolated by villagers.[78] The Augustinians tell us that in Guamachuco, an idol referred to as Guallio was located in a shallow cave between two towering crags; *quwis* were slain there and their blood smeared on the *waqa.*[79]

The Huarochirí manuscript describes several episodes where people worship Parya Qaqa by dispatching guinea pigs,[80] and relates a story where Maca Uisa receives sacrifices of rodents.[81]

METALS

Among the ritual materials offered to peaks were metals such as gold, silver, and copper. The metals took a variety of forms: everything from gold dust and nuggets to ingots and manufactured goods. The latter items included figurines, both anthropomorphic and zoomorphic, and vessels. A common way to sacrifice a metal article was to bury it at the site of a *waqa.*[82]

Cobo and Polo list numerous idols on hills in the Cuzco area that received metal offerings. In most of these cases, however, the metal goods were intended for more prominent deities—the Creator, Sun, and Moon—rather than the *waqas* themselves.[83] There are three exceptions. A pebble called Picas, situated on a peak in the northeastern quarter of the Cuzco Valley, was believed to influence the hail. Round bits of gold were bestowed on it.[84] A large stone referred to as Guamansaui that sat on a hill in Qulla Suyu received gold and silver.[85] Wana Kawri also was proffered metallic riches; when the Spaniards reached this *wanqa,* they found an enormous amount of gold and silver around it.[86]

Cieza discusses the offering of men and women, along with metal goods, on Wana Kawri Hill. He asserts that male victims were buried with all kinds of gold accoutrements and offerings, including headbands, large medallions, bracelets, and pitchers. Females were sent to their graves bearing other types of gold items such as pins, spoons, bowls, and plates.[87] In the legend about the three hundred men from Upatari, they are interred on Pachatusun with a large quantity of gold in the form of dust and ingots.[88]

According to Guaman Poma, many pinnacles in the provinces received sacrifices of metals, among them Canchi Cira, a summit in Qulla Suyu. An ethnic group called the Poma Canche venerated Canchi Cira by burying gold and silver for it.[89] In Kunti Suyu, the populace bestowed these same metals on Qhuru Puna.[90] Other peaks in the provinces that were given gifts of gold and silver included Zupa Raura, Parya Qaqa, Caruancho, Wallullu, Ayza Bilca, Carua Razo, Razu Bilca, Saua Ciray, Pitu Ciray, Ausan Cata, Willka Nuta, and Putina.[91]

Bello Galloso says the people living around Cuenca, Ecuador, worshipped hills and volcanoes, to which they dedicated precious metals.[92] Dávila reports that while in the province of the Yauyo, he confiscated fourteen silver cups used in the monthly sacrifices to Parya Qaqa.[93] While Ulloa asserts the inhabitants of southern Peru offered figurines of gold and silver to their principal *waqas,* five high peaks,[94] Albornoz states the Inkas honored Sara Sara, Sulimana, Ampato, Putina (El Misti), and other summits by bestowing gold and silver cups on them.[95] This author lists major *waqas* in the provinces, a large percentage of which were mountains, that received gold and silver statuettes.[96]

The chroniclers tell us that in the hinterlands of the empire, sacrifices of metals were made to structures and idols associated with peaks.[97] The temple on the slopes of Qhuru Puna was given numerous loads of gold and silver;[98] the *wanqas* situated on adjacent hills in Cajatambo were offered small silver vessels;[99] gifts of gold were left for the Aymara idol Pisi;[100] and the *waqa* at the base of Tantalluc Hill received figurines executed in copper and gold.[101]

The Augustinian priests relate the story of Catequil, set during the war of succession between Atawalpa and Waskar. This idol and oracle, located on a crag in Guamachuco, told Atawalpa that his half-brother was the rightful king. In response, Atawalpa sent troops to destroy Catequil and to plunder the gold and silver it had accumulated through the years, a considerable amount.[102]

Noboa mentions a case where silver continued to be sacrificed at a hilltop *waqa* even after the arrival of the Europeans. Before the Conquest, the inhabitants of Cajatambo immolated the two boys on the crest of Nabincoto, and in Colonial times, seven silver coins were left there.[103] Arriaga asserts that the Spanish coins current in the early seventeenth century when he was writing, known as *reales*, were common offerings to idols.[104]

SHELL

Another item sacrificed to mountains was *mullu*, shell. Depending on their color, seashells were known by different names and could be presented to a variety of deities for different purposes. They were offered in a number of forms: whole, broken to pieces, carved into figurines, made into beads called *chaquira*, and ground to a powder. Shells were considered to be appropriate gifts for gods associated with water, as they were thought to be the "daughters" of Mama Qucha, Mother Sea, the ultimate source of all terrestrial liquid.[105] Arriaga says that in the early seventeenth century, *mullu* was still moving from the coast to the highlands, where it was being sacrificed to *waqas*. He tells of an Indian who paid four *reales*, a fair sum of money at the time, for a fragment of shell no larger than a fingernail.[106]

The term *mullu* has often been equated with Spondylus, a type of mollusk found, among other places, in the warm waters off the coast of Ecuador and sometimes northern Peru. A subspecies, *Spondylus princeps*, or "spiny oyster," has a shell that is white on the inside and that varies from orange to red on the outside.[107] Gonçález Holguín probably had this subspecies in mind when he defined *mullu* as a "red shell of the sea."[108] It is likely, however, that the word once had a broader meaning encompassing other kinds of seashells, including Strombus.[109]

In the area around the Inka capital, *mullu* was offered to peaks and to idols and stones situated on hills. For some examples, let us consult Cobo and Polo. They tell us that in the southeastern quarter of the Cuzco Valley, a summit called Sumeurco received shells,[110] while a knoll known as Chuquimarca was given pulverized shell.[111] In Anti Suyu, there was a *waqa* referred to as Cuipan that consisted of six stones on a hill with the same name. It was honored with red *mullu*.[112] Returning to the southeastern quarter, three stones on a hillock called Quiquijana were offered shells,[113] and a stone pillar on a small peak received ground *mullu*.[114]

According to Molina, the Inkas celebrated special rites on two pinnacles near Cuzco, Wana Kawri and Achpiran. These rites involved the sacrifice of red and yellow seashells carved in the shape of corn.[115]

In the provinces, worshippers also offered *mullu* to mountain-*waqas*. Guaman Poma states that while the Yauyo, who lived in Chinchay Suyu, gave shells to Parya Qaqa,[116] the Huanca and other ethnic groups from this quarter left thorny oysters for Wallullu,[117] their volcano-god and the arch enemy of Parya Qaqa. The folk of Anti Suyu sacrificed *mullu* to Saua Ciray and Pitu Ciray, high summits topped by anthropomorphic images, and the inhabitants of Kunti Suyu honored Qhuru Puna with gifts of shells.[118] Albornoz catalogues a number of peaks, many with idols on them, that received figurines carved from shell.[119]

The Huarochirí manuscript contains several references to the sacrifice of Spondylus to deities associated with mountains. In one myth, Parya Qaqa sees a man carrying an infant, some spiny oyster shells, and other offerings. The man is weeping. When Parya Qaqa asks him why he is so sad, he replies that it is because he has to offer up his child to Wallullu. Parya Qaqa tells him to stop worshipping the volcano-god and to quit practicing human sacrifice, whereupon the *waqa* takes the Spondylus and eats it, producing a loud "cap cap" sound.[120] In another story, Maca Uisa, who is being served by the emperor, demands he be brought spiny oysters, which he devours all at once. As he consumes them, he makes a deafening crunching noise.[121]

TEXTILES

Yet another item commonly offered to mountain-*waqas* was clothing. According to Cobo, fine textiles called *qumpi* were considered an integral part of almost every important sacrifice and included various sizes of both men's and women's garments. Each type of clothing was intended for a specific purpose and woven differently, during which process special rites were observed. Miniature pieces were often used to attire the statuettes of gold and silver that were bestowed on *waqas*. Some textiles—which were of excellent quality, brightly colored, and occasionally decorated with feathers—were made to fit the idols themselves. Such a piece would have been worn by the *waqa* or folded and placed next to it as an offering. The vast majority of garments were burned.[122]

Clothing was sacrificed to several peaks and mountaintop idols near the capital. Cobo and Polo tell us that in the northeastern quarter of the Cuzco Valley was the much venerated hill Mantocallas, where a ceremony took place during the shelling of the maize that involved the cremation of carved logs dressed in male and female garments.[123] In the same part of the valley, the sacred stones on the summit of Cariurco were honored with gifts of clothing.[124] Among the *waqas* of Qulla Suyu was a stone known as Guamansaui that was located on a peak and received offerings of tiny textiles.[125] Also in the southeastern quarter was Quiquijana. This knoll had three *wanqas* on it, which were allotted small garments.[126] When the Spaniards arrived in the Cuzco area, they found offerings of clothing, executed in miniature, on the pinnacle of Wana Kawri.[127]

Mountain-*waqas* in the provinces also received gifts of textiles. Bello Galloso states that the people living near Cuenca bestowed garments on sacred hills and volcanoes,[128] while the Anonymous Jesuit reports that the Aymara honored Pisi with sacrifices of clothing.[129] The Augustinian priests assert that the inhabitants of Guamachuco left textiles on Mount Guacat, which were intended for Catequil, their prominent *waqa*.[130]

COCA

Coca was a universal sacrificial material that could be offered to any *waqa* on any occasion. It was grown in the warmer and wetter parts of the empire, often in fields designated for a particular idol or deity.[131] Gifts of coca took a number of different forms, among them whole leaves, quids (what remains of the leaves after they have been chewed and the juices sucked out),[132] and small baskets of leaves.[133]

Coca was sacrificed to the majority of mountain-*waqas* in the Cuzco area, if not to all of them. Because it was such a ubiquitous offering, though, the chroniclers rarely mention it in connection with specific hills or peaks. An exception is Tampuvilca. Cobo and Polo say that this round hill, which was located in Qulla Suyu and had five stones on its pinnacle, received baskets of coca that were burned.[134] Molina tells us that baskets of leaves referred to as *paucar-runcus* were offered to Wana Kawri and Achpiran.[135]

Mountains and hilltop idols in the provinces were honored with gifts of coca.[136] Polo states that when highlanders went walking in the hills, they often discarded quids as simple sacrifices,[137] while Ayala asserts that in Chinchaycocha, the inhabitants proffered leaves to representations of the peak Raco.[138] Guaman Poma notes that a number of ethnic groups in Chinchay Suyu gave coca to Wallullu,[139] that the populace of Anti Suyu worshipped Saua Ciray and Pitu Ciray by providing them with leaves,[140] and that the natives of Kunti Suyu bestowed coca on Qhuru Puna.[141] In his drawing titled "Idolos i vacas de los Colla svios" (see Figure 2.3), Guaman Poma portrays a provincial noble holding a basket of leaves intended as an offering for Willka Nuta.[142]

The Huarochirí manuscript contains several examples of coca being sacrificed to a mountain-god. Consider the legend where Parya Qaqa encounters the man carrying gifts for Wallullu, including a child and coca, which are meant as food for the volcano-deity. Parya Qaqa takes the leaves and eats them.[143] In another part of the document, it says that before the Conquest, the Yunca would walk to Mount Parya Qaqa to proffer the *waqa* coca.[144] And we are informed that people used to trade away their wealth to get the leaves, which were used in festivals connected with Parya Qaqa.[145]

CORN AND CORN PRODUCTS

Like coca, maize was highly esteemed and frequently given to mountain-*waqas*. It was presented in several forms, including whole,[146] chewed,[147] toasted,[148] and ground to a flour.[149] Depending on its color, the flour could be blended with various substances and the mixture used for a specific ritual; for example, ground white corn was combined with red ocher and other ingredients to make an offering for the Sea. Maize flour also was mixed with fat and wool to produce a dough that was burned as a sacrifice,[150] was blended with llama blood to make *yawar sankhu*,[151] and was combined with *tikti* (the thick residue that remains at the end of the maize-beer brewing process)[152] to produce *sakaya*.[153] The resulting corn dough was often formed into little balls before being left for a *waqa*,[154] while the maize-beer residue, itself considered an appropriate gift for a mountain-deity, was made into tiny cakes.[155]

Mountain-*waqas* in the Cuzco area received not only ears of corn, but representations of ears. According to Molina, during the festival of Inti Raymi, which fell in June,[156] the Inkas made sacrifices on Wana Kawri and Achpiran of toasted maize and corncobs carved from red and yellow sea-shells.[157] Cobo and Polo tell us that maize ears made of wood were burned on Mantocallas.[158]

Mountain-*waqas* in the provinces were honored with offerings of corn too.[159] Whereas Polo asserts that highland people sometimes tossed pieces of chewed maize as minor presents for the hills,[160] the Anonymous Jesuit reports that the Aymara left different colored corn for Pisi.[161] Ayala states that the inhabitants of Chinchaycocha kept effigies of Raco, to which they made gifts of foods derived from maize; among the gifts were little balls known as *parpas* prepared from cornmeal, tiny cakes called *tantallas* concocted from maize flour and seeds, and *tikti,* the corn-beer residue.[162] Guaman Poma claims that the natives of Chinchay Suyu proffered *sankhu,* ground maize rolled into balls, to Parya Qaqa.[163] Accompanying this chronicler's text is his drawing of child sacrifice, "Idolos i vacas de los Chinchai svivs" (see Figure 4.6), in which a woman off to the side holds a plate piled with small oval-shaped offerings, most likely representing *sankhu*.[164] Guaman Poma also says that the folks who lived in Anti Suyu prepared maize cakes for Saua Ciray and Pitu Ciray,[165] while the inhabitants of Kunti Suyu sacrificed *sankhu* to Qhuru Puna.[166]

The Huarochirí manuscript refers to the presentation of *tikti* to Parya Qaqa. In the myth where the mountain-god encounters the man bearing gifts, the man gives the *waqa* some corn-beer residue.[167] In a chapter describing the veneration of the mountain-*waqa,* the narrator reports that in the old days, the Yunca would gather at Mount Parya Qaqa to proffer *tikti*.[168] At the end of the document, it is asserted that the day before a special rite, people would show their respect for the mountain-deity by bestowing maize-beer residue on it.[169]

A corn product closely related to *tikti* and commonly sacrificed was *chicha*. Arriaga calls this drink "the principal offering" because it was so ubiquitous and was employed to open festivals held for the *waqas.* Sometimes the beer was produced from maize grown especially for an idol; at other times it was brewed from the first ears to ripen. Girls and women would chew the kernels, spit the masticated mush into a vessel, and let it ferment, during which process they had to fast, which meant abstinence from salt, pepper, and sexual relations. As the brew matured, it became strong and thick. Arriaga reports that when the Peruvians gave *chicha* to a *waqa,* they believed they were providing the deity with a drink.[170] The oblation could be made in different ways (see Figure 5.2): a priest could take a cup of beer, dip his fingers into it, sprinkle the liquid onto an idol, and take a draught;[171] he might pour part of a tumbler of brew over the *waqa* and drink the rest himself;[172] or he could drain a cup onto the ground in front of an image.[173]

Chicha was probably sacrificed to most mountain-*waqas,* but again, perhaps because it was such a standard offering, few chroniclers discuss it in relation to specific peaks or idols. Molina, who is an exception, states that during the initiation of Inka youths, they would climb to the top of Raurana, where a priest dedicated to the service of the *waqa* would pour corn beer onto the ground. At the same time, he would invoke the Creator, Sun, Moon, and Thunder.[174] Ulloa says that the five sacred summits around Arequipa received libations of maize brew.[175] Ayala asserts that the people of Chinchaycocha routinely proffered *chicha* to their effigies representing Raco,[176] while the Augustinian priests claim that the natives of Guamachuco left oblations of corn beer on Mount Guacat for Catequil.[177] Guaman Poma tells us that the people of Chinchay Suyu honored the mountain-deities Aysa Uilca and Parya Qaqa with gifts of maize brew.[178]

FIGURE 5.2.   *Emperor making a toast/offering of* chicha *to the Sun (Guaman Poma 1980a: 220).*

FEATHERS

Among the items occasionally bestowed on *waqas* were feathers.[179] The color of a plume appears to have been significant: Andean peoples sacrificed red feathers known as *astop tuctu* that came from parrots and other jungle birds,[180] white plumes called *wachiwa* from the geese that made their homes on the lakes of the altiplano, and pink feathers referred to as *pariwana* from flamingos that also lived on high lakes.[181] Rhea plumes were used as offerings as well.[182]

Feathers were sometimes left on mountains or at shrines associated with peaks. According to Polo, highlanders occasionally dropped plumes as presents for the deities that dwelt in the hills.[183] Guaman Poma reports that the natives of Anti Suyu proffered feathers to Saua Ciray and Pitu Ciray,[184] and that the inhabitants of Kunti Suyu offered pink and white plumes to Qhuru Puna.[185] Cieza says that the temple on Qhuru Puna and another dedicated to Willka Nuta received whole birds, not just their plumage.[186]

COOKED FOOD

Sacrifices of cooked food were made to *waqas* related to peaks and hills. Guaman Poma claims the Yauyo offered comestibles to Parya Qaqa,[187] and the Huanca left food for Wallullu,[188] while Ayala writes that the people of Chinchaycocha provided Raco with victuals.[189] It is maintained by Ulloa that the natives of the Arequipa area honored their mountain-*waqas* with oblations of food.[190]

MISCELLANEOUS

Additional offerings are mentioned only rarely in the ethno-historic sources, either because they were uncommon or the Spanish did not have much interest in them. One such item is carved firewood. Cobo and Polo assert that Mantocallas was given numerous bundles of wood to be ritually burned.[191] They also refer to a summit called Puncu, the last *waqa* on the ninth *siq'e* in the southeastern quarter of the Cuzco Valley, to which were proffered leftovers from the other sacred sites on the line.[192]

Guaman Poma observes that Aysa Uilca, one of the most prominent *waqas* in Chinchay Suyu and possibly a mountain,[193] received odd gifts, including cotton, fruit, and "colors."[194] I am not sure what the chronicler means by "colors" ("colores" in the original text), but it may be an allusion to sacred powders of different hues that were sacrificed to idols and at shrines. One such powder, called *paria,* was vermillion and consisted of ground mercury sulphide obtained from the mines of Huancavelica; a green powder known as *llacsa* was comprised of pulverized copper oxide. There was also a blue powder referred to as *binço,* and a yellow one bearing the name *carvamuqui.* These powders were blown toward the *waqas* as offerings.[195]

Regarding other unusual items, Torres says that during an eruption of

Putina (actually Huayna Putina)[196] in 1600, the people living near Arequipa sacrificed birds to appease the volcano.[197] Polo notes that when Andean natives had nothing else to leave for a hill or peak, they would make an oblation of an old sandal, eyelash, or eyebrow hair,[198] the latter items being blown toward the object of veneration.[199] Some sacrificial materials were closely linked with particular mountain-*waqas.* In the Huarochirí manuscript, it says that after Wallullu was defeated by Parya Qaqa, the volcano-god was condemned to receive immolations of dogs from the Huanca.[200] The Augustinian priests tell us that the *waqa* Guallio, situated in a cave between two crags, was proffered specific articles such as weaving tools (see Figure 5.3), fashioned from horn and bone, and spindle whorls.[201]

OFFERINGS TO *APACHITAS*

Apachitas were a special kind of *waqa* located on the tops of hills and at mountain passes. Consisting of great piles of rocks amassed by travelers over the years, they received an assortment of offerings, all of which were humble, and some of which were mentioned above. A wayfarer might leave a coca quid among the stones or a piece of chewed corn or a feather. A few oblations came from the human body itself: people would pluck an eyelash or an eyebrow hair and blow it toward the *apachita.* A wanderer could also cast onto the mound any item he or she was carrying and wanted to discard, such as a sandal, a piece of rope, a rag, or a sling. If a person had nothing else, he would pick up a stick, rock, or clod of dirt and add it to the accumulation, or he might grab a handful of *ichu* grass, twist it into a coil, and spit into it before tossing it onto the growing heap.[202]

BRIEF DISCUSSION OF SACRIFICIAL MATERIALS

Although each type of offering is discussed separately above, perhaps giving the impression that the Cuzqueños would leave a single type of offering for a mountain-*waqa,* this was rarely the case. As Cobo observes, "It should not be understood that the sacrifices . . . were made alone, with only one kind of thing, because it was not done in this way."[203] The Inkas had a hierarchy of imperial oblations, at the pinnacle of which were human lives, and at the bottom, goods such as feathers. The kinds of ritual materials that a peak received partly depended on its status. The most

FIGURE 5.3.   *Young woman weaving on a typical backstrap loom; note the different tools of her trade (Guaman Poma 1980a: 191).*

significant *waqas* were given children and/or young women for immolation, as well as llamas, gold and silver, clothing, *mullu*, coca leaves, and so
forth.[204] A summit of secondary importance might have merited clothing
as its principal offering and have been proffered lesser articles such as shells,
coca, feathers, and so on.

Were any oblations identified specifically with peaks? One way to
answer this question is to compare the types of materials contributed by
the lords of Cuzco to mountain-*waqas* with the kinds of items awarded

another class of *waqa:* fountains and springs. Of all the sacred sites Cobo and Polo list for the Cuzco area, over a quarter fall into the latter category, and of these, there is a subset for which we learn the types of offerings they received. As it turns out, 88 percent of the fountains and springs falling into the subset were provided with both *mullu* and other items, while 67 percent were given only shell, and only 1 percent was allotted human victims.[205] It would seem that these *waqas* were of moderate significance as they awarded few human immolations and were closely linked with *mullu*. The most likely explanation for the association is that fountains/springs were worshipped primarily for water; *mullu,* as the daughters of Mother Sea,[206] were thought to be appropriate gifts for water-related *waqas*.

Mountain-*waqas*—including venerated hills and peaks with sacred stones, shrines, and temples on their slopes—make up about 22 percent of the hallowed sites around the capital. For a small subset of these, we are told the types of sacrifices made to them by the Inkas.[207] If we look at the *waqas* comprising the subset, we find that, in contrast with the fountains/springs, 56 percent were proffered infants for sacrifice. The figure may be misleading, though, for several reasons. Some of the immolations that took place at mountain shrines were dedicated not to the *waqas* themselves but to prominent gods such as the Creator and/or Sun.[208] Also, because the killing of a child was so abhorrent to the chroniclers, they were more likely to report it than they were the offering of more mundane items. Taking the first factor into account (I have no way to compensate for the second), I have found that perhaps a third of the mountain-*waqas* were offered human sacrifices. This percentage, which is significant, is indicative of the general holiness of mountain sites.

Examining the relationship between hilltop shrines and other kinds of sacrificial materials, I have made the following determinations: about 20 percent of mountain sites in the Cuzco area received textiles, while another 20 percent were given *mullu*. Neither association seems particularly noteworthy; what they suggest is that mountain-*waqas* were not linked exclusively with clothing, shell, or any single item. Nor does there seem to be a correlation between hilltop shrines and fixed sets of offerings. This lack of association may be significant, however, the most plausible explanation being that—unlike fountains/springs, which were worshipped for water—mountain-*waqas* were venerated for a variety of reasons. Consequently, the oblations allotted them were not always the same, but varied from peak to peak, and perhaps from occasion to occasion. I will further explore these possibilities in Chapter 6.

Although there does not appear to be a close correspondence between hilltop shrines and particular offerings, it does not follow that any goods could have been left for such *waqas*. As noted earlier, there is considerable repetition in the types of items said to have been donated to them.

I have compared and contrasted the inventory of materials sacrificed by the Inkas at mountain shrines in the Cuzco area[209] with the list of goods proffered by royal officials at similar *waqas* in the provinces.[210] There do not seem to be any substantial differences between them; prominent mountain-*waqas* near the capital and in the hinterlands received essentially the same types of imperial items, which may mean that regardless of where they were located, peaks and hills were venerated by the lords of Cuzco for the same reasons. I also have looked at the similarities and differences between royal oblations made in the provinces and local offerings. It would seem that in many cases, Inka and provincial priests were sacrificing the same general types of things to mountain shrines.[211] Sometimes the local immolations were simpler than the imperial ones, though not substantially different.[212] The most important distinction between them may be that royal oblations could include human victims, whereas regional offerings could not, at least not without the consent of the emperor.[213] These findings probably indicate that the Cuzqueños and provincial peoples worshipped at hill shrines for similar reasons, and that the former were intent on regulating human immolation. Such ideas will be further developed in Chapter 6.

NON-MATERIAL CONTRIBUTIONS TO MOUNTAIN-*WAQAS*

According to ethnohistoric sources, after the Inkas subjugated a region, they assumed responsibility for venerating the principal *waqas* there, a large percentage of which were associated with peaks. Honoring a mountain-*waqa*, however, required more than contributing materials for sacrifice. It entailed making a labor pool available to the shrine or idol, establishing a llama herd in its name, ensuring that fields and pastures were available to it,[214] and appointing priests to serve it.

Albornoz claims that in Kunti Suyu, there was a very sacred snow-capped summit known as Sara Sara (the spelling in the document is "Caraçara," which literally translates as "corn corn," but means "a heap of maize"[215]). After conquering the area where the peak is situated, the lords of Cuzco settled two thousand *mitmaq-kuna*, colonists moved en masse from a province that had been pacified earlier, there. Among the colonists there may have been *kamayuqs*[216]—a term that refers to skilled professionals, including bureaucrats and craftsmen—as well as unskilled laborers. The bureaucrats may have been charged with keeping track of and managing the materials to be offered to the *waqa,* the artisans with manufacturing items for sacrifice to it, and some of the workers with cultivating its fields. The produce raised in these fields would have been used to "feed" the mountain-deity. Two hundred female llamas of breeding age along with their parents (possibly six hundred animals) were made part of Sara Sara's holdings as well. This sizable herd was likely self-sustaining and was grazed in pastures assigned to the *waqa.* Animals were regularly picked from it for immolation. Albornoz writes that several peaks in Kunti Suyu were venerated by the Inkas in the same fashion as Sara Sara—including Sulimana, Qhuru Puna, Ampato, and Putina[217]—and that there were numerous mountain-*waqas* in the other quarters that they so honored.[218]

According to the Augustinians, in Guamachuco there was an anthropomorphic statue that sat on a boulder, which was itself situated on a pinnacle. This mountain-*waqa,* called Apocatequil, was venerated throughout the province. Near the peak was a village with buildings and fields dedicated to the *waqa;* all the village's residents—including five priests, two servants, and many others—were consecrated to its service.[219] The same sources tell us that the populace of Guamachuco venerated Yanaguanca and Xulcaguanca, two summits that had their own retainers.[220] Cieza notes that Wana Kawri Hill was provided with fields and a llama herd, and that it was served by various categories of people,[221] including *mama-kuna* (who were similar to European nuns in that they dedicated their lives to a particular god and were kept cloistered),[222] *yana-kuna* (male retainers[223] who probably cultivated the *waqa's* fields and tended its herd), and priests.[224] Cieza also writes that the temple on Qhuru Puna, like Wana Kawri, was assigned agricultural land, llamas, *mama-kuna,* laborers, and priests.

Guaman Poma states that the Cuzqueños established a hierarchy of religious officiants to serve their deities, including those related to mountains. Among the highest-ranking officials was one assigned to Wana Kawri. Below him were "bishops" who attended non-Inka *waqas* known throughout the empire, such as the peaks Parya Qaqa, Ayza Bilca, and Muchuca Billca. At a still lower level were "clergymen" who honored significant provincial gods, many of them mountains and volcanoes: Saua Ciray, Pitu Ciray, Ausan Cata, Qhuru Puna, and Suri Uillca. All these religious officiants were supported by the state.[225]

In the Huarochirí manuscript is a story about the Yauyo, an ethnic group whose members were divided into two social units, an "upper" and "lower" moiety. After the Inkas subjugated them, the emperor decreed that they worship Parya Qaqa. He instructed the upper moiety to send thirty men to serve and make offerings to the *waqa* for fifteen days, subsequent to which they were replaced by thirty men from the lower moiety for the next fifteen days. Thus, the two social groups alternated in providing retainers for Parya Qaqa.[226] In another myth, the king assigns fifty servants to the mountain-deity[227] and gives it a llama herd.[228]

SECONDARY RITES ASSOCIATED WITH SACRIFICE AND MOUNTAIN WORSHIP

Sacrifices to mountain-*waqas* were accompanied by secondary acts of reverence, among them confession, bathing, fasting, face painting, paying homage to the *waqa,* praying, singing, dancing, playing music, and drinking. The first four of these lesser rites took place before an offering was made, the final six during or subsequent to the oblation.

Cobo maintains that confession was a nearly universal ritual act, and that people who were going to honor a *waqa* with gifts would first disclose their transgressions to priests in the service of the sacred entity. The priests, which included men and women, were categorized according to rank. It is probable that nobles confessed only to the higher-status members of the "clergy," while commoners revealed their trespasses to priests with a lower social stature. If a commoner had committed a grave sin, however, he or she had to disclose it to a supreme confessor. All members of the clergy, regardless of rank, were bound to secrecy, though within certain limits. The Inkas supposedly considered the following to be serious transgressions, albeit some of them sound much like Catholic sins: murder through violence, witchcraft, or poisoning; theft; failure to take part in a major festival; negligence in venerating the *waqas* properly; cursing the king; and trying to cover up a sin in confession.[229]

After admitting his trespasses, but before making a sacrifice to an idol or peak, an individual might be directed to bathe in a stream so the current would carry away his sins. He might be required to give penance too, perhaps by fasting, which usually involved abstinence from salt and chile peppers for a short time. Depending on the gravity of the transgressions and/or the importance of the immolation, fasting could mean giving up meat, *chicha,* and sex for extended periods.[230] It was not only sinners who were required to fast, but priests as well. The Augustinians tell us that when there was drought in Guamachuco, the local religious officials would climb a high mountain to carry out a ceremony involving the two *waqas* called *magacti*. First they fasted for several days.[231] A final act of reverence related to the sacrifice that took place prior to the oblation was face painting. The Anonymous Jesuit—discussing rites performed by the Aymara for Pisi—asserts that villagers intent on bringing offerings to the *waqa* often prepared themselves beforehand by smearing red coloring made from the seeds of the annatto tree or the mineral cinnabar on their faces.[232]

Some secondary rituals were carried out at about the same time as or following the sacrifice. One such rite entailed paying homage to a *waqa*. Cobo reports that as Peruvians approached a temple, idol, or shrine, they honored it by going through the following motions: they faced it and bowed in a show of humility; stretched their arms out in front of themselves, being careful to keep these limbs parallel and a little higher than their heads; opened their hands with the palms pointing toward the *waqa*; made a kissing sound with their mouths; and brought their hands to their lips in order to kiss their fingertips.[233] Ulloa notes that the natives of the Arequipa area observed this custom when venerating the five peaks.[234] The Aymara showed their respect for Pisi in much the same way, the only difference being that they kept their left hands on their heads with their right arms extended.[235]

Another ritual act associated with immolation was prayer. People invoked the *waqas* both silently and aloud. To consecrate an oblation, an officiant would say a prayer that varied according to the deity being addressed, the type of offering, and the purpose it was meant to serve.[236] Ayala states that the inhabitants of Chinchaycocha made offerings to and invoked the mountain-god Raco during planting season.[237] Singing was also a secondary rite connected with immolation and high peaks.[238] When the Aymara gathered on the unnamed summit to honor their *waqa*, they were divided into four groups, each with its own dirges, which its members chanted as part of the ceremonies,[239] and when the Inkas put men and women to death on Wana Kawri, there was much singing.[240] Oblations for mountain-*waqas* were sometimes accompanied by dancing[241] and/or music. We are informed not only that the Aymara danced for Pisi, perhaps to the sound of drums and small flutes,[242] but that the human sacrifices on Wana Kawri were associated with dancing.[243] Polo reports that when miners carried out rituals venerating a peak—during which they would ask it to give up its silver, mercury, or other metals—they would spend the night keeping vigil and dancing.[244] The Huarochirí manuscript mentions that the Yunca made sacrifices to Parya Qaqa, after which they danced for at least five days.[245] The Augustinians say they found some trumpets in Guamachuco that were composed of silver and a base metal, were affiliated with the mountain/storm god Catequil, and were likely played during sacred ceremonies. Said ceremonies may have involved leaving offerings on the pinnacle Guacat.[246]

The final ritual act identified with immolation and mountain-*waqas* was drinking.[247] Returning to the example from Polo on the rites performed by miners for summits, these included imbibing.[248] According to Murúa, when a traveler safely reached his destination, he would give thanks to a local peak by proffering it a gift and by drinking,[249] probably corn beer. In his discussion of Wara Chicuy, Molina reports that the participating youths climbed to the top of Raurana, where they proceeded to imbibe, following the order of their social rank.[250] As part of their initiation ceremonies, the adolescents participated in a footrace on Anahuarqui too. Starting from its summit, they ran down the slope to a finish line at the base, where they were met by maidens holding jars of *chicha*.[251]

Six

REASONS FOR
WORSHIPPING MOUNTAINS

The chroniclers give numerous reasons for worshipping mountains. For the most part, the explanations fall into fifteen categories: (1) the extraordinary nature of peaks; (2) their prominent role in Andean mythology; (3) their role as "stepping stones" to higher gods; (4) their capacity to control meteorological phenomena; (5) their association with water; (6) their connection with human health; (7) their association with economic production; (8) their link with travel; (9) their capacity to frighten or intimidate; (10) their oracular functions; (11) their incorporation into sight-lines; (12) their function as markers of limits and boundaries; (13) their role as unifiers of diverse people; (14) their symbolic role in the empire's well-being; and (15) their manipulation to create and reinforce power relationships. These categories are not mutually exclusive, there being a fair amount of overlap between them.

1. THE EXTRAORDINARY NATURE
OF PEAKS

Andean groups revered mountains that were higher than others or unusual in some other way.[1] According to Cobo,[2] a hill was considered sacred when it was "different in shape or substance from those nearby, being formed of earth or sand, where the rest were rocky, or vice versa."[3] Acosta tells us that in the Nazca area, on the south coast of Peru, was a hillock regarded as the principal *waqa* of the Hacari people. This peak was special and worthy of homage in that it consisted of sand, while the summits around it were of stone.[4]

As discussed in Chapter 4, Garcilaso denies that the inhabitants of Peru considered mountains to be gods, but admits that high pinnacles that far surpassed nearby peaks were much esteemed, as were summits covered with snow.[5] Cobo discusses a mountain that probably had both of these characteristics. Referred to as Raurao Quiran, it was situated in the southeastern quarter of the Cuzco Valley and was venerated because of its large size;[6] given that the word *rao,* which translates as "snow,"[7] comprises part of the peak's name, it very likely bore a mantle of white. Ulloa maintains that the Collagua revered Collaguata Volcano because it was snow-capped and stood out from adjacent pinnacles.[8] Other mountains that were worshipped in southern Peru include Suquilpa, Omascota, and Gualcagualca, all of which were lofty and blanketed in white.[9] Cabeza de Vaca notes that the people living around La Paz, Bolivia, adored a high and perpetually snow-covered peak called Hillemana (Illimani).[10] Albornoz asserts that the Yauyo and Huanca had Wallullu as their principal *waqa,*[11] the Atavillo had Mount Yarovilca,[12] and the Quito had Piccinca (Pichincha),[13] each of which was large and occasionally snow-covered.

There are numerous references in the ethnohistoric literature to Parya Qaqa. Dávila mentions that a greatly esteemed summit by this name, situated in the province of the Yauyo, not far from Lima, was the loftiest point in the local mountain range and had a snowy mantle.[14] The Huarochirí manuscript says that the god Parya Qaqa was closely identified with one or more pinnacles blanketed in white.[15]

Why were the inhabitants of the Andes preoccupied with snow? One explanation is that when a peak was covered in white, it looked more impressive, and probably seemed more worthy of reverence. Also, water from the melting snows was used to irrigate the crops.[16] I will explore the latter idea later in the chapter.

2. THE PROMINENT ROLE OF MOUNTAINS IN ANDEAN MYTHOLOGY

Another reason for worshipping mountains was because they played significant roles in the mythical histories of Andean peoples,[17] particularly in origin stories. This subject is discussed at length in Chapter 4, so I will summarize the main points here. Several authors tell us that high summits were conceived of as living and divine beings. Paz reports that the natives of the Quito area considered the sacred volcanoes Chimborazo and Tunguragua to be, respectively, male and female, husband and wife, and lovers.[18] Some pinnacles represented the projection of a local legend onto the landscape. In a story from Huarochirí, after Parya Qaqa defeats Wallullu and chases him to the lowlands, he makes sure that the volcano-god never returns by posting a brother at a pass overlooking the tropical region. The brother turns into a snow-capped peak.[19]

Many a mountain-*waqa* was venerated as a *paqariku,* the spot where the legendary ancestors of an ethnic group were thought to have first emerged into this world.[20] The Collagua revered Collaguata as their *paqariku,* while the Cavana considered Gualcagualca to be their place of origin.[21] Similarly, the inhabitants of Parinacocha traced their roots to Sara Sara,[22] the populace of Tomebamba to Guasaynan,[23] the members of a group living near Tomebamba to Chimborazo,[24] the Indians of Guamachuco to Guacat,[25] and the residents of Urcos to Awsan Qata.[26]

Whereas some summits were worshipped as *paqarikus,* others were esteemed because they saved the ancestors from a primordial flood. The Cañari believed they were descended from the two brothers who took refuge from a deluge on the sacred hill called Huaca Yñan;[27] part of the population of Huarochirí traced their lineage back to a herder delivered from certain drowning by Mount Villca Coto, which was greatly revered.[28] Origin myths of this type also were recorded in the provinces of Tomebamba and Ancasmarca, and involved, respectively, the mountain-*waqas* Puna[29] and Ancasmarca.[30]

Wana Kawri figures prominently in the creation legends of the Cuzqueños. According to Sarmiento, the mythical ancestors of the Inkas—four brothers and four sisters—appeared from their *paqariku* and climbed the hill from whose crest they saw a rainbow arching over the Cuzco Valley. They interpreted the rainbow as a sign that this was where they should build their capital. The youngest of the brothers then turned into a *wanqa.*[31] Each year, the Inkas honored Wana Kawri by carrying out initiation rites on its summit[32] and by sacrificing men and women there.[33] Another peak esteemed by the lords of Cuzco was Anahuarqui, said to have run as fast as a puma during the primordial flood, and down whose slopes Inka youths had to sprint. This race was one of the ritual trials by which they became men.[34]

3. MOUNTAINS AS "STEPPING STONES" TO HIGHER GODS

A third explanation for why Andean peoples performed solemn ceremonies on pinnacles may have been to reach their principal gods; the Cuzqueños may have believed that by ascending a high and revered summit, they were getting as close as possible to Wira Qucha, Inti,

Illapa, and Mama Killa,[35] and that any rite carried out on the peak to honor one of these deities would have special efficacy. This idea is somewhat speculative, but many ethnohistoric sources mention rituals that took place on pinnacles but that were intended for gods other than the mountain-*waqas*. Having described such ceremonies in Chapter 4, I will review the pertinent information here.

Cobo and Polo assert that on Chuquipalta, a revered summit in the Cuzco Valley, offerings were made to the Creator, Sun, and Thunder rather than to the mountain-spirit.[36] They tell of another peak near the capital called Churuncana where human sacrifices were carried out to glorify Wira Qucha.[37] Molina notes that during the initiation rites for Inka youths, the llamas slaughtered on Anahuarqui were dedicated to the Creator, Sun, Thunder, and Moon, and that the camelids put to death on Raurana were likewise intended to benefit the major Inka deities.[38]

Several sacred ceremonies performed on mountains in the provinces honored the Sun. Noboa claims that the immolation of two brothers on Nabincoto in Cajatambo was meant to venerate Inti,[39] while Hernández says that Tanta Carhua's sacrifice on the summit in Aixa was intended to glorify the Sun.[40]

4. THE CAPACITY OF MOUNTAINS TO CONTROL METEOROLOGICAL PHENOMENA

An important motive for worshipping peaks was because they were thought to control meteorological phenomena.[41] Cobo and Polo maintain that in the northeastern quarter of the Cuzco Valley was a hill on whose crest sat a small stone called Picas. The Inkas left offerings there so it would not hail.[42] Pachacuti relates the tale of the three hundred men from Antis who arrived at the capital just as the temperature plummeted. To prevent the crops from freezing, the emperor had them and their gold taken to the top of Pachatusun and immolated,[43] the implication being that this pinnacle had some influence over the weather and could reverse the cold spell. Paz tells us that on the slopes of Chimborazo were numerous llamas; the local inhabitants left these animals alone because they believed that if any harm came to them, the volcano-god would destroy the harvest with frigid temperatures and hail.[44]

Stories in the Huarochirí manuscript link Parya Qaqa to hail, wind, fog, snow, and lightning. One legend tells how the mountain-deity got angry at the people of Huauqui Usa and bombarded them with red and yellow hail,[45] while in another myth he is offended by the Colli and sends them flying with a violent wind.[46] There also is a story in which the *waqa* causes a cloud of fog to appear over a summit before he wipes out the populace of San Damián.[47] Other parts of the Huarochirí document identify Parya Qaqa as a peak covered with snow[48] and as a god who fights with lightning.[49] Given that hail and snow could devastate crops by flattening and freezing them, lightning could kill people, and wind and fog could make life miserable, peaks such as Parya Qaqa were venerated to placate them so they would not call up foul weather and violent storms.

5. THE ASSOCIATION OF MOUNTAINS WITH WATER

A primary impetus for paying homage to pinnacles was that they were believed to regulate rainfall and the movement of water.[50] According to Murúa, the Cuzqueños sacrificed camelids and scattered their blood among the mountains to bring snow to high summits and rain to the surrounding area.[51] Albornoz asserts that white-clad peaks and volcanoes often received offerings because the water that flowed from them was used for irrigation.[52] Ulloa notes that the natives of Cavana worshipped Gualcagualca and bound the heads of their infants to give them the same shape as the mountain; Gualcagualca provided meltwater that was crucial for agriculture.[53] Other mountains in the region—including Collaguata, Suquilpa, Apoquico, and Omascota—were venerated for the same reason.[54] Ramos claims that the Yunguyo, an ethnic group whose members dwelt by Lake Titi Qaqa, had an idol called Copacati that was situated on a hill with the same name. During times of drought, the people gathered on the pinnacle and asked for water for their crops.[55] Bibar relates that in the area around Santiago, Chile, at the southern extreme of the Inka state, the Pormocae revered snow-capped summits because they supplied water for the fields.[56]

An example from Velasco's chronicle illustrates the connection between mountain worship and flowing water. He talks about a sacred pinnacle in Ecuador, at the opposite end of the empire from where the Pormocae lived, which was called Ashuay. It was covered with snow for part of the year and had various constructions on its slopes, including two stone baths, a lake, and most intriguing of all, a serpentine channel. Water from high on the peak would run into the channel, follow its more than three hundred twists and turns, and empty into the lake.[57] In form, the watercourse resembled a *paccha,* a type of vessel that existed during the Late Horizon and in Colonial times. Either water or *chicha* would be poured in one end of the *paccha* and flow through it—often following a zigzag course—and out the other side. The gushing of fluid through the piece represented the circulation of water through the terrestrial and celestial spheres, considered vital for human life.[58] Thus, the movement of water through the serpentine channel on the flank of snow-capped Ashuay may have symbolized the mountain's role as a circulator of water for human use.

Parya Qaqa is closely associated with rain and flowing water, most of it uncontrolled. In the Huarochirí manuscript, the god is said to have castigated the residents of Huauqui Usa by causing a downpour that washed them away,[59] to have battled Wallullu by employing rain as a weapon,[60] and to have destroyed the hamlet of San Damián with colored rain.[61] There is, in fact, only one myth linking the *waqa* to regulated water. It begins with Parya Qaqa watching a beautiful woman named Chuqui Suso. She is crying because her maize fields have withered from lack of water, so Parya Qaqa tells her that he will make the water flow in her irrigation channels if she will sleep with him. She agrees. He then clears an obstruction at the point where one of her ditches leaves a pond, widens an old canal originally built by the Yunca, and extends it from the river to her lands. When he finishes his labors and water is coursing to her fields, they sleep together.[62] This final image makes explicit the idea that the union of controlled fluid and earth is analogous to sex.

The Huarochirí document includes another legend about a mountain-*waqa* closely identified with flowing water, both unregulated and regulated. This *waqa* is called Collquiri. As the story opens, Collquiri, standing on a summit overlooking the hamlet of Yampilla, spies a lovely woman called Capyama and falls in love with her. He sends a servant to fetch her under the pretext that one of her llamas has given birth on the pinnacle. She arrives at the spot where he is waiting, whereupon the deity changes himself into a grasshopper, jumps into her dress, and begins to grow. Then he appears to her as a young man. They sleep together, and he takes her as his wife and priestess.[63] Meanwhile, Capyama's relatives, worried because she has disappeared, set out to look for her. They find her and threaten to take her away from her husband, but finally relent when he promises to give them what he calls the "Thing-that-goes-into." Five days later, true to his word, Collquiri burrows into the earth and heads toward Yampilla, popping out of the ground near the village. He is followed by a gush of water. At this point, the answer to the riddle of the "Thing-that-goes-into" becomes clear, for it refers to the mountain-*waqa* himself, who goes into

Capyama's dress as a grasshopper and into the earth as a spring; the riddle makes apparent the symbolic connection between sex and the movement of water through soil. Returning to the myth, the gushing spring created by Collquiri washes away the hamlet's tubers, quinua (high-altitude grain), and other crops, threatening to completely destroy the fields. The villagers desperately shout at the *waqa* to stop the flow, but when he tries to oblige them, water spurts everywhere, so he jumps into the hole and uses his body and cloak to plug it. He seals it so well, however, that nothing can get through, and the inhabitants of Concha, a nearby hamlet, start complaining that they are experiencing drought. At the end, Collquiri has an irrigation system built and puts Llacsa Misa, a priest, in charge of operating it, which is significant in that irrigation authority and priestly power become vested in a single individual.[64]

These stories exemplify important principles underlying the belief system of Huarochirí. There is the notion that the earth, particularly valleys and flat, irrigable lands, are female, while high peaks, with their mantles of snow and ice, are male. The physical substance of the earth, the soil—especially the deep fertile soil of a river valley—is conceived of as being like a womb and is thought to have "female" characteristics: solidity, dryness, stability, and potential fecundity. The fundamental essence of the mountains is that of uncontrolled water that comes from melting snow and glacial ice. Water is likened to semen and is believed to have such "male" properties as fluidity, wetness, movement, and virility.[65] Because it is unregulated, the liquid that flows from lofty summits is dangerous, as illustrated by Parya Qaqa's destruction of the villages of Huauqui Usa and San Damián, by his defeat of Wallullu, and by Collquiri's devastation of Yampilla's crops.

A second principle reflected in the myths is the idea that the combination of moving fluid and dry soil is analogous to the union of male and female elements. In other words, water soaking into the parched earth is akin to intercourse, the result being fertility and new life. But, before it can be used, runoff from the heights must be controlled, which brings us to the third principle illustrated by the Huarochirí manuscript: that water is managed through irrigation and sacrifice. Irrigation takes place in the physical world and involves mobilizing human labor to create networks of canals that channel meltwater from the peaks to the fields so it can flow evenly over them, impregnating the soil (see Figure 6.1). Sacrifice affects the spiritual realm and entails making offerings to mountain-deities to placate them so they will not employ water for destructive purposes.[66] In the story about Collquiri, the irrigation system is entrusted to Llacsa Misa, a

FIGURE 6.1.   *Young woman irrigating the corn fields; note the network of ditches (Guaman Poma 1980c: 1059).*

priest,[67] suggesting that irrigation and ritual immolation are different sides of the same proverbial coin.

6. THE CONNECTION BETWEEN MOUNTAINS AND HUMAN HEALTH

One reason that pinnacles were venerated was because they were thought to influence human health and fecundity.[68]

Cobo and Polo cite several examples of summits near the capital that were worshipped for the salutary effect they had on people. In the north-eastern quarter of the Cuzco Valley was a hill called Illansayba. On its crest sat several stones where sacrifices were offered for the health of anyone entering Andes province.[69] In the northwestern quadrant was a knoll bearing the name Sonconancay, where it was customary to make oblations to ensure the king's good health.[70] A peak in the southeastern part of the valley had a large stone on top known as Guamansaui. The Inkas left gold, silver, and miniature garments at this *waqa* so the monarch would remain physically strong.[71] Returning to the northeastern quarter, on one hillock was a *wanqa* called Sanotuiron where gifts were left to ensure the well-being of the prince.[72]

The folk in the hinterlands likewise venerated peaks and beseeched them for health and long life.[73] Ayala relates that in Chinchaycocha, the inhabitants made sacrifices to Raco and invoked it for their salubrity.[74]

Mountain-*waqas* were also thought to have a role in controlling disease. According to the Anonymous Jesuit, the adoration of Pisi began to decline during the Colonial period, whereupon this *waqa* threatened to decimate the Aymara with an epidemic if they did not resume their ancient practices, including the sacrifice of animals in its honor.[75] Arriaga, citing a letter from Father Luis de Teruel, reports that when a person became sick, he often consulted a sorcerer. The sorcerer would make his way to a summit, propel stones at it with his sling, complain that it was responsible for the illness, and beg it to make the patient better.[76] Ayala maintains that highlanders who went walking in the hills and who came upon an *apachita* would occasionally grab a handful of straw, spit into it, and toss it onto the pile. In this way, they got rid of their sins,[77] which could cause not only disease, but the death of family members.[78]

Another factor in the well-being of a group was the ability of its members to avoid getting killed. The Augustinian priests assert that the inhabitants of Guamachuco respected and feared Catequil because it produced thunder and lightning with its sling, which compelled these people to leave offerings so it would not slay them.[79] Murúa tells us about the eruption of the volcano near Arequipa that destroyed the city and wiped out most of its residents. To placate the pinnacle and stop its slaughter of his subjects, the emperor hurled little balls containing sacrificial blood at it.[80] A number of chroniclers—among them Ayala, Murúa, Polo, and Ramos—declare that Andean folks would offer simple gifts to summits and/or *apachitas* while journeying through hilly terrain so the mountain-spirits would allow them to pass safely and do no harm.[81] Albornoz relates that travelers would discard coca quids at *waqas* known as *ormaychicos,* situated at the bases of peaks, to prevent deadly rockfalls.[82]

Pinnacles were adored not only because they were partly responsible for human health, but because they influenced fertility.[83] The Agustinos mention that the populace of Guamachuco honored Catequil, and in exchange it gave them children.[84] Similarly, Polo notes that before a woman bore a child, she and her husband would venerate local summits to guarantee a successful delivery.[85] The Huarochirí manuscript says that the reason the Yunca and other coastal groups started dying out during the Colonial era was they no longer worshipped and carried out immolations for Parya Qaqa; the highland Indians were flourishing because they still performed ceremonies on behalf of this mountain-deity.[86]

7. THE ASSOCIATION OF MOUNTAINS WITH ECONOMIC PRODUCTION

Many motives for paying homage to peaks were related to economics.[87] The economy of the Inkas—which included the production, distribution, and consumption of goods and materials—was based primarily on agriculture. Mountain worship was linked to cultivation in several ways: rituals were employed to ensure adequate water for irrigation, to keep the crops from freezing, to signal when the different steps in the agrarian cycle should take place, and to guarantee success in all phases of agricultural production. (The connection between lofty pinnacles and water and the role of mountain-deities in controlling weather are noted above.)

Sacred summits also played a crucial role in the calendrical rites employed to coordinate each stage of cultivation. Herrera tells us that twelve pillars were placed on hills around the capital in such a way that when the Inkas saw the sun set or rise behind a specific one, it was time to sow. When the sun reached another column, the harvest could begin.[88] Cobo and Polo provide similar, though more detailed, data. They assert that in the northwestern quarter of the Cuzco Valley was the knoll called Sucanca on whose slopes sat two markers, and that when a person standing at a particular spot witnessed the sun rise between these structures, the maize could be planted.[89] In the southwestern quadrant was a hill known as Chinchincalla with two pillars that served to indicate the time for sowing another crop.[90]

Peaks were worshipped and offerings made to them to ensure a favorable outcome for each phase of agricultural production.[91] Ayala mentions that in Chinchaycocha, just as planting was getting underway, the inhabitants sacrificed food and drink to Raco, invoking the mountain-*waqa* for an abundant crop.[92] Velasco says that every year the Cañari climbed to a cave on Supayurco to immolate a hundred children. The rite took place toward the end of the agricultural season and was intended to guarantee a good harvest.[93] Cobo and Polo claim that during the shelling of the maize, Mantocallas received offerings of children, llamas, carved firewood, and wooden ears of corn.[94]

Another significant component of the Andean economy associated with mountain worship was herding. The Inkas maintained vast flocks of llamas, while provincial groups had smaller herds. The camelids were raised for their meat and wool, and to serve as beasts of burden; long trains comprised of hundreds or even thousands of animals were employed to transport goods and materials around the empire.[95] In the minds of the Andean people, there was a close relationship between summits and livestock. According to Paz, the natives of the Quito area, who believed Chimborazo protected the llamas living on its lower flanks, never killed the camelids, nor got close enough to harm them, lest the pinnacle retaliate by destroying their crops with cold and hail.[96] Avila's document relates that in Huarochirí, the populace periodically raced to a peak from which Parya Qaqa could be seen. As the participants made their way up the slope, they drove their llama bucks before them, and the first animal to reach the top was considered the darling of the mountain-god.[97]

Pinnacles were also associated with the fertility of livestock.[98] The Augustinian priests assert that in Guamachuco, the inhabitants had three prominent *waqas*—Apocatequil, Mamacatequil, and Pigueroa—which consisted of large stones on the summit of a hill. They were partly honored so they would provide "sheep [of the land]," llamas.[99] The Huarochirí manuscript says that the Checa and Yunca, who had intermingled through conquest and marriage,[100] celebrated a special festival. As part of it, each family decorated its animals with bells and ear tassels, walked to a peak called Curri, and carried out a rite involving its *caullama* (a statuette of a household deity that guaranteed the llamas' fecundity).[101] Monzón tells us the Rucana had a similar practice. They would climb sacred pinnacles where they kept idols made of stone and clay representing livestock; on these pinnacles, they would immolate llamas and guinea pigs, probably so their animals would become more fertile and their herds grow.[102]

Labor was an essential component of the Inka economy. The empire had no currency, thus all taxes were paid in the form of service to the state. Much of the work contributed by the *runas* (peasants) as part of their tax obligations consisted of sowing, tending fields, harvesting, and storing crops for both the polity and Inka religious institutions. In regions where raising camelids was important, people grazed and cared for flocks owned by the king and "church." Occasionally, the taxpayer had to do *mit'a* service, a type of labor obligation that men fulfilled on a rotating basis and that lasted up to several months. A *runa* whose turn it was to serve might man a garrison, fight as part of the army, attend to the needs of a noble, work as a messenger on a royal road, or care for and maintain a sacred shrine. If the emperor or one of his governors had plans for a massive project such as the construction of a fortress or palace, taxpayers provided the labor (see Figure 6.2). In this way, the Inkas employed about thirty thousand *mit'a* workers at a time to build the fortress of Sacsahuaman in Cuzco.[103] Labor was as vital at the provincial level as it was at the state level. Given the importance of human labor in the Andes, it may have been desirable to increase the size of the workforce by getting people to multiply quickly, an objective they could pursue by honoring *waqas* and offering them sacrifices. The number of laborers was not the only consideration, though, since the strength of the workforce also depended on the health of its members. As noted above, it was generally believed that a community's well-being could be improved by glorifying sacred shrines, especially those associated with peaks.[104]

Specialized production was crucial to the Inka Empire, and one type of craftsman and skilled worker, known as a *kamayuq*, was exempt from *mit'a* service. These weavers, miners, smiths, potters, and wood-carvers produced goods that went directly to the state, and the surplus was distributed by the emperor to nobles whom he wished to honor.[105]

According to the chroniclers, there was a connection between certain kinds of specialized production and mountain veneration. Cobo, Murúa, and Polo[106] all mention mining and give us the same information: before a man went to the gold, silver, mercury, or other type of mine where he worked, he carried out a ritual that lasted the night and that was meant to pay homage to the hills.[107] The rite consisted of drinking, dancing, and beseeching local peaks to give up their metal. Cabeza de Vaca relates that the inhabitants of Chuquiapo, a town near La Paz, worshipped a pinnacle known as Choque-Guanca around which there were several gold mines, including one at its base. These mines were worked from precontact times through the Colonial period.[108] The Augustinian priests tell us that before specialized weavers in Guamachuco made fine *qumpi* cloth for the king, they honored Guallio. They offered not only guinea pigs to this mountain-*waqa*, but spindle-whorls and weaving tools made from horn and bone.[109]

159

ELUOVEUOCAPITÃ
IUGAVRCOU•

FIGURE 6.2.   Runas *moving a large stone, perhaps as part of their* mit'a *service (Guaman Poma 1980a: 138).*

8. THE ASSOCIATION BETWEEN MOUNTAINS AND TRAVEL

Another reason for paying homage to summits and conducting rituals on their behalf was because they were connected with travel and trade.[110]

In the Inka Empire, peasants were generally restricted in their movements to local travel, which meant they were tied to their lands, and the

royal roads were less congested. On the other hand, certain imperial officials could move around the polity more freely, as could military personnel
and *mit'a* laborers on their way to and from projects. Since ordinary people
were limited in the amount they could travel, it was impossible for them to
engage in long-distance trade. Hence, the state, along with certain ethnic
groups, may have had a near monopoly on the transportation of raw materials and finished goods from one region to another.[111] The distribution
of products, an integral part of the economy, was carried out mostly by
means of the llama trains mentioned above, with each of the hundreds or
thousands of animals carrying up to 45 kilos.[112]

When *runas* did travel in the hills, perhaps going to neighboring villages
or making pilgrimages to nearby shrines, they would come upon *apachitas*.
On such occasions, they would make simple sacrifices and recite prayers
to these *waqas*—and to the spirits connected with local peaks—so they
might pass safely and in peace.[113] The pile of rocks often would be located
where a royal road, after climbing for many kilometers, leveled off at the
top of a knoll or pass. By the time a peasant reached the *apachita,* he was
exhausted from the arduous ascent and would add a stone to the ever-
growing heap to get rid of his fatigue. It also was believed that in exchange
for the small oblation, the mountain-deities would give him the strength
to continue.[114]

Runas who engaged in trade venerated pinnacles at different stages of
their journeys. An anonymous priest discusses the people of Chapi, a village near Quito. He says that before these folks went on business trips, they
would make their way to the crown of a hill, accompanied by area "sorcerers," to carry out sacrifices. They would ask the mountain-spirit about their
fates, being especially keen to learn if they would die before they returned
home.[115] Ayala mentions that when the inhabitants of Chinchaycocha went
on excursions involving trade, they would invoke and make simple offerings to the summits they passed on their way, asking the mountain-deities
for success in their commercial ventures, for health, and for safe passage.[116]
Polo and Murúa declare that upon reaching their destinations, some Andean
natives would stay up all night and honor a hill by performing immolations
on its behalf and toasting it.[117]

As noted above, the Cuzqueños needed vast numbers of camelids for
moving raw materials and finished goods around the empire; thus, they
tried to get their animals to multiply, as did various ethnic groups, by worshipping peaks related to fertility.[118]

9. THE CAPACITY OF MOUNTAINS
TO FRIGHTEN OR INTIMIDATE

A significant motive for revering pinnacles was to appease them in an effort to avoid their wrath.[119] Hills, crags, and volcanoes were considered powerful deities that could harm human beings in many different ways: by burying them in volcanic eruptions; infecting them with diseases; wiping out their crops by causing drought, floods, or frost; crushing them in landslides; and striking them with lightning. Murúa and Ulloa say that oblations were made to summits to placate them when they got angry.[120] If a mountain-deity was not appeased, it could cause serious damage and/or injury. Molina maintains that the Inkas carried out sacrifices for hills, at least in part, because otherwise these *waqas* would become enraged and punish the emperor.[121] In the Huarochirí manuscript, it sounds like the Yunca paid homage to Wallullu for one major reason: they were scared of him. He was, it seems, a man-eater who forced them to offer their children to him as food.[122]

10. THE ORACULAR FUNCTIONS
OF MOUNTAINS

Yet another reason why Andean peoples honored and left offerings for peaks was because of their connection with oracles.[123] Matienzo, writing about the myriad ethnic groups incorporated into the Inka state, maintains that many of them had *waqas* situated on mountains that served a common function: augury. These *waqas* received gifts of llamas, guinea pigs, coca leaves, gold, silver, and so on.[124] An anonymous priest claims that before going on long journeys, the inhabitants of Chapi carried out immolations on a hill and asked the mountain-spirit about their fates.[125] According to Cieza, one of the most sacred spots in Kunti Suyu was snow-capped Qhuru Puna, on whose slopes was a prominent oracle said to have spoken freely and to have given prophesies continuously rather than periodically. Buried near the oracle were sacrificial materials such as gold, silver, and jewels.[126]

Cieza also talks about Wana Kawri, the Inkas' second most important *waqa,* which was visible from the capital. He tells us there was an oracle on this hill that made predictions about the future, and that interred around the revered site were offerings, including numerous treasures and the bodies of victims ritually slain by the lords of Cuzco.[127] Guaman Poma confirms that

Wana Kawri was connected with divination. His picture titled "Capítvlo de los ídolos" (see Figure 4.1) shows Thupa Yapanki consulting a group of *waqas* about the past and about events to come, especially the arrival of the Spanish. Dominating the left-hand side of the drawing and positioned directly opposite the king is the peak with an idol on top.[128]

The relationship between the Inkas and mountain oracles was not always cordial. Several chroniclers discuss an incident that took place in Guamachuco during the civil war between Atawalpa and Waskar. In Betanzos's account, Atawalpa consults a *waqa* situated on the crest of a pinnacle about his fate, and when the idol's answer displeases him, he destroys it, kills its attendant, and has the summit burned.[129]

There are several instances in the ethnohistoric literature where a mountain-deity reveals its prophesies not through an idol, but by some other means. One such case involved Cotopaxi. When this volcano erupted in 1532, it was taken by the Cuzqueños as a portent that their empire would soon fall to foreign invaders.[130] In a story from Huarochirí, thirty retainers are assigned to serve Parya Qaqa for fifteen days. During this time, they ritually slaughter a llama belonging to the mountain-*waqa* and remove its heart and lungs so they can be examined; based on his reading of various signs, a character called the "Mountain Man" announces that the worship of Parya Qaqa will eventually end. He claims that the source of the prediction is the peak itself.[131] Another myth from the Huarochirí document is concerned with Maca Uisa, who also discloses the future to an old man by means of a camelid's entrails.[132]

11. THE INCORPORATION OF MOUNTAINS INTO SIGHT-LINES

According to the chronicles, mountain worship was connected with two types of sight-lines.[133] One involved an observer who would stand some distance from a peak and look toward it, and in the other, the viewer was located on the pinnacle itself and would gaze away from it.[134]

There are numerous examples of the former type of sight-line. Garcilaso says that the natives of Peru considered a summit to be a *waqa* if it greatly exceeded the neighboring peaks in height,[135] which implies that people were looking at sacred mountains and visually comparing them. Avila, Hernández, and Guaman Poma provide clearer evidence for sight-lines oriented toward pinnacles. The first author relates that during a specific festival, the inhabitants of Checa would ascend to the top of Ynca Caya, where they had an unobstructed view of Parya Qaqa, which they would venerate.[136] Likewise, the Concha people would climb Huaycho, the Suni Cancha would go up an unnamed crag, and the Chauca Ricma (along with the residents of such towns as Santa Ana and San Juan) would make their way to the summit of Acu Sica. From their respective vantage points, these groups would gaze directly at Parya Qaqa and carry out rituals honoring it.[137] Hernández discusses the case of Tanta Carhua, after whose sacrifice pilgrims gathered on hills with a clear view of the peak where she was buried to perform special rites.[138] Guaman Poma has a series of drawings illustrating the link between mountain veneration and sight-lines. One such picture, "De los ídolos Ingas" (see Figure 4.2), shows the king and queen honoring their holiest *waqas*. The king, who has assumed a position of great humility and respect, faces Wana Kawri and has an unobstructed view of its pinnacle.[139] A second sketch, "Idolos i vacas de los Chinchai svivs" (see Figure 4.6), depicts a noble from the northwestern quarter of the empire offering a sacrifice to Parya Qaqa. Like the king in the previous drawing, he is on his knees and gazes at the top of the sacred summit.[140]

Sight-lines directed toward peaks were also used for calendrical purposes.[141] Cobo cites the case of the two pillars on Quiangalla: when an observer standing at a designated point in the Cuzco Valley saw the sun rise or set between them, it was the beginning of summer.[142]

Turning to Andean lore, the view toward a pinnacle could serve as a metaphor for an autochthonous group's loss of independence. In one Inka legend, Manqu Qhapaq, the first king, emerges from Lake Titi Qaqa and makes his way to the Cuzco Valley. He sends messengers ahead to tell the original inhabitants that the son of the Sun is coming. Then, as he nears the valley, he puts a sheet of polished silver on his chest, another on his back, and a diadem of the same metal on his head. Showing himself from a high hill, the sunlight reflecting off the silver makes Manqu Qhapaq appear so radiant to the natives staring up at the pinnacle in wonder that they agree to become his vassals.[143]

Although Andean peoples regarded unobstructed views toward sacred summits as significant, they sometimes considered the point where such a view was blocked to be important too: the Cuzqueños had a *waqa* called Atpitan that was located at the very spot where one lost sight of Wana Kawri.[144]

The ethnohistoric sources mention not only sight-lines directed toward mountain-*waqas,* but lines pointing away from them. Arriaga provides an instance of the latter type. Citing a letter from a Spanish priest, he declares that near the town of Hilavi was a pinnacle with a *waqa* on it that was notable, at least in part, because a person standing in front of it faced the rising sun.[145]

In the Andean belief system, the view from a peak could be used to claim land. Cobo recounts a myth in which Manqu Qhapaq and his siblings leave Pakariq Tampu, the cave considered their place of origin, and head north. Upon reaching Wana Kawri, Manqu Qhapaq climbs to its summit, whereupon he gazes out over the Cuzco Valley, visually traces its boundaries, and uses his sling to hurl stones toward the four corners of the earth. Thus, he takes possession of the area.[146] Oberem's two documents from Ecuador make explicit the connection between sight-lines and territorial rights. The first one is the will of the *kuraka* named Sancho Hacho in which he affirms that as part of the ceremony by which he acquired his high status, he was ritually buried on top of a round knoll. Appearing from his "grave," the emperor awarded him control of all the land he could see.[147] The second record is the will of Sancho Hacho's wife, Francisca Sinasigchi, who states that she too took part in a rite meant to confirm her political position; this rite involved being interred on the crest of a hill. When she left her symbolic crypt, she was given jurisdiction over the area that fell within her field of vision.[148]

A sight-line from the top of a peak could portend the seizure of an indigenous group's territory by an invader. The Huarochirí manuscript contains a story illustrating the idea: during the reign of Thupa Yapanki, there was a revolt in one of the provinces, and the emperor asked the *waqas* for their aid in squelching it. Only Maca Uisa agreed to help. The mountain-god was carried in a litter to the crown of a hill—from which vantage point he could look out over the rebellious country and see the inhabitants and their villages—whereupon he conjured up a violent storm. The villages were washed away by heavy rains, and most of the people were killed by lightning. The few who survived were taken prisoner by Maca Uisa and marched to Cuzco, leaving the land pacified for the Inkas.[149]

In parts of the Huarochirí myth-cycle, a sight-line from a summit serves as a symbol of the union between invaders and aborigines. According to Salomon,[150] the invading group is often identified with a male mountain-deity, while the original inhabitants are linked to an earth-goddess. In the legend of Collquiri, this masculine and foreign *waqa* appears on a pinnacle overlooking the village of Yampilla, where he spies the dancing Capyama, an autochthonous earth-mother who will become his wife.[151] The brief story of Rucana Coto begins with this male god standing on a peak with a view toward the native town of Mama. It is in Mama that the stone idol representing Chaupi Ñamca, an indigenous earth-goddess and Rucana Coto's future lover, is kept.[152]

Just as summits associated with sight-lines were often revered, so pinnacles on whose slopes significant sight-lines were obstructed could be holy. Cobo tells us that the lords of Cuzco had a *waqa* known as Curauacaja, a hillock from which the view of the capital was blocked.[153] Another hallowed hill of the Inkas was Mascata Urco; it too was notable because one lost sight of Cuzco from its crest.[154]

12. MOUNTAINS AS MARKERS OF LIMITS AND BOUNDARIES

Mountain worship was connected with lines denoting limits;[155] sacred peaks were employed in the Andes to indicate territorial, social, religious, environmental, and temporal boundaries. Nonetheless, I would like to note that parts of the following section are speculative.

The Inka state consisted of a hierarchy of nested territorial units, and high summits demarcated the borders between units at all levels of this hierarchy. At the macro scale, a pinnacle could denote the imperial frontier: according to Hernández, Tanta Carhua was immolated by the Cuzqueños on a mountain marking the edge of the kingdom at that point in time.[156] At a lower level of political organization, the polity was divided into *suyus,* quarters, which were called Qulla Suyu, Anti Suyu, Chinchay Suyu, and Kunti Suyu. Cobo and Polo tell us there was a large hill and *waqa* in the Cuzco Valley with the name Pantanaya that had a cleft in the middle. It separated the road to Chinchay Suyu from the one going to Kunti Suyu,[157] and physically demarcated the border between these quarters. The veneration of sacred peaks could conceptually divide the kingdom into *suyus* too. In the drawings of Guaman Poma, each quarter is associated with the worship of a primary mountain-*waqa:* in Chinchay Suyu, Parya Qaqa is the most important object of devotion;[158] in Anti Suyu, it is the double-crag of Saua Ciray and Pitu Ciray;[159] in Qulla Suyu, it is Willka Nuta;[160] and in Kunti Suyu, it is Qhuru Puna.[161] By honoring a different summit, the inhabitants of each quarter created social boundaries that set their *suyu* apart from the others.

At a finer level of organization, mountain worship could be used to define regions within a quarter. The conceptual lines separating areas could have been established and maintained through the veneration of a distinct pinnacle in each area. Guaman Poma states that the most hallowed peaks—each of which should correspond to a particular region—in the northwestern *suyu* were Zupa Raura, Parya Qaqa, Wallullu, Carua Razo, and Razu Bilca. The most notable summits in the northeastern quarter and around Cuzco were Wana Kawri, Saua Ciray, and Pitu Ciray. Among those in the southeastern *suyu* were Awsan Qata and Willka Nuta, while in the southwestern quarter they included Qhuru Puna and Putina.[162] At the local level, an *ayllu* (a lineage that controlled its own land) would honor a nearby and relatively minor pinnacle,[163] a practice whose cumulative effect throughout a region could have been to divide it into small territorial units.

There is another possible link between the veneration of hills and the division of territory in the Inka state. Cobo and Polo list numerous peaks that marked the ends of *siq'es,* the sight-lines, in the Cuzco area: Chuquipalta was the last *waqa* on the fourth *siq'e* in Chinchay Suyu,[164] a knoll called Curauacaja was the final point on the sixth sight-line in the quarter of Anti,[165] and a small hill referred to as Llulpacturo indicated the end of the third *siq'e* in Qulla Suyu.[166] As the central core of the empire consisted of the capital and the surrounding system of sight-lines, the summits situated at the ends of *siq'es* indicated the boundary between the Inka homeland and hinterlands.

Closely related to—and probably inseparable from— territorial limits were the social boundaries between peoples. A pinnacle could be symbolically manipulated as part of the process to fix such a boundary and legitimate its existence. This process could involve projecting a group's origin myth onto the landscape, especially onto a nearby peak, to establish the permanent and exclusive rights of the group to the region. An origin myth would not only reflect the tie between a people and the land, but would reinforce this bond. It could take various forms, including a story in which a local crag serves as the *paqariku* of the legendary ancestors, or a fable in which a nearby summit saves the progenitors from a primordial flood. For an example, we turn to Albornoz. He gives the impression that the Cañari of Tomebamba province were divided into moieties: the "upper" moiety was called Hanan, while the "lower" one was referred to as Hurin. But just as the members of the upper group venerated Guasaynan because they believed the pinnacle had delivered their ancestors from the mythical flood, so the lower moiety worshipped Mount Puna for the same reason.[167] It is likely that each group had its own territory, claimed on the basis of its origin legend; also, it is possible that Guasaynan and Puna were somehow employed to fix the border between territories.

In Chapter 4, I mention a practice from the sixteenth century related to the worship of peaks that completely separated the members of two ethnic groups, the Collagua and Cavana. The former had Collaguata as their *paqariku*, which they honored by binding their babies' heads to give them the shape of the volcano. The Cavana thought their place of origin was Gualcagualca, and they too showed their devotion by wrapping cords around their infants' crowns so they would have the same form as the pinnacle. Ulloa tells us it was easy to distinguish the Collagua from the Cavana because of this practice.[168]

In Andean lore, a mountain could be employed as a dividing line and as a symbol of conquest. A fragment of a story in the Huarochirí manuscript concerns a character named Tutay Quiri, the strongest child of Parya Qaqa. Tutay Quiri seizes two river valleys from the Yunca by setting his golden staff on Unca Tupi, a black summit.[169] The legend legitimates the appropriation of one group's territory by an invading people and fixes a new boundary between them, represented by the black peak.

Earlier I describe how various groups in Huarochirí—the Colli (?), Concha, Suni Cancha, and Chauca Ricma—venerated Parya Qaqa from different pinnacles,[170] which reinforced the ethnic divisions in the province.

Summits also were associated with the establishment of religious boundaries; we can use mountain worship to trace theological variation across the Inka Empire. At the level of the *suyu,* each quarter had a distinct cult based on the adoration of a particular crag,[171] while at a lower level, many provinces had their own spiritual practices tied to the veneration of specific peaks. These peaks were of lesser significance than the ones honored by entire quarters.[172] At the local level, religious boundaries were created through the worship of nearby[173] and minor pinnacles.

Summits were also seen as markers of environmental and temporal limits. A legend from the Huarochirí manuscript illustrates the link between mountains and ecological borders. Wallullu is associated with the lowlands and with jungle animals such as snakes and parrots,[174] Parya Qaqa with the highlands.[175] The latter character defeats the former and banishes him to the tropical country of Anti Suyu. To make sure the volcano-god never returns, Parya Qaqa leaves his brother, Paria Carco, at a pass separating the two regions. Paria Carco turns into a snow-covered pinnacle marking this transition zone.[176] As noted above, summits were likewise related to calendrical sight-lines that indicated the passage of time.

13. MOUNTAINS AS UNIFIERS OF PEOPLE

Mountain worship was employed not only to establish boundaries in the Andes, but to promote unity:[177] any belief or practice that deepens the division between groups can at the same time increase solidarity within a group. Considered in relation to the Inka Empire, this dictum may have been true at many levels of territorial organization. As discussed above, the peak where Tanta Carhua was sacrificed highlighted the line[178] separating the people who lived within the polity from the "barbarians" on the outside; it also gave the *runas,* who were "citizens" of the state, a certain amount of cohesion, since they only existed as a social entity in opposition to the outsiders. Likewise, the veneration of a summit in each *suyu* served to split, at least conceptually, the population of the empire into quarters. Within a *suyu,* however, the specific cult found there acted as a common bond among the populace.[179] Avila demonstrates how a practice that separated people at the local level unified them on the regional level. He tells us that the inhabitants of Huarochirí were divided into distinct ethnic groups based partly on their diverse mountain rites, which they performed on different peaks. At the same time, they were symbolically tied together as natives of the province by their shared experience of honoring Parya Qaqa during his festival.[180]

The ethnohistoric literature tells of several cases where the worship of a pinnacle promoted interethnic solidarity. When the people from the four villages congregated before Pisi to offer sacrifices,[181] they probably strengthened their identity as Aymara. The same can be said of head-binding. This practice, common among the Collagua and Cavana, created strong bonds, both visual and psychological, between the respective members of the two groups, helping to consolidate them.[182]

Cobo and Polo mention several rituals carried out by the Inkas on summits around Cuzco that probably promoted unity. They celebrated a ten-day festival on a knoll and *waqa* called Raquiancalla, made noteworthy by the idols on its slopes from all four *suyus;*[183] they may have been venerated together as a symbol of imperial solidarity. Another ceremony, which took place on a hill known as Picho during Qhapaq Raymi, was significant in that it involved all the *ayllus* of Cuzco[184] and may have been intended to strengthen the social ties between them.

The Inkas consolidated their empire through force of arms, and war sometimes had a ritual component associated with the adoration of high peaks. Cobo and Polo state that the Cuzqueños left oblations on Toxan, a pinnacle near the capital, to ensure that the king be victorious in all his military campaigns,[185] and that he unify the state. The link between conquest, imperial unity, and the veneration of summits is found in Andean mythology. Consider the legend of Maca Uisa recounted above. After agreeing to assist Thupa Yapanki in putting down a revolt, this mountain-*waqa* goes to the crest of a hill and unleashes a terrible storm that destroys several rebel villages; he firmly incorporates the region into the empire, for which service he is revered by the king.[186]

14. THE SYMBOLIC ROLE OF MOUNTAINS IN THE EMPIRE'S WELL-BEING

Pinnacles were honored because they were considered indispensable to the well-being of the Inka polity. As we have seen, they could contribute to the welfare of the state by guaranteeing its success in war.[187] It was not only the lords of Cuzco who made this connection between the worship of peaks, warfare, and the fortunes of society. According to the Augustinians, when the natives of Guamachuco were attacked, they would carry out rites for two *waqas* linked to summits—Yanaguanca and Xulcaguanca—to build up their military strength. Hence, they thought they could repulse the invaders and save their homeland.[188]

Deities associated with mountains could be vengeful and destructive; the safety of the empire was often contingent on their being placated,[189] which usually involved venerating them and making offerings. Murúa recounts how Pacha Kuti tried to appease the volcano near Arequipa that was erupting violently.[190]

Given that Cuzco was the heart of the Inka Empire, ensuring the prosperity of the polity as a whole meant preserving the city. Cobo and Polo say that the Inkas carried out "universal" immolations on a hill called Capi for this purpose.[191]

The Sapa Inka (emperor) was the embodiment of the state, so it was imperative that he stay healthy if the polity was to remain vital. For this reason, the Inkas performed numerous rites on peaks around the capital that were supposed to guarantee his salubrity:[192] Cobo and Polo tell us the lords of Cuzco had an ancient custom of leaving oblations on a hill known as Sonconancay for the ruler's well-being;[193] they likewise made sacrifices on a pinnacle called Cuipan.[194]

The emperor's health was thought to be closely related to sin in the polity. The Inkas held that the misdeeds and transgressions of their subjects caused illness and suffering in the ruler.[195] Any ritual act, no matter how small, that dissipated a person's sins tended to increase the vitality of the king and contributed to the welfare of the state. A simple ceremony of this sort, involving pilgrims, consisted of grabbing a handful of grass, spitting into it, and tossing it onto an *apachita*.[196]

Molina states that the Cuzqueños made offerings on hills because they feared that otherwise these *waqas* would punish the king,[197] which would harm the polity.

Cobo and Polo claim that the Inkas carried out sacrifices on a knoll near the capital for the health of the crown prince.[198] I imagine his strength was linked to the future vitality of the empire.

15. THE MANIPULATION OF MOUNTAINS TO CREATE AND REINFORCE POWER RELATIONSHIPS

There is a final explanation for why various Andean peoples, especially the Inkas, considered the adoration of summits important: they knew that they could manipulate the practice to justify and strengthen their power over others.[199] According to Giddens, a dominant group will often employ a strategy of "naturalization" when exercising authority, which entails symbolically linking its authority to divine law, mythological history, the cosmological order, and/or the natural environment. The purpose is to make its influence appear completely "natural"; that is, inevitable, beyond question, and permanent.[200]

In several legends recounted by ethnohistoric authors, a cultural hero plants a staff on or near an important mountain as a sign of conquest. Cobo narrates an Inka story in which Inti sends his children, Manqu Qhapaq and Mama Uqllu, to the Andes to teach the barbarians there how to live properly. Appearing from Lake Titi Qaqa, the two head north. When they reach the foot of Wana Kawri, they take a golden staff given to them by the Sun and thrust it into the soil, whereupon it disappears. This is a sign that they can claim the valley as the site of their capital and subjugate the local people as their vassals.[201] There is also the myth from Huarochirí about Tutay Quiri, who represents an invading group. He seizes control of two river valleys by setting his golden staff on the black peak called Unca Tupi, at the same time cursing the Yunca, the indigenous population from whom he has taken the land.[202] Each story legitimates the power of a dominant people by naturalizing it: tying it to a mythic past and the natural environment. The fables involve images of high summits that are manipulated and transformed into symbols of conquest. As symbols, which embody such qualities as permanence and dominance, the pinnacles not only reflect power, but help to constitute it.

As discussed above, sight-lines—ones pointing toward and those directed away from peaks—could be used as metaphors for subjugation. Cobo relates the tale in which Manqu Qhapaq travels to the Cuzco area and shows himself from the crest of a hill wearing sheets of silver. When the inhabitants of the valley look toward the hilltop, they behold him glowing with reflected light and agree to become his subjects.[203] The same author recounts the Inka creation myth relating to a sight-line that points away from a sacred mountain. In this story, Manqu Qhapak climbs Wana Kawri and surveys the land below him, after which he takes his sling and sends stones flying in the four cardinal directions, thus claiming the region.[204] Avila, too, has a fable concerned with a sight-line directed away from a pinnacle: the story in which Maca Uisa helps the emperor put down a revolt while standing on a hill overlooking the rebellious province.[205] The three legends—which link Inka authority and imperial expansion to mythic heroes, lines-of-sight, and high summits—were meant to justify and strengthen their power. The images of peaks, employed as metaphors for domination, are critical in the process of naturalization.

Bello Galloso discusses Coxitambo, the pinnacle situated near the town of Pueleusi in Ecuador. He tells us the Cuzqueños turned Coxitambo into an explicit emblem of their hegemony: while in the process of conquering the surrounding territory, they constructed a fortress on its summit. Once the region had been firmly incorporated into the empire, the king ordered that the mountain—perhaps along with the fort on top—be worshipped by the local people.[206]

Alcayá explains how another set of peaks came to symbolize Inka power and retribution. He relates how the emperor condemned the two hundred Chiriguano to death by ordering that they be taken to some snow-capped pinnacles and forced to spend the night.[207]

Molina has an example of a rite that took place on a crag and was directly concerned with social hierarchy; this rite highlighted and reinforced the unequal power relationships that existed within a particular group. During Wara Chicuy, Inka youths ascended Raurana Hill and drank following the order of their social ranking.[208]

There are several instances in the ethnohistoric literature where a hierarchical structure seems to have been projected, either consciously or unconsciously, onto the landscape. Such a projection could have been used to rationalize the social hierarchy in the Inka state. Before describing a few examples, though, some background information is in order. The empire was characterized by a social/political structure with a pyramidal form, at the pinnacle of which was the king. Below him were his royal kin, followed by the Inka people, many of whom filled posts in the imperial bureaucracy. At the base of the pyramid were provincial groups that had been subjugated and incorporated into the polity. The lords of Cuzco may have tried to make this system of unequal power relationships appear natural—immutable, beyond question, and relating to the nonhuman world—by locating the symbolic model for it in the landscape. In other words, they could have equated their social system with a hierarchical system imposed on the topography of the countryside. The natural hierarchy could have had at its apex a high and very important mountain that was associated with the emperor, below which would have been lower and less significant summits. At the bottom of the pyramid could have been local hills with clear lines-of-sight toward the most notable peak,[209] linking the native inhabitants to the capital.

Several examples from the chronicles of topographical hierarchies more or less match this description. Hernández relates how the Inkas buried Tanta Carhua alive on a lofty pinnacle. What is significant about her sacrifice is that it was sanctioned by the king and was dedicated to the Sun, the king's "father." Her immolation linked the mountain to the top level of the social hierarchy. Situated around the central summit were lesser hills. The provincial people would gather on the crests of these hills, from which they could see Tanta Carhua's final resting place and carry out sacred rites.[210] The hills were equated with the lowest strata of the social system.

A second case where a topographical hierarchy may mirror the social pyramid is found in the Huarochirí manuscript. Avila tells us Parya Qaqa was the highest point in the province of the Yauyo,[211] was one of the holiest *waqas* in the northwestern quarter of the state,[212] and was personally venerated by the emperor.[213] It was associated with the upper echelon of Cuzqueño society. Around this peak were lesser pinnacles whose crowns offered unobstructed views of the main *waqa,* and which served as places where local groups congregated to worship.[214] Hence, the minor summits were connected with conquered peoples at the bottom of the Inka social system.

There is a third instance where a pyramidal structure appears to have been projected onto the landscape. It is somewhat different from the other two, since in this case the hierarchical system is based on offerings: the higher-status peaks in a region received the most important sacrificial materials and greatest diversity of goods, and tended to be associated with imperial gods such as the Sun and/or with the king. Lower-status pinnacles were given not only more trivial oblations, but fewer kinds of materials; they were often connected with local deities and provincial groups. It seems that many summits in the Cuzco Valley which were part of the *siq'e* system were ranked in the manner described. Near the apex of the hierarchy was Chuquipalta, on whose slopes "universal" immolations were made of children, llamas, anthropomorphic figurines made of gold, and clothing. It was linked to the three most notable Inka gods: the Creator, Sun, and Thunder.[215] Occupying a tier below Chuquipalta was Sucanca, a hillock associated with the Sun[216] that received camelids, zoomorphic statuettes of gold and silver, and clothing. Still lower on the hierarchy was Cariurco; this hill was offered spotted llamas and clothing, and was not connected with any major deities.[217] Below Cariurco was Quiquijana, a knoll to which small garments and shells were sacrificed,[218] while near the bottom of the stratified system was Sumeurco, which received shells.[219] As with the other examples of mountain hierarchies, the one from the Cuzco area reflects the imperial social system and may have been intended to naturalize the asymmetrical power relationships between different classes of people in the empire.

The Cuzqueños may have employed yet another stratagem for turning crags into material symbols of their authority. It entailed building solar temples and/or carrying out immolations dedicated to the Sun on sacred peaks in the hinterlands. Inti was considered the patron god of the polity and father of the emperor. Reinhard, based on his reading of Garcilaso, believes that solar worship was peculiar to the Inkas and was not practiced much by other groups—at least not until they were conquered and had the cult imposed on them. What is certain, though, is that before they were subjugated, many autochthonous peoples venerated high pinnacles, which were thought of as local deities.[220] So, by consecrating a temple and/or a sacrifice to the Sun on a prominent summit, the Cuzqueños were setting up the following analogy: Inti lorded over the mountain-god as they ruled over the provincial folk.

There are a number of instances from the ethnohistoric literature of the possible use of this strategy, including the immolation of Tanta Carhua on the peak in Aixa to honor Inti[221] and the offering of the two brothers on Nabincoto in Cajatambo. The latter sacrifice was ordered by the king to glorify the Sun.[222] Velasco asserts that a solar temple constructed on the slopes of Cayambe in Ecuador was very celebrated among the local inhabitants.[223] Although he does not specifically say this structure was Inka, if

Reinhard is correct in his conviction that the lords of Cuzco were responsible for the spread of the Sun cult to the provinces, then it may have been. Velasco also mentions a solar temple on Ashuay.[224] In the myth recounted by Cobo, Manqu Qhapaq assumes the role of his father, the victorious Inti, by climbing to the top of a hill wearing sheets of silver. He is so resplendent with the reflected light of the sun that the local populace agrees to accept his authority.[225] Unfortunately, we are not told if the summit where Manqu Qhapaq stands is considered sacred. In each case cited above, it appears that the Cuzqueños naturalized their power by tying it to the might of the Sun.

When one ethnic group defeated another, there were two strategies available to the victor for strengthening its authority over the vanquished, both of which involved manipulating cults relating to summits. The conquering people could wipe out the religion of the conquered and impose its form of mountain worship on them, or the victorious group could usurp, perpetuate, and even aggrandize the practices of the other group.

According to Avila, the Yunca, the aboriginal inhabitants of Huarochirí,[226] were originally associated with Wallullu.[227] Then they were subdued by a highland people referred to as "Parya Qaqa's children."[228] The conflict between the Yunca and highlanders, and the eventual defeat of the former, is represented in Andean lore by the fight between Wallullu and Parya Qaqa.[229] Subsequent to their conquest, the Yunca were forced to honor the mountain-*waqa* of the highlanders.[230]

The Inkas often employed the second strategy for augmenting their power; after subjugating an ethnic group and incorporating it into the empire, they usurped its adoration of a peak. In this way, they gained the good will of the mountain-god. And the vanquished people—who were dependent on their revered crag for water, fertility, fair weather, and so on—became reliant on and symbolically indebted to the lords of Cuzco.[231] Hence, Albornoz tells us that after conquering the province of Parinacocha in southern Peru, the Inkas took over the worship of Sara Sara, a notable snow-covered pinnacle. They moved two thousand *mitmaq-kuna* to the region to serve the *waqa* and established a llama herd for its benefit. This herd consisted of as many as six hundred animals. They probably allotted pastures to the sacred summit where the camelids could graze, fields where the settlers could raise crops, and gold and silver cups for rituals.[232]

The Cuzqueños subdued other parts of southern Peru too, whereupon they assumed from the aboriginal groups the responsibility for honoring Sulimana, Qhuru Puna, Ampato, and Putina (El Misti). They aggrandized the worship of these peaks, assigning to each its own retainers and/or llama herds.[233] I get the impression from Guaman Poma that the inhabitants of the empire's four *suyus* had their respective mountain cults that predated the foundation of the state. As part of the process by which the Inkas unified each quarter, they took control of the major cult there, offering the principal summit gold and silver, assigning it priests,[234] and consequently increasing their authority over the people.

Sometimes the power of a *kuraka* was directly dependent on a ceremony involving a pinnacle. As the rite could not take place unless it was sanctioned by the lords of Cuzco, they could exert control over the local ruler. The chroniclers provide examples of this form of governance. Hernández relates how the decision of Caque Poma, leader of the community of Urcón, to have Tanta Carhua sacrificed to the Sun on a peak led to the Inkas making him lord of the whole region.[235] In his will, Sancho Hacho, the Ecuadorian *cacique* (regional leader), states that the Cuzqueños carried out a special ritual for him on a provincial summit. The purpose of the ceremony was to confirm his political power.[236] Francisca Sinasigchi says she took part in a similar rite, which ratified her position as *cacica,* "headwoman."[237] In each case, the Inkas employed a mountaintop ritual to bind a *kuraka* to the polity. Since the ruler would have been connected to his/her own people by traditional ties, the result would have been to indirectly link the whole group to the empire.

Seven MATERIAL CORRELATES OF
MOUNTAIN WORSHIP

As an archaeologist, I am interested in the following questions: How would we recognize a site where a mountain was worshipped in the past? What are the distinct features of this practice, and what are its material correlates? What remains might we find in the archaeological record that would give us a hint as to why a summit was venerated? I will try to answer these queries.

I would expect a peak adored in the prehispanic era to stand out from the surrounding pinnacles in some way: it may have an unusual shape, be snow-capped, be much higher than the others, or be made of a different material. People often carried out ceremonies honoring a mountain on its crest, on its slopes, or at its base; in such an instance, there might be an idol, sacred *wanqa* stone, altar, temple, burial crypt, or other structure on it. If a populace revered a prominent peak from a lesser hill, there might be a ritual site on the latter's summit; in this case, there would probably be an unobstructed sight-line between the site and the hallowed peak. A pinnacle also could be worshipped from the plaza in a village or city, from a field, or from any other open space. Again, the holy mountain would likely be visible from the spot where the rites held in its honor took place. A group might also pay homage to a summit indirectly; rather than venerate the crag itself, either from its own slopes or from a site with an unimpeded view of it, the people could worship and bestow offerings on a representation of it. For such an effigy to survive in the archaeological record, it would most likely have to be made of stone. Its outline should unmistakably echo the shape of a local peak.

SACRIFICIAL MATERIALS

A review of the ethnohistoric literature informs us that we might find many different kinds of offerings at a site connected with mountain worship. There could be the body of a sacrificial victim, perhaps entombed like Tanta Carhua; she was found in a small space at the bottom of a 5 m deep shaft, curled up in a fetal position and wearing fine clothes. In a rare instance, we might discover the corpse of a llama that had been immolated and interred. The animal would probably have a slit in its throat or an incision in its side where its heart was removed. I think it more likely, however, that we would unearth its charred bones, since most chronicles say that after a llama was ritually slaughtered, it was cremated in a bonfire. We also might come upon the buried remains of guinea pigs, sometimes intact, but usually burned. A site linked to the veneration of a pinnacle might have a variety of gold, silver, and/or copper goods: gold dust and nuggets; ingots and little pieces of metal; anthropomorphic figurines, both male and female; zoomorphic statuettes; jewelry and other personal adornments; and an assortment of vessels and utensils. These materials would be interred. Sometimes metal items, such as the gold and copper idols discovered by Martínez, were placed in a small chamber at the bottom of a shaft (see Figure 4.4). Other oblations we might find include shells, textiles, coca leaves, corn, corn products, feathers, food, and so on.

The Inkas organized the things they sacrificed into a hierarchy, with human beings and llamas at the top, feathers and food at the bottom. The types of offerings they awarded a particular mountain depended on the *waqa's* status, their specific reason(s) for worshipping it, and the urgency of their petition to it. It should be simple to determine the prominence of a peak by examining collections of materials from the archaeological record: in general, the higher the *waqa's* rank, the greater the diversity of items it should have received, and the more prestigious the goods. The reverse would be true as well. If we were to discover the corpse of a sacrificial victim buried on a high pinnacle, we could reasonably conclude this *waqa* had been significant in the past. If we were to disinter the remains of textiles, coca leaves, feathers, and food from around an altar with a clear line of sight toward a crag, we could deduce the *waqa* had been moderately sacred.

The relationship between the materials left for a summit and their intended purpose is less straightforward. Part of the problem is that there does not appear to be much of a one-to-one correspondence between individual oblations and specific motives, which is to say that the same types of goods could be given to different peaks for different reasons. The ethno-historic sources mention only a few exceptions to this rule, one of which is *mullu*, especially Spondylus.

Mullu made an appropriate gift for a mountain-*waqa* when petitioning for water, since it was considered the daughter of Mother Sea, the source of all terrestrial liquid. The symbolic association between Spondylus and rain has a solid basis in climatology. The waters off of Peru's north coast are ordinarily too cold for the mollusks. However, during years when there are strong El Niño events—unusually warm ocean conditions that cause heavy rains and flooding along the coast—the water temperature rises enough to support Spondylus. Early on, people on the north coast began to link the appearance of the bivalves with rain.[1]

The connection between shells and water can be demonstrated using information from Cobo and Polo, who list numerous springs and fountains that were venerated in the Cuzco Valley. They tell us that 88 percent of these *waqas* received *mullu*.[2] The correspondence is less than perfect, though. Cobo and Polo mention the pinnacle Cuipan, situated near the Inka capital, that had six sacred stones on it. This *waqa* was given red *mullu*—most likely Spondylus—not for water, but for the king's health.[3] The conclusion we can draw from this discussion, not an altogether satisfying one, is that we will likely discover shells on a crag known to have been petitioned for rain. But just because we find *mullu* associated with a summit does not necessarily mean the *waqa* was adored for water.

Representations of agricultural products like maize made suitable oblations to peaks when asking for a bountiful harvest, as there seems to have been a link between a plant's image and its fertility; the Inkas left corncobs carved from seashells on Wana Kawri and Achpiran, and burned maize ears fashioned from wood on Mantocallas. It is possible the same relationship existed between statuettes of llamas and the fecundity of herds. Alternatively, the statuettes, which were not uncommon gifts for mountain-*waqas*, may have been regarded as "substitute sacrifices" that took the place of real animals. It is conceivable the anthropomorphic figurines offered to pinnacles were meant to augment human fertility[4] or were substitute immolations.[5] Tools employed in specialized production were sometimes offered to summits to make sure the manufacturing process went well. Weavers left spindle whorls and other weaving implements for Guallio.

It would be difficult to determine the urgency of a petition made to a hallowed crag based solely on oblations. In general, the more critical the supplication, the more important the materials being sacrificed. In a specific case, though, it would be almost impossible to say whether the rich goods provided to a peak represented an urgent request or reflected the *waqa*'s high status.

MATERIAL CULTURE AND SPECIFIC
REASONS FOR MOUNTAIN WORSHIP

What types of remains—such as offerings, ritual paraphernalia, idols, altars, temples, crypts, and so on—might we find at a site connected with mountain worship that would enable us to understand the reasons behind the practice? The extraordinary nature of the pinnacles themselves has already been noted. Also significant is the prominent role of summits in Andean mythology. If this was the primary motive for venerating a peak, there could be a shrine dedicated to it with a physical reference to a hallowed legend. The Cañari of Ecuador traced their ancestry back to a pair of brothers who were saved from a primordial flood by Huaca Yñan and who mated with a parrot-woman. Given this story's significance, we might discover a Cañari structure oriented toward a crag and containing a stone idol shaped like a parrot. In such a case, we could conclude the structure was a place to pay homage to the pinnacle, which was linked to the origin myth. It would only be possible to make this association, though, if we already knew the legends of a region or ethnic group; unfortunately, few stories concerning summits were recorded by the chroniclers.

Consider another likely reason to worship mountains—their use as stepping stones to more notable deities like the Sun. Possible material correlates include physical allusions to the higher gods. The Augustinians state that people participating in ceremonies for Inti sometimes painted their faces red and smeared yellow on their noses.[6] If we were to come upon the remains of a victim interred in a crypt on a pinnacle, whose face was colored red and yellow, we might deduce that he had been immolated to honor the Sun. And the summit where he was buried may have been considered a stepping stone. A reference to Inti also could take the form of a sight-line, directed toward or away from a mountain. In the former case, we might uncover an altar, temple, or building located some distance from the peak, but whose long axis pointed in its direction. An observer positioned next to the structure might see the sun rise or set behind the top of the pinnacle on the summer or winter solstice, on the equinoxes, and on other significant days. With respect to a sight-line directed away from a mountain, we might find a shrine or temple on its crest or slope. A viewer standing at the structure who followed its long axis to a point on the horizon might have been able to observe the rising or setting sun at this point on a solstice, equinox, or other important day.[7]

Venerating a summit because of its control over meteorological phenomena and because of its regulation of water are related, so I will consider them together. If a crag was revered for one of these reasons, we might discover a material reference to water at an altar, temple, or crypt situated within sight of or on the peak. An allusion of this sort could take various forms, among them *mullu*, especially Spondylus. Alternatively, a physical reference to fluid could take the form of a container for water or *chicha*, such as a jug, *maka* (Cuzco bottle), or *kero* (beaker). Or we might find a *paccha*, the vessel through which liquid flowed in a zigzag or serpentine channel, like the one on Ashuay.

Pinnacles were revered due to their perceived influence on human health and fertility; a summit esteemed for this reason might be associated with a structure containing an anthropomorphic *qunupa*, which was a figurine believed to be responsible for the fecundity of whatever it represented,[8] in this instance humans. It is worth noting that an idol of this type was usually accessible to worshippers, so unlike sacrificial materials, it would not have been buried at a site.

Among the more significant motives for venerating peaks were those related to economics. The Inka economy was based on agriculture, whose success depended on the availability of water, the fertility of cultigens, and the timing of the stages of production. Each component of farming was connected with mountain worship and has specific material correlates. As noted above, at a place where a crag was petitioned for water, we might uncover Spondylus shell, vessels for carrying liquids, *pacchas*, and/or zigzag-shaped canals. At a site where a mountain-deity was supplicated for the fecundity of the crops, we might discover representations of agricultural products (e.g., ears of maize) interred as oblations. We might also come upon *qunupas* shaped like corncobs, potatoes, or other cultigens. A sacred peak employed as part of a calendar for farming might be incorporated into a sight-line, evidence for which could take the form of a structure located on the pinnacle and oriented toward a spot on the horizon, or situated some distance from the crag but aligned with its summit. In either case, a person sighting along the *siq'e* would observe the rising or setting sun on the day when planting, harvesting, shelling, and other activities took place.

Herding was likewise integral to the imperial economy, and mountains were thought to have the power to increase the fecundity of llamas. If the primary objective in paying homage to a summit was to build up the royal and/or local flocks, the peak might be linked to a site with camelid idols situated on an altar or inside a temple.

Another critical part of the Inka economy was specialized production. Before a craftsman started working, he might offer some tools of his trade to a pinnacle to ensure the manufacturing process went smoothly. What would we find if we excavated a site where a mountain was worshipped because of its connection with the making of fine cloth? Perhaps spindle whorls and weaving implements. Skilled workers who engaged in the exploitation of a natural resource often venerated samples of the raw material and/or their specialized equipment. Miners would adore nuggets of gold, silver, or other metals, which they called *mama*. They also would revere *corpa*, pieces of ore from which valuable metals were extracted, and *guayras*, braziers used in the smelting process.[9] Given that minerals were thought to be under the control of mountain-deities, I would not be surprised to find an archaeological site located in a rich mining area and associated both with a summit and a sacred structure containing *mama*, *corpa*, and/or a *guayra*.

Some crags, as noted above, were honored because they were connected with travel and trade. The Cuzqueños employed enormous numbers of llamas for transporting raw materials and finished goods and considered the fertility of the beasts to be regulated by peaks. To get their camelids to multiply so they could continue traveling and moving loads, the Inkas venerated mountain-*waqas*. In terms of material culture, the place where such worship took place might consist of a shrine or temple with *qunupa* idols shaped like llamas. Sites where individuals worshipped sacred pinnacles while engaged in long-distance exchange might have exotic offerings from distant places and thus stylistically different from locally produced ones. A person journeying far from home—as, for example, a pilgrim—would often add a stone to an *apachita* situated on a hill or at a pass. A traveler might also leave a modest gift for the mountain-deity, such as a coca quid, piece of chewed corn, feather, sandal, bit of rope, rag, or sling. I would expect *apachitas* to be more ubiquitous along major trade routes and beside trails frequently used by pilgrims.

It would be difficult to establish that a pinnacle was venerated out of fear. We might uncover evidence for a natural disaster at a site associated with a prominent summit. There could be an altar with a clear sight-line toward an active volcano, around which were buried the charred bones of numerous llamas that had been ritually dispatched. If the spot were covered with a layer of volcanic ash—and if the ash were mixed in with the bones, indicating the eruption and immolations took place at the same time—then we could conclude the sacrifices were intended to pacify the mountain-god,[10] and we might infer that the people feared the volcano's destructive power.

We might also discover the remains of an Inka temple offering an unobstructed view of a snow-capped peak. In front of this structure we might unearth the body of a victim who had been put to death and buried with numerous offerings. If this victim were sealed in his/her crypt with a layer of mud that later dried, and if there were evidence of flooding and erosion at the site, we could deduce the immolation took place to mollify the crag during a period of excessive rain, perhaps when there was a major El Niño event.[11]

It would be hard to demonstrate that a hallowed pinnacle served an oracular function. According to Cobo, the lords of Cuzco sometimes practiced divination by fire, for which purpose they employed a pair of braziers of silver, copper, or clay. Each vessel had a large opening at the top from which flames issued, and many smaller apertures around the body to let in air. Slivers of wood soaked in fat were burned in the braziers. To aid combustion, attendants blew into them using long tubes made partly of silver and partly of copper. Around the vessels were set little bowls of gold, silver, wood, and clay that held food and drink to attract spirits.[12] In the unlikely event we were to discover any of this ritual paraphernalia at a spot linked with a sacred summit, we could conclude the summit was connected with an oracle.

Given the previous discussion of the material correlates of sight-lines, I offer only a brief summary here. Suffice to say that we should recognize a regional system of lines in the archaeological record: such a system could take the form of a significant *waqa* sitting atop a revered peak and surrounded by lower hills, each of which has its own shrine and clear view toward the main *waqa*. I would expect to find higher-status offerings and a greater diversity of goods at the central temple than in the surrounding shrines.

What evidence might we discover in the archaeological record that would demonstrate a pinnacle was used to mark or create boundaries, either social or territorial? At the local level, several ethnic groups that wanted to emphasize the social boundaries separating them could play up the differences in the way they worshipped a mountain. The Huarochirí manuscript describes how various peoples paid homage to Parya Qaqa from their respective sites, and possibly with exclusive rituals. If these rites really were meant to highlight the distinctions between them, we would expect to find variation between sites in the types of remains that are present, and the diversity of artifacts would be a direct reflection of the variability in the sacred ceremonies. Or consider the information provided by Ulloa on the Collagua and Cavana, who molded the heads of their children to resemble two different summits. Burial grounds of the two populations would probably exhibit much homogeneity in cranium shape within them, but little between them. Some groups may have employed burial practices relating to the adoration of peaks to set themselves apart from others; certain populations are said to have interred their dead with the heads turned toward their respective *paqarikus,* the high crags from which they came at birth and to which they returned at death.[13] In terms of the orientation of the heads, graveyards of the different groups would manifest little diversity within them, but much between them.

At the state level, the Inkas could have used pinnacles to indicate the limits of their territory. The empire is said to have expanded out from the capital in waves of conquest, and after each victory the Cuzqueños may have made oblations to summits to mark their new boundary with the outside world. If this really happened, there should be a series of concentric circles around Cuzco, each of which should be larger than the preceding one, consisting of sacrificial materials left at sites connected with mountain worship. Since all the artifacts found along a circle would date to the same period, there should be no stylistic differences between them. On the other hand, each subsequent wave took place a little later in time, so there should be some variation between items from successive circles.[14]

The final three motives for honoring peaks—because they could be employed to unify peoples, because they played a symbolic role in the well-being of the state, and because they could be manipulated to create and reinforce imperial power—are related, so naturally their material correlates overlap. I will conclude this chapter by considering them together.

After the Inkas subjugated a region, they may have left materials linked to imperial authority on or near local crags. In such cases, I would expect them to have emphasized the superiority of Inka culture over those of vanquished groups, which means that most of the offerings, especially the high-status ones, would be purely Inka in style. Among the items might be generic symbols of power in the Andes, such as staffs and slings, or representations of royal insignia (see Figure 7.1): the *suntur pawkar,* a standard that was completely covered with small feathers of various colors and that had three large plumes sticking up out of the top;[15] the *waman chanpi,* a star-shaped mace with a long handle;[16] and the *maskha paycha,* imperial fringe.[17] There also could be an idol in the form of a *ñapa,* a llama with white fur wearing a red cloth on its back,[18] or a male tunic called an *unku* that is covered with *tukapus,* square pieces of cloth bearing special designs.[19] As

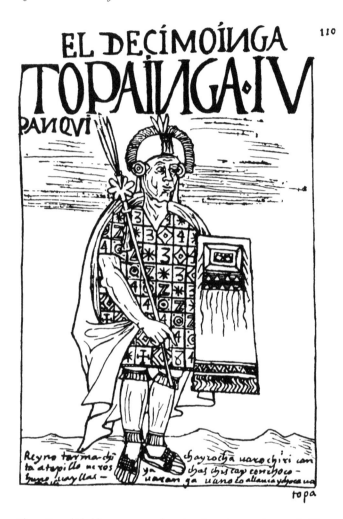

FIGURE 7.1.   *Thupa Yapanki holding a* waman chanpi *and wearing a tunic covered with* tukapus *(Guaman Poma 1980a: 90).*

these items were emblems of the king's authority, their presence on a pinnacle would signify his domination of the region and of the autochthonous people.

The Cuzqueños offered not only objects, but human lives. I cannot think of a more potent expression of imperial control than the *qhapaq hucha:* the child or young woman chosen from among the provincial nobility, taken from his or her community, and dispatched by the state. A *qhapaq hucha* sacrificed to a summit would be buried in a crypt or pit, either on the crest, on the slopes, or some distance from the mountain, but with a clear sight-line toward it. A boy often would be dressed in his native clothing, whereas a girl or post-pubescent female would wear the costume of an *aqlla,* which was similar to the garb of a noble woman in Cuzco. All of them would be interred with imperial goods. A lesser, though still significant symbol of imperial power, was the immolation of prisoners on a peak. I would expect these captives, who might have been warriors or other folks captured by the Inkas during the conquest of a province, to be stripped, bound hand and foot, and buried.

Another strategy the Inkas may have employed to turn hallowed peaks into monuments to their authority involved building special structures on the pinnacles. Such structures would have included *pukarás* (hilltop fortresses), shrines, and temples devoted to imperial gods. A *pukará* was a manifestation of Inka power in both a symbolic and real sense: it could be venerated as a *waqa* while simultaneously housing a garrison charged with keeping the indigenous population from revolting. The fort would have been manned by Inka soldiers and/or *mitmaq-kuna,* meaning the artifacts discovered there would be imperial in style and/or non-Inka, but foreign to the region.

By putting a shrine or temple devoted to a state deity on a mountain, the Cuzqueños could have naturalized their authority over a provincial folk by equating it with the metaphoric domination of the local mountain-god by an imperial one. If the temple was associated with the Sun, we might expect its long axis to be oriented toward a solstice or equinox. Alternatively, though unlikely, we might find an idol inside representing Inti, which probably would have the following characteristics: it would be anthropomorphic, made of gold,[20] purely Inka in style, and dressed in the finest imperial clothing.[21] It would sit on a bench or in a niche where it would have been accessible to priests.

As hypothesized earlier, the Inkas may have usurped and aggrandized the worship of summits in the hinterlands as a means of tying native populations to the state. If this was indeed a strategy, there should be archaeological evidence for the pre-Inka adoration of a crag as well as a pattern of remains suggesting that the total resources dedicated to the cult of the peak increased dramatically under the Inkas.

Hernández tells us the power of every *kuraka* was directly based on the immolation of a *qhapaq hucha.* Since a sacrifice of this type could only take place if it was sanctioned by the empire, the Cuzqueños could exert a certain amount of control over a *kuraka.* The *qhapaq hucha* sacrifice that Hernández describes in detail, Tanta Carhua's, took place on a mountaintop; the implication is that in every former province of the empire, there could be the remains of a child or young woman who was ritually slain by the Inkas. A corpse would only have survived for about five hundred years, though, if the conditions for preserving it were right, and if it was so well hidden that neither the colonial priests nor modern treasure hunters could find it. It is likely that there are still bodies on high pinnacles that remain intact.

Yet another Inka method for naturalizing their authority entailed projecting concepts of social hierarchy onto the landscape. In archaeological terms, an area where the strategy was used should be marked by a lofty summit surrounded by lower ones; from each of the lesser peaks, an observer should have an unobstructed view of the central one. Associated with the primary crag should be a great quantity and diversity of high-status goods, all of Inka manufacture. The secondary peaks, which should be more or less equal, will have offerings that are relatively poor in quality, provincial in style, and of lower prestige. The differences in material culture between the central summit and surrounding ones should be a reflection of the inequality of the imperial social system. Alternatively, there could be a complete hierarchy of pinnacles in a province. The most notable mountain, both in terms of sacredness and visual impact, would be associated with the lion's share of sacrificial materials, most of which would have been produced by the state. There could even be a *qhapaq hucha* buried on its slopes. A secondary peak would have gifts of a correspondingly lower status, including llamas, gold and silver, Spondylus shell, and other offerings; further down the scale, a tertiary summit might merit a mixture of goods, some Inka in style, others provincial. At the bottom of the hierarchy could be hills venerated by indigenous people who offer them locally produced materials.

Eight   CONCLUSIONS

According to Rowe, in the 1470s Emperor Thupa Yapanki led a large army down to southern Peru, northern Chile, and northwestern Argentina,[1] where he subjugated numerous peoples. They included the Quilca, Tampo, Moquehua, Locumba, Sama, Tarapaca,[2] Atacameño, Colla, Chango, Diaguita, Chiquillane, and Picunche.[3] Once his conquests had been completed, he faced a major dilemma: how best to incorporate these ethnic groups into the state and consolidate the vast territories they occupied. Since it would have been too costly in terms of manpower for him to have relied exclusively on military means, Thupa may have decided to manipulate human immolation[4] and mountain worship[5] to unify what would become the southern quarters of the empire.

ETHNOHISTORIC RESEARCH

One goal of this work is to model a systematic method for dealing with the Andean chronicles. I have relied extensively on these sources, written during the sixteenth through the eighteenth centuries, in my research on human sacrifice and mountain worship. On a general level, I brought together all the ethnohistoric texts I could find, written by as many authors as possible, and extracted information on the two topics. I then organized the large data-set and searched for patterns. In those instances where I discovered patterns that contradict accepted "facts" about the Inkas or that are at variance with one another, I account for them.

FINDINGS ON HUMAN IMMOLATION
AND MOUNTAIN WORSHIP

Another goal of this book is to shed light on two religious practices that were crucial during the Late Horizon. Only two of my ethnohistoric sources, Garcilaso and Blas Valera, deny that the Cuzqueños offered human beings in sacrifice (see Chapter 2), but both had indigenous (possibly Inka) mothers and were proud of their Andean roots. Also, Garcilaso wanted to demonstrate to the Spanish that his maternal ancestors had a civilizing effect on the peoples they had subjugated. Given their backgrounds and motivations, I think we can disregard their denials about immolation.

From my reading of other authors—among them Cieza, Polo, Hernández, and Cobo—I conclude there were at least five types of sacrificial victims in the Inka Empire (see Chapters 2 and 3). They were the *runa,* a "citizen" of the state; the *necropampa* victims, who could have been servants, blood relatives, or the spouse of a deceased ruler; the warrior captured in battle; the "substitute" victim, who was put to death so that another might live; and perhaps most important, the *qhapaq hucha.* *Runas* were males between the ages of twenty-five and fifty, *necropampa* victims could be of either gender and of any age from pre-adolescence to elderly, prisoners were able-bodied men between early adulthood and middle age, substitute victims tended to be boys when sacrificed at the local level, and *qhapaq huchas* were children and young women. Male citizens, *necropampa* victims, and *qhapaq huchas* were dressed in their finest clothing and were often given lavish adornments and goods before meeting their ends. Warriors were usually stripped naked, their weapons confiscated. There is little information on the attire of the substitutes, though it seems likely each wore clothing befitting his social status. In terms of the actual immolation, there were certain methods used to dispatch *runas, necropampa* victims, and *qhapaq huchas,* including cutting their throats, strangling them, hitting them on the head, and burying them alive. Regardless of the method employed, these three types of victims, along with the substitutes, were otherwise treated with respect. Once dead, their bodies were carefully interred with grave goods, among them precious metals, fine cloth, various kinds of vessels, and food. In contrast, the warriors were bound, tortured, and killed. Their corpses were mutilated and/or haphazardly dumped.

Concerning the purpose(s) each served, the most distinct of the five categories were the *necropampa* and substitute sacrifices. Whereas victims of the former type were sent to the other world to serve their lord or provide companionship, a substitute was meant to appease a deity or *waqa* so it would spare the life of another person. At the community level, a father who was very sick would occasionally offer the life of his son so that he might recover. At the imperial level, when the king was gravely ill, the Lords of Cuzco would sacrifice *runas* and/or *qhapaq huchas* in his name, which indicates an overlap between the categories. Common reasons for the immolation of *runas,* warriors, and *qhapaq huchas* included honoring the Sun, the patron god of the empire, and promoting fertility. Having too little or too much water was also a significant reason for slaying *runas* and *qhapaq huchas*—but not war prisoners, *necropampa* victims, nor substitutes. Finally, *qhapaq hucha* sacrifice may have been connected with mountain veneration, the Inka economy, the social structure and political organization of the polity, imperial boundaries, the statewide network of sight-lines, and the asymmetrical relationship between the capital and provinces.

Only Garcilaso and Valera are at odds with what many chroniclers declare: that the Inkas considered lofty summits to be gods, which they adored (see Chapter 4). By making their denials, the two authors hoped to convince Europeans that Andean religion was not very different from Christianity, but as explained above, I discount what they say because of their backgrounds and motives for writing.

From the rest of my ethnohistoric sources—among them Albornoz, Avila, Guaman Poma, and Cobo—I extracted a wealth of descriptive data on mountain worship that provided the basis for my generalizations on the practice. The chroniclers tell us that Andean peoples conceived of high peaks in several ways, including as divine beings, the fossilized remains of mythical heroes, the residences of powerful deities, oracles, and the origin-places of ethnic groups. As a god, a summit could assume various guises, such as a feature of the landscape, a human or animal, a violent storm, or uncontrolled water. Many pinnacles in the Cuzco area and hinterlands were considered sacred *waqas* and had hallowed stones or idols on their slopes. According to several authors, both cyclic and one-of-a-kind rites were carried out on these peaks. Instances of the former include the yearly sacrifices made by Inka initiates on Wana Kawri, the regular distribution of llama blood to peaks throughout the empire, the offering of items on Pisi by the Aymara, and the immolation of children by the Cañari on Supayurco. Among the one-of-a-kind rituals were the ceremonial killing of three hundred men on Pachatusun to save the crops, the dispersion of camelid blood on the slopes of El Misti to pacify it, and the veneration of water pitchers on the summit in Guamachuco for rain. Rites relating to peaks did not have to take place on the peaks themselves, as demonstrated by Guaman Poma's picture of the emperor worshipping Wana Kawri from Cuzco. Another drawing of his shows two people from Chinchay Suyu paying homage to Parya Qaqa from an open space with a clear view of the pinnacle. As an indication of the significance of mountain worship in the Inka polity, consider the following statistics: about 22 percent of the known *waqas* near the capital were closely identified with summits,[6] while about 54 percent of the sacred places that Albornoz lists for the provinces were related to peaks.[7]

A variety of items were offered to/on pinnacles (see Chapter 5). They included human lives, llamas, guinea pigs, metals, anthropomorphic and zoomorphic statuettes, shells (especially Spondylus), textiles, coca leaves, corn, corn products, feathers, food, and a number of miscellaneous goods. The Cuzqueños did more to honor a mountain-*waqa* than just contribute materials for sacrifice: they appointed priests to serve it, established camelid herds in its name, assigned it fields and pastures, and made a labor pool available to tend the herds and crops.

The ethnohistoric sources give many reasons why the inhabitants of the Andes venerated high summits (see Chapter 6). The most important motives relate to controlling the weather, regulating the flow of water, improving specialized production, creating a system of sight-lines, indicating limits and boundaries, unifying people, and establishing/reinforcing power relationships. The sets of material correlates derived for these motives (see Chapter 7) often overlap.

Human sacrifice and mountain worship were not completely distinct and unrelated rituals. Hernández describes an event that represents the union of the two practices: the sacrifice of Tanta Carhua, the girl who was taken to a high summit and then lowered into a shaft about 5 m deep and made to sit in a fetal position as she was surrounded by offerings and buried alive.[8]

IMPLICATIONS OF THIS STUDY FOR ARCHAEOLOGY

Some scholars are critical of the ad hoc approach of many archaeologists when it comes to working with ethnohistoric sources. Randall, for example, maintains that these scholars often sift through sixteenth- and seventeenth-century texts, select the bits of data that best support their reconstructions of the past, and disregard the rest.[9] It is my hope that this work represents an improvement over such an approach since I synthesized the information from the chronicles to create the analytical framework for interpreting materials from the archaeological record.

Researchers might find this volume useful in interpreting sets of human remains discovered on pinnacles in southern Peru, northwestern Argentina, and northern Chile. It can help scholars confirm whether materials are from human sacrifices and determine whether they are connected with mountain worship. It can be utilized to reach an understanding of the symbolism behind immolations and/or mountain offerings, and to ascertain the purpose(s) they served. It also provides insight on how the Inkas may have manipulated the two ritual practices to incorporate subjugated peoples into the empire.

Twenty-seven bodies and a variety of artifacts have been recovered from sites on such peaks as El Misti, Ampato, Pichu Pichu, Sara Sara, Chachani, Chuscha, Quehuar, El Toro, Chañi, Llullaillaco, Aconcagua, Esmeralda, and El Plomo (see Map 1.3). Some sets of materials, among them the ones from Llullaillaco[10] and Aconcagua,[11] have been exhaustively analyzed. The scholars who conducted the research—Reinhard, Ceruti, and Schobinger—have made tremendous contributions to our knowledge of human immolation and mountain veneration in the southern Andes. Other collections of remains, including the one found on Chañi, have not been completely studied nor adequately interpreted.[12] Still others—for example, the materials recovered from El Plomo[13] and Esmeralda[14]—have been thoroughly examined but remain imperfectly understood. The problem, as I see it, with a number of the original interpretations of the remains from El Plomo and Esmeralda is that they are incomplete, outdated, or wrong.

Cerro El Plomo is a high, snow-capped mountain visible from Santiago, the capital of Chile. In 1954, the body of an eight-year-old boy was discovered within a structure called the Enterratorio—which is situated at 5,400 m on the peak's secondary summit—where he had been buried alive. The child wore an *unku* (sleeveless tunic), a *yaqolla* (mantle) over his shoulders, and moccasins on his feet. He also had a black headband and headdress of condor feathers on his crown, an H-shaped pendant under his chin, and a silver bracelet on his right forearm. Accompanying the victim were two figurines depicting llamas, a pair of woven bags, one of them crammed with coca leaves, and five pouches. Somewhere in the Enterratorio, though not in direct association with the body, was found a silver statuette representing a woman. It was dressed in its own clothing. The boy undoubtedly had been a *qhapaq hucha* dispatched by the Inkas as an offering to the pinnacle.[15]

Esmeralda is an impressive hill located on the north coast of Chile near the city of Iquique. On the 905 m high crest of this peak is an archaeological site where the corpses of two females were unearthed. One was approximately nine years old, the other about twenty at the time of death. Each had on a fine *aqsu* (dress), *chumpi* (wide belt), and *lliklla* (shawl). The young woman also wore a pubic cover, a headdress with a semicircular fan of white feathers, a tubular cord to which were attached a pair of silver pins, and a feathered cape. One forearm was adorned by a gold bracelet, the other by a silver bracelet, and over each breast was a ground and polished Spondylus shell. Buried with the victims were numerous artifacts, including additional textiles, twenty-one ceramic pieces, several silver objects, a wooden spoon, two small containers made from gourds, seven cloth bags, a cylindrical box fashioned from a reed, coca leaves, burnt shell, seeds, and powdered cinnabar. It is fairly certain the females from Esmeralda represent *aqllas* who were put to death as *qhapaq huchas,* probably as offerings for the mountain-*waqa*.[16]

It is beyond the scope of the present work to present my interpretations of the materials from El Plomo and Esmeralda, but I plan to apply the analytical framework derived from the chronicles to these collections of remains as well—the subject of my next volume. To bridge the gap between the two types of information, ethnohistoric and archaeological, I will use arguments relating to analogy. I will compare—looking for similarities, but being sensitive to differences[17]—the material correlates of human sacrifice and mountain worship with the data on the bodies and artifacts from the two peaks. I will confirm that the three victims—the boy, girl, and young woman—were *qhapaq huchas* and that they were immolated to honor the mountain-*waqas.* I also will assess the degree of "fit" between the material correlates and the archaeological information: I will determine how closely the generalized descriptions of the Inka practices match what was found in the archaeological record. The better the fit, the more confident I can be that my interpretations relating to less tangible aspects of the analogy—such as the symbolism, meaning, and purpose(s) of the sacrifices/mountain offerings—are correct. And I will ascertain if and how the Cuzqueños manipulated the immolations on El Plomo and Esmeralda as part of the process to unify the state's southern quarter.

The interpretive framework can be applied not only to sacrifices from mountains, but to immolations from other contexts (see Map 1.3). The corpse of a boy of about six was recovered from a salt-flat called Salinas Grandes in northwestern Argentina. He had been placed in a hole dug into the salt, along with a red tunic, a copper bracelet and ring, a scepter made from the bone and wool of a camelid, and a gold ornament.[18] He was probably a *qhapaq hucha.* At the site of Pachacamac, situated on Peru's central coast, Uhle found the remains of at least 46 adult women who had been strangled. Buried with them were numerous textiles, ceramic and wooden vessels, ornaments, highland foods, utensils and implements, pins, and the body of a dog. There can be little doubt that the women were *aqllas* who had been ritually killed.[19]

The results of the present study can be employed to reach a better understanding of Inka figurines. Examples representing males and females are known. They are usually of gold, silver, copper, or Spondylus, and often wear miniature clothing and headdresses. They have been discovered in many contexts, including at high-altitude sites (both with the bodies of sacrificial victims[20] and alone[21]), on the summits of lower hills,[22] and in other settings.[23]

According to Andean scholars, there are four major theories concerning the meaning of the statuettes: (1) they could represent deities;[24] (2) the male figurines could depict the Sapa Inka, and female figurines the queen;[25] (3) they could be proxies for human immolations;[26] and/or (4) they could be human *qunupas* (idols thought to increase the fertility of whatever they resemble).[27] The generalizations distilled from the ethnohistoric sources can be utilized to assess the plausibility of each interpretation. If they were meant to serve as surrogate sacrifices, the masculine statuettes should be similar to *runas:* they should represent males in the prime of their lives and should have garments that resemble — in terms of quality, decoration, and style — the ones worn by citizens of the polity. They also should be recovered from the same contexts as immolated *runas.* If the female figurines were conceived of as substitutes, they should share many traits with the *aqlla-kunas* who were ritually put to death as *qhapaq huchas.* They should depict mature women, wearing clothing, headdresses, and accoutrements identical to those of the chosen women, and they should be found in the same settings as the sacrificial victims.

FINAL WORDS

In writing this book, it has not been my intention to devise a radically new method for dealing with the Andean chronicles; rather, I have tried to find a reasonable approach for collecting and exploring ethnohistoric information, some of it contradictory, relating to the Late Horizon. I have also attempted to create a more solid foundation on which archaeologists can build their arguments concerning the Andean past. My ultimate goal has been to elucidate what were notable religious practices in the Inka Empire: human sacrifice and mountain worship.

EPILOGUE

Dedicated to María Constanza Ceruti

Early the next morning, the day of her immolation, one of the priests awakened the fourteen-year-old girl. He gave her something to eat and told her, "It's nearly time to begin the sacred ceremony."

Thirty minutes later, a slow procession made its way from the stone hut to the top of the lofty peak, following a trail delineated by rocks.[1] The procession consisted of a high priest, the *qhapaq hucha,* two lesser priests, and the Inka official. Once on the summit, they mounted a low platform that was rectangular in shape, about 6 × 10 m.[2] Whereas the previous afternoon the wind had been howling, now the air was perfectly still, though the cold was intense. Drawing her *lliklla* (shawl) closely around her shoulders and wrapping the corners of the garment around her fingers for warmth, the young woman stared out at the sea of mountains around her. The sun, just peeking over the horizon, gave their snowy caps a pinkish-orange glow, similar to the color of Spondylus shell.

The sacrificial victim was wearing the clothing of an *aqlla* and looked very beautiful. Her shiny black hair, which had been plaited into hundreds of tiny braids, hung down her back. Draped over her shoulders and fastened over her heart with a silver pin was her *lliklla.* Beneath the shawl was an *aqsu,* a long dress made of fine alpaca wool that extended from her underarms to her ankles. Girding her narrow waist was a wide *chumpi,* on her feet leather moccasins, on her head the stunning headdress with a semicircular halo of white feathers.[3]

Standing on the sacred platform and facing the rising sun, the five people bowed as a gesture of humility. The priests lifted their arms with forearms parallel, hands slightly above their heads and open, palms forward. Each one made a kissing sound with his mouth, bringing his right hand to his lips and kissing his fingertips, thus paying homage to the mountain-

waqa. Then, while the imperial official and the two lower-ranking priests chanted, the higher-status officiant raised an Inka jug and consecrated the *chicha* it contained. He poured some of the corn beer onto the platform and handed the vessel to the young woman, telling her to drink deeply. She complied. Though it had a low alcohol content, the *chicha* went to her head quickly due to the extreme altitude[4] and her nearly empty stomach. The high priest dedicated the ritual objects, brought with the sacrificial victim, to the mountain-god; finally, he consecrated the young woman herself. Lifting his arms in supplication to the *waqa,* he addressed it directly.

"Powerful *apu,* accept these humble offerings, including the life of the *qhapaq hucha*. In return, make our fields fertile. Send us plentiful water and fair weather so our plants will not wither, nor be destroyed by frost, but will grow large and produce a bountiful harvest. Bestow on the emperor health and long life. Grant that his realm, especially the vast lands visible from your lofty summit, be peaceful and prosperous. I beseech you, in his name and in the name of Inti, the Sun."

With these words, the officiant produced a cloth bag from which he selected several perfect coca leaves. He put them in his open palm, gently blew across them, and gave them to the young woman, instructing her to chew them with a little crushed lime to release their narcotic effect. He took her hand and led her, since by this time her brain was numb from the drugs she had consumed, to a hole at the northern end of the platform. It had been excavated with pointed sticks several days earlier by the laborers, who had been prohibited from using metal tools. The high priest lowered her into the shaft as the other three individuals taking part in the ceremony began a solemn song. At the bottom of the shaft was a flat, cramped space where she sat, drawing her knees toward her chest so she would fit, and crossing her ankles[5] for warmth. The officiant arranged the ceramic vessels, wooden spoon, wooden cups, cloth bags, and statuettes around her. As the song continued, he adjusted the headdress and placed a beautiful tunic—that of a mid-level noble, which was also intended as an offering for the mountain-*waqa*—on the right side of her body.[6] He was draping another textile over the young woman's face when he noticed some tiny pieces of coca leaf under her nose;[7] he momentarily paused and stared, but then finished wrapping the piece around her head and upper body.[8] As the song reached its climax, he grabbed a wooden shovel and began to fill in the hole. The others followed suit. Despite the extreme altitude, the work went quickly and easily since the soil was loose and sandy.[9] First to disappear under the rising tide of dry earth were the offerings. Next, it covered the *qhapaq hucha's* legs, reached the level of her torso, enveloped her shoulders, and gently shrouded her head. Last to vanish was the halo of white plumes. Within fifteen minutes they had completed the job, whereupon they said a final prayer and hurried back to the hut; the wind was beginning to pick up.

By the following morning, the weather had turned sour: thick clouds had settled onto the upper slopes of the peak, and it was snowing. The high priest emerged from the stone hut, intending to return to base camp. Before setting off, he turned toward the sacred platform for a last look at the tomb of the *qhapaq hucha*. Nothing could be seen. The summit was completely blanketed in white, the platform buried, the tomb concealed, and all signs of human presence gone.

"The mountain jealously guards its offerings," he thought.

NOTES

PROLOGUE

1. See Reinhard 1999a: 42.
2. See Reinhard and Ceruti 2000: Photos 13a, 13b.
3. See Reinhard and Ceruti 2000: 163/no. 51, Photos 50–52.
4. See Reinhard 1999a: 42.
5. Reinhard and Ceruti 2000: 96–99.
6. Reinhard and Ceruti 2000: 111–113.
7. See Reinhard 1999a: 42, 47.
8. Reinhard and Ceruti 2000: 163/no. 50, Photo 50.
9. Reinhard and Ceruti 2000: 115.
10. Reinhard 1999: 47.
11. Reinhard 1999a: 45–46.

CHAPTER ONE

1. Rowe 1946: 205/Map 4, 208.
2. Silva 1978: 211, 220.
3. Rowe 1946: 205/Map 4.
4. Rowe 1946: 204–206.
5. See Rowe 1946: Map 3 between pages 184 and 185, 205/Map 4, 206–208.
6. Larrain 1987: 232–234, Map 1.
7. Rowe 1946: 205/Map 4, 208.
8. Rowe 1946: 205/Map 4, 208.
9. Moseley 1992: 11.
10. Kurtz 1978: 169.
11. Kertzer 1988: 2–3, 24–25, 174.
12. Kertzer 1988: 12.
13. See Acuto 2004: 107–123, 166, 239–242; Beorchia 1985: 391; Ceruti 2004: 119; Gose 1986; Reinhard 2005, 1999a: 47, 1993: 48, 1992a: 110, 1985: 310, 314, 1983a:

62, 1983b: 55; Salomon 1991: 10; Schobinger 1998: 389, 390, 1991: 66, 67, 1986: 301; Topic, Topic, and Melly 2002: 328–332.

14. See Acuto 2004: 107–123, 241; Beorchia 1985: 391; Bray et al. 2005: 85, 97–98; Ceruti 2003: 166–167; Duviols 1976: 29–30; Farrington 1998: 55; MacCormack 1991: 201–202; McEwan and Silva 1989: 180–182; McEwan and Van de Guchte 1992: 362, 366, 368, 370–371; Reinhard 2005, 1999a: 42, 47; Reinhard and Ceruti 2000: 85; Schobinger 1998: 390, 1986: 302, 304; Silverblatt 1987: 94–100; Zuidema 1982: 429, 1977–1978: 141–143.

15. See MacCormack 1991: 189–191; also see Reinhard 2005: 12, 119–120, 1985: 306, 1983b: 27.

16. Albornoz 1967: 33.

17. Albornoz 1967: 31.

18. Albornoz 1967: 30.

19. Albornoz 1967: 33.

20. Albornoz 1967: 21.

21. Hernández 1923: 41; also see MacCormack 1991: 416.

22. Hernández 1923: 28–29.

23. Associated Press 1998; Reinhard 1999b, 1999c; Reuters 1998.

24. National Geographic 1997; Reinhard 1998: 130, 134–135, 1997, 1996: 62–81.

25. Beorchia 1985: 161–164; Linares 1966: 20–46; Reinhard 1998: 128–131; 1992: 95, 101; Schobinger 1982: 82.

26. Horizon 1997; Nova 1996; Reinhard 1998: 132–133.

27. Beorchia 1985: 65–66; Conway 1901: 56–57.

28. Beorchia 1985: 40–46; Schobinger 1995: 43–46.

29. Beorchia 1985: 188–200; Haskel 1999; Reinhard 1992a: 99; Schobinger 1982: 92.

30. Beorchia 1985: 224–237; Reinhard 1992a: 95, 102–103; Schobinger 1995: 33–34, 1982: 84–89, 1966.

31. Beorchia 1985: 67–70; Millán 1966: 81–84; Pérez n.d.; Schobinger 1995: 33, 1982: 76; Martínez 1966: 85.

32. Begley 1999: 48–49; Blank 1999: 60–61; Noble 1999: A-1, A-19; Reinhard 1999a; Reinhard and Ceruti 2000; Sawyer 1999: A-1, A-10.

33. Bárcena 1989: 62–65; Beorchia 1985: 18–20; Reinhard 1992a: 95, 103; Schobinger 1995: 3–24; Schobinger, Ampuero, and Guercio 1985: 175.

34. Beorchia 1985: 171–180; Mostny 1957; Schobinger 1995: 31–32, 1982: 78–79.

35. Beorchia 1985: 77–84; Checura 1985, 1977.

36. See Beorchia 1985: 15–245.

37. Reinhard 1985: 302, 1983a: 62.

38. See Biggar 1999: 37–126.

39. See Biggar 1999: 127–180.

40. Reinhard 1985: 302; also see 1983a: 64.

41. Reinhard 1985: 302.

42. Silverblatt 1987: 99; Hernández 1923: 62.
43. Reinhard 1985: 302–303.
44. D'Altroy 1992: 14.
45. Silverblatt 1987: xxiii, 231.
46. Salomon 1991: 3.
47. Silverblatt 1987: xxiii.
48. Silverblatt 1987: 231.
49. Silverblatt 1987: 232.
50. MacCormack 1991: 149.
51. "Justicia 413" 1988: 66.
52. Salomon 1991: 28.
53. Silverblatt 1987: 232–233.
54. Silverblatt 1987: xxii–xxiii.
55. Silverblatt 1987: xxiii.
56. Silverblatt 1987: xxix.
57. Rowe 1946: 195.
58. MacCormack 1991: 80.
59. Means 1928: 342–345.
60. MacCormack 1991: 80–83.
61. MacCormack 1991: 84, 187.
62. Rowe 1946: 195.
63. MacCormack 1991: 186–188; Means 1928: 428–430; Rowe 1946: 195.
64. MacCormack 1991: 187.
65. Means 1928: 352, 357; Rowe 1946: 194.
66. Means 1928: 349–350.
67. MacCormack 1991: 393–394.
68. MacCormack 1991: 392–393; Rowe 1946: 194.
69. Means 1928: 349.
70. MacCormack 1991: 401–402.
71. Silverblatt 1987: xxiv; Rowe 1946: 197.
72. See Duviols 1980; also see Silverblatt 1987: xxiv–xxv.
73. Silverblatt 1987: xxiv–xxv, 231–232.
74. MacCormack 1991: 318–319; Silverblatt 1987: xxiv.
75. Salomon 1991: 1; Silverblatt 1987: xxiv.
76. See Silverblatt 1987: xxiv–xxv.
77. Silverblatt 1987: xxiv; Means 1928: 308.
78. Salomon 1991: 1–3.
79. Salomon 1991: 1–2.
80. Salomon 1991: 5.
81. Cobo 1979: 94–96.
82. See Cobo 1979: 261/no. 2.
83. Randall 1990: 3–4.
84. Rowe 1946: 196.

85. Means 1928: 367.
86. MacCormack 1991: 333.
87. MacCormack 1991: 342.
88. Garcilaso 1961: 91–92.
89. Randall 1990: 3–4.
90. Randall 1990: 3–4.
91. Randall 1990: 4.
92. Urton 1990: 5–6.
93. Urton 1990: 9.
94. Guaman Poma 1980a: xx–xxii.
95. Guaman Poma 1980c: 1075–1108.
96. Hyslop 1984: 14–15.

CHAPTER TWO

1. Cobo 1979: 235–238.
2. Garcilaso 1961, 1945; Valera 1968.
3. Rowe 1946: 196.
4. Means 1928: 371, 378.
5. Means 1928: 367.
6. Garcilaso 1961: 120, 141, 208–209, 308.
7. Means 1928: 497–498.
8. Valera 1968: 155–156; Means 1928: 505.
9. Cobo 1979: 235; also see Acosta 1880: 344; García 1981: 98; Herrera 1730: 92; Murúa 1964: 137/fol. 280, 1946: 342; Polo 1916a: 26.
10. Cobo 1979: 236.
11. Cobo 1990: 112; Guaman Poma 1980a: 236; Ruiz 1904: 181.
12. Calancha and Torres 1972: 176; Cobo 1990: 99; Ramos 1976: 56.
13. Acosta 1880: 332; Calancha and Torres 1972: 155; Cobo 1979: 236–238; García 1981: 181; Las Casas 1967: 237–238; Paz 1897: 150; Polo 1916b: 92, 1873: 166; Román 1897: 226.
14. Cobo 1979: 238.
15. Betanzos 1996: 78, 132, 1987: 84, 142, 1968: 284; García 1981: 98; Murúa 1946: 265; Paz 1897: 150.
16. Molina 1873: 54; also see Betanzos 1996: 46, 1987: 51, 1968: 247.
17. Cobo 1990: 111, 1979: 235; Díez 1964: 39, 92.
18. Molina 1873: 54.
19. Cobo 1979: 235–236.
20. Cobo 1990: 112, 1979: 236.
21. Cobo 1979: 235–237; also see Polo 1916b: 91–94, 1873: 165–167.
22. Hernández 1923: 61.

23. Molina 1873: 54.

24. Hernández 1923: 61; MacCormack 1991: 416; Silverblatt 1987: 96–97; Cieza 1967: 100, 1959: 191.

25. Guaman Poma 1980a: 221, 1978: 63.

26. Hernández 1923: 61.

27. Betanzos 1996: 77, 132, 1987: 84, 142, 1968: 284.

28. Molina 1873: 54–59.

29. Murúa 1946: 265–267.

30. Polo 1917: 28.

31. Guaman Poma 1980a: 233, 245, 246.

32. Cieza 1967: 96, 1959: 150–151; Murúa 1946: 266.

33. Cieza 1967: 96, 1959: 150.

34. Molina 1873: 55, 58.

35. See Cobo 1990: 110, 51–83; Polo 1917: 3–42.

36. Cobo 1990: 156; Molina 1873: 57–58.

37. See, for example, Betanzos 1996: 132, 1987: 142; García 1981: 98.

38. Murúa 1964: 110/fol. 259v, 1946: 271–272.

39. Molina 1873: 54–55.

40. See "Justicia 413" 1988: 200/fol. 256v; also see Molina 1873: 54–55; Rostworowski 1988: 66.

41. "Justicia 413" 1988: 195/fol. 245v, 197/fol. 250r, 200/fol. 256v; also see Rostworowski 1988: 66.

42. Cobo 1990: 156; Molina 1873: 57–58.

43. Murúa 1964: 110, 1946: 271–272.

44. Cobo 1990: 156; Molina 1873: 59.

45. Albornoz 1967: 20–21, 26–34; Avila 1991: 43/sec. 3, 67/sec. 99; Bello 1897: 189/sec. 14; Cieza 1967: 95–98, 1959: 150–151; Cobo 1990: 65 [An 3:6]; Dávila 1881: 72; Guaman Poma 1980a: 239, 240, 242, 243, 245–247; Molina 1873: 57; Murúa 1964: 113/fol. 261v, 1946: 281; Paz 1897: 150; Polo 1917: 20, 1916c: 193/sec. 8.

46. Albornoz 1967: 26, 33; Cobo 1990: 58 [Ch 5:10]; Polo 1917: 10.

47. Albornoz 1967: 29, 30, 33; Guaman Poma 1980a: 245; Hernández 1923: 41.

48. Albornoz 1967: 26–29; Cobo 1990: 78 [Cu 1:13]; Polo 1917: 36.

49. Albornoz 1967: 26–35; Bello 1897: 189/sec. 14; Cobo 1990: 59 [Ch 7:3], 64 [An 2:9], 69 [An 8:11], 72 [Co 3:7], 76–77 [Co 9:11], 78 [Cu 1:10], 79 [Cu 4:4]; Polo 1917: 12, 19, 24–25, 28, 34, 35–36, 37.

50. Cobo 1990: 73 [Co 4:8], 78 [Cu 1:6]; Polo 1917: 29, 35.

51. Albornoz 1967: 26; Cobo 1990: 54 [Ch 2:1], 70 [Co 1:4]; Polo 1917: 4, 26.

52. Albornoz 1967: 34.

53. Bello 1897: 189/sec. 14; also see Dávila 1881: 75.

54. Albornoz 1967: 26, 33.

55. Cobo 1990: 71 [Co 2:3], [Co 3:4]; Polo 1917: 27, 28.

56. Albornoz 1967: 27.

57. Cobo 1990: 81 [Cu 8:2]; Polo 1917: 39.

58. Albornoz 1967: 25–27, 33; Cobo 1990: 65 [An 3:4], 80 [Cu 7:1], 82 [Cu 10:2]; Polo 1917: 19–20, 38, 40.

59. Cobo 1990: 80 [Cu 5:1]; Polo 1917: 37.

60. Albornoz 1967: 26–30, 33, 34; Cobo 1990: 54 [Ch 2:3], 78 [Cu 1:7]; Polo 1917: 5, 35.

61. Cobo 1990: 45–46.

62. Albornoz 1967: 26, 34.

63. Cobo 1990: 51–83; Polo 1917: 3–42.

64. Hernández 1923: 28, 41.

65. Hernández 1923: 61–62.

66. Molina 1873: 58.

67. Calancha and Torres 1972: 174; Hernández 1923: 62; Cobo 1990: 157.

68. Murúa 1964: 104–105/fol. 256.

69. Betanzos 1996: 46, 77, 132, 1987: 51, 84, 142, 1968: 247, 284; Carabajal 1965: 218; Cieza 1967: 96, 1959: 150–151; Murúa 1946: 265.

70. Murúa 1946: 265.

71. Agustinos 1918: 39; San Pedro 1992: 202–203.

72. Cobo 1990: 112; Molina 1873: 55.

73. Cieza 1967: 96, 1959: 150–151; Cobo 1990: 112, 1979: 236; Murúa 1946: 266.

74. Calancha and Torres 1972: 156.

75. Jesuíta Anónimo 1944: 80; Oviedo y Valdez 1959: 101.

76. Cieza 1967: 96, 1959: 150.

77. Cobo 1990: 112.

78. Cieza 1967: 96, 1959: 150; Zárate 1968: 50.

79. Agustinos 1918: 15–16; Arriaga 1968: 37; Cobo 1990: 124–125.

80. Murúa 1946: 266.

81. Cieza 1967: 96, 1959: 150; Herrera 1730: 92; Molina 1873: 54, 55; Murúa 1964: 104/fol. 256.

82. Cobo 1990: 112; 1979: 235.

83. Cobo 1979: 235.

84. Calancha and Torres 1972: 156; Ramos 1976: 25.

85. Acosta 1880: 344; Betanzos 1996: 132, 1987: 142; García 1981: 98.

86. Calancha and Torres 1972: 173; Carabajal 1965: 218; Cobo 1990: 112; Herrera 1730: 92; Molina 1873: 55; Ramos 1976: 62.

87. Cobo 1990: 112; Molina 1873: 55–56.

88. Calancha and Torres 1972: 174; Cobo 1990: 112; Ramos 1976: 62.

89. Avila 1991: 112/sec. 280; Betanzos 1996: 46, 77, 132, 137, 162, 1987: 51, 84, 142, 147, 177, 1968: 247, 284; Hernández 1923: 61, 62; Montesinos 1920: 37; Sarmiento 1907: 102.

90. Cobo 1990: 112.

91. Hernández 1923: 62.

92. Hernández 1923: 62; Molina 1873: 54, 55; Murúa 1946: 266.

93. Cieza 1967: 96, 1959: 150; Hernández 1923: 61, 62; Noboa 1986: 248/fol. 117.

94. Hernández 1923: 62.

95. Carabajal 1965: 207; 1881: 149/sec. 14; Cieza 1967: 215; Montesinos 1920: 43; Murúa 1964: 113/fol. 261v, 1946: 281.

96. Carabajal 1965: 218, 1881: 167; Cobo 1990: 57 [Ch 4:8], 58 [Ch 6:2], 60 [Ch 7:7], 72 [Co 3:9], 99, 111, 155–156; Las Casas 1967: 237–238; Murúa 1964: 137/fol. 280; Pachacuti Yamqui 1873: 79; Polo 1917: 8, 10, 12, 28.

97. Acosta 1880: 304; Betanzos 1996: 46, 1987: 51, 1968: 247; Calancha 1972 and Torres: 153, 168, 173, 174; Carabajal 1965: 218–219, 1881: 167; Cobo 1990: 57 [Ch 4:8], 65 [An 3:4], 70 [Co 1:3], 73 [Co 4:8], 82 [Cu 10:2]; Guaman Poma 1980a: 236; Hernández 1923: 30, 41, 60, 61; Herrera 1730: 91; Las Casas 1967: 238; Montesinos 1920: 43; Murúa 1964: 109/fol. 258v, 113/fol. 61v, 137/fol. 280, 1946: 286; Noboa 1986: 248; Oliva 1895: 34; Pachacuti Yamqui 1873: 101; Polo 1917: 8, 19–20, 26–29, 40, 1916: 7; Ramos 1976: 26, 61, 62; Sarmiento 1907: 126.

98. Acosta 1880: 304; Cobo 1990: 54 [Ch 2:3], 57 [Ch 4:8]; Hernández 1923: 27, 41, 46; Herrera 1730: 91; Jesuíta Anónimo 1944: 71; Murúa 1964: 109/fol. 258v, 113/fol. 261v; 1946: 281; Polo 1917: 5, 8, 1916a: 6–7/sec. 3, 193, 1916c: 193/sec. 8.

99. Calancha and Torres 1972: 174; Murúa 1964: 113/fol. 261v; Ramos 1976: 26, 65.

100. Carabajal 1965: 219; 1881: 167.

101. García 1981: 98.

102. Anónimo 1904: 227; Albornoz 1967: 26, 35; Arriaga 1968: 88; Cabello 1920: 31; Carabajal 1965: 207, 1881: 149/sec. 14; Cobo 1990: 54–82, 111; Díez 1964: 92/fol. 45r; Gutiérrez 1905: 438; Hernández 1923: 32, 41, 46; Jesuíta Anónimo 1918: 186, 196; Matienzo 1967: 9; Molina 1873: 54, 55; Murúa 1964: 113/fol. 261v, 1946: 267, 281, 286, 291; Polo 1917: 4–40, 1916a: 37, 1916c: 193/sec. 8; Ramos 1976: 25; Rocha 1891: 8; Sarmiento 1907: 102.

103. Guaman Poma 1980a: 239; Murúa 1964: 216/fol. 338v; Ramos 1976: 88; Santillán 1968: 392.

104. Cobo 1990: 12.

105. Guaman Poma 1980a: 245; Hernández 1923: 41.

106. Cieza 1967: 95–96, 1959: 150–151; Guaman Poma 1980a: 239; Molina 1873: 57.

107. Murúa 1964: 99/fol. 252v.

108. Albornoz 1967: 20–21, 26–34; Ávila 1991: 43/sec. 3, 67/sec. 99; Bello 1897: 189/sec. 14; Cieza 1967: 97–98; Dávila 1881: 72; Guaman Poma 1980a: 240, 242, 243, 245–247; Herrera 1730: 93; Murúa 1964: 113/fol. 261v, 1946: 281; Paz 1897: 150; Polo 1916c: 193/sec. 8.

109. Albornoz 1967: 26–35; Bello 1897: 189/sec. 14.

110. Murúa 1964: 216/fol. 338v; Ramos 1976: 88; Cieza 1967: 95–98; 1959: 150–152; also see Bray et al. 2005: 85; MacCormack 1991: 103–105.

111. Cobo 1990: 170.

112. Murúa 1964: 11/fol. 188v.

113. Hernández 1923: 41, 62.

114. Acosta 1880: 344, 412–413; Cobo 1990: 69 [An 8:11], 112; García 1981: 98; Herrera 1730: 92; Molina 1873: 55; Montesinos 1920: 65; Murúa 1964: 137–138/fol. 280–280v, 1946: 266, 342; Polo 1917: 24–25, 1916a: 26/sec. 3; Ramos 1976: 26.

115. Cobo 1990: 156; Molina 1873: 55; Murúa 1946: 267.

116. Acosta 1880: 344; Calancha and Torres 1972: 155/sec. 4; Cobo 1990: 112, 1979: 237; García 1981: 98; Herrera 1730: 92; Polo 1916b: 92, 94; Ramos 1976: 26; Rocha 1891: 9.

117. Acosta 1880: 332; Carabajal 1965: 219; Cobo 1990: 54 [Ch 2:3], 59 [Ch 7:3], 155–156, 1979: 237; García 1981: 98, 181; Molina 1873: 55; Murúa 1964: 137/fol. 280–280v; Polo 1917: 5, 12, 1873: 166; Ramos 1976: 26.

118. Murúa 1946: 291; Polo 1916a: 37; Ramos 1976: 26.

119. Acosta 1880: 332, 344; Cobo 1990: 60 [Ch 7:7], 112, 155–156; 1979: 237; García 1981: 98, 181; Herrera 1730: 92; Murúa 1964: 137–138/fol. 280v, 1946: 123; Polo 1917: 12, 1916b: 92, 1873: 166; Ramos 1976: 26; Sarmiento 1907: 122.

120. Betanzos 1996: 77–78, 1987: 84, 1968: 283–284.

121. Sarmiento 1907: 123.

122. Acosta 1880: 332; Betanzos 1996: 132, 137, 162, 1987: 142, 147, 177; Cobo 1979: 237; García 1981: 98, 181; Montesinos 1920: 65; Murúa 1964: 99/fol. 252v, 137/fol. 280; Rocha 1891: 9.

123. Cobo 1990: 112.

124. Calancha and Torres 1972: 175/sec. 6.

125. Guaman Poma 1980a: 221.

126. Ramos 1976: 65.

127. Guaman Poma 1980a: 233.

128. Guaman Poma 1980a: 221, 233, 1978: 63, 67–68.

129. Cobo 1990: 111–112, 151, 170; Gutiérrez 1905: 490; Las Casas 1967: 237; Murúa 1964: 104/fol. 256, 1946: 281; Polo 1916a: 193, 1916b: 92, 1916c: 193/sec. 8; Román 1897: 225.

130. Murúa 1964: 137–138/fol. 280v.

131. Cobo 1990: 54 [Ch 2:1]; Gutiérrez 1905: 490; Polo 1917: 4–5; 1916b: 92; 1873: 166.

132. Cobo 1990: 27; Montesinos 1920: 37; Polo 1916b: 92, 1873: 166.

133. For contemporary scholars, see Beorchia 1985: 390, 391; Reinhard 1999a: 38, 1985: 313; Reinhard and Ceruti 2000: 86; Schobinger 1998: 382, 390, 1991: 67.

134. See Ruiz 1904: 181; also see Bray et al. 2005: 85; Silverblatt 1987: 100; Velasco 1978: 194; Zuidema 1977–1978: 146–147, 168.

135. Herrera 1730: 93.

136. Cobo 1990: 156.

137. Cobo 1990: 71 [Co 2:3]; Polo 1917: 27.

138. Polo 1917: 20; also see Cobo 1990: 65 [An 3:6].

139. For contemporary scholars, see Beorchia 1985: 390; Bray et al. 2005: 85; MacCormack 1991: 417; Reinhard 1999a: 38, 1998: 130, 1996: 70, 1992: 99–101, 1985: 312–313; Reinhard and Ceruti 2000: 86; Schobinger 1998: 382, 390; Velasco 1978: 194; Zuidema 1982: 429, 1977–1978: 148–149, 168.

140. Ulloa 1885: 44–45.

141. Murúa 1964: 113/fol. 261v, 1946: 281; also see Polo 1916c: 193/sec. 8.

142. Polo 1917: 10; also see Cobo 1990: 58 [Ch 5:10].

143. Hernández 1923: 60–62; also see Zuidema 1982: 429, 1977–1978: 142–143, 148–149, 168.

144. Herrera 1730: 93.

145. Murúa 1964: 113/fol. 261v.

146. Murúa 1964: 109/fol. 258v.

147. Cobo 1990: 156.

148. Betanzos 1996: 77–78, 132, 1987: 84, 142, 1968: 284; García 1981: 98.

149. Ruiz 1904: 181.

150. Hernández 1923: 34; also see Zuidema 1977–1978: 138.

151. Cieza 1967: 215.

152. For contemporary scholars, see Acuto 2004: 107–123, 241; Beorchia 1985: 391; Bray et al. 2005: 85, 97–98; Ceruti 2003: 166–167; Duviols 1976: 29–30; Farrington 1998: 55; MacCormack 1991: 201–202; McEwan and Silva 1989: 180–182; McEwan and Van de Guchte 1992: 362, 366, 368, 370–371; Reinhard 2005, 1999: 42, 47; Reinhard and Ceruti 2000: 85; Schobinger 1998: 390, 1986: 302, 304; Silverblatt 1987: 94–100; Zuidema 1982: 429, 1977–1978: 141–143.

153. Calancha and Torres 1972: 156/sec. 5.

154. Hernández 1923: 27; also see Zuidema 1977–1978: 137.

155. Hernández 1923: 60–62.

156. Hernández 1923: 62; Molina 1873: 57–58; Murúa 1946: 267. For contemporary scholars, see Bray et al. 2005: 85; Ceruti 2004: 167; Duviols 1976: 24–25, 29; MacCormack 1991: 201–202; McEwan and Silva 1989: 180–182; Reinhard and Ceruti 2000: 85; Zuidema 1982: 429–432.

157. See "Justicia 413" 1988: 200/fol. 256v; also see Molina 1873: 54–55; Rostworowski 1988: 66.

158. Bray et al. 2005: 85; Ceruti 2004: 171.

159. "Justicia 413" 1988: 195/fol. 245v, 197/fol. 250r; also see Ceruti 2004: 171; Rostworowski 1988: 66.

160. Cobo 1990: 51–83; Polo 1917: 3–42; also see Zuidema 1990: 73.

161. Cobo 1990: 156; Molina 1873: 57–58; also see Zuidema 1982: 431.

162. See Zuidema 1982: 439.

163. See Duviols 1976: 29.

164. See Beorchia 1985: 390; Reinhard 1985: 312.

165. Hernández 1923: 62; also see Zuidema 1982: 429, 1977: 146.

166. See Cobo 1990: 60–61 [Ch 8:7], 67 [An 6:7], 81 [Cu 8:6], 83 [Cu 13:3]; Polo 1917: 13–14, 23, 39, 41; also see Bauer and Dearborn 1995; Urton 1981: 196–197; Zuidema 1990: 73–75, 1982: 435.

167. Cobo 1990: 111; 1979: 235–238.

168. Silverblatt 1987: 94–95.

169. Molina 1873: 54–55; also see Rostworowski 1988.

170. Hernández 1923: 61, 62; Noboa 1986: 248/fol. 117.

171. Guaman Poma 1980a: 272.

172. See Mostny 1957: 55–57; Schobinger 1995: 18–22.

173. Guaman Poma 1980a: 148, 244, 268, 299.

174. Guaman Poma 1980a: 144, 264, 295.

175. Guaman Poma 1980a: 95, 128.

176. Guaman Poma 1980a: 168, 316, 324.

177. Guaman Poma 1980a: 315, 316, 324, 326, 328.

178. Guaman Poma 1980a: 148, 244.

179. Guaman Poma 1980a: 144, 240.

180. Guaman Poma 1980a: 316, 324, 326, 328.

181. Cobo 1979: 236–238.

182. Guaman Poma 1980a: 198, 216, 273; also see Rowe 1946: 235.

183. See Pachacuti 1873: 82 and fn. 4; Gonçález 1952: 271, 372; Guaman Poma 1980a: 101, 103, 105, 109, 111, 113, 115, 119.

184. Guaman Poma 1980a: 273.

185. DiMaio and DiMaio 1993: 236–241; Galloway 1999: 79, 80; Pollanen and Chiasson 1996; Ubelaker 1992: 1219, 1220.

186. DiMaio and DiMaio 1993: 231–236; Pollanen and Chiasson 1996; Ubelaker 1992: 1219, 1220.

187. Galloway 1999: 66–69.

188. Cartmell et al. 1991; Cartmell 1994.

189. Acosta 1880: 343; Murúa 1964: 106, 1946: 294.

CHAPTER THREE

1. See Cobo 1979: 194; Guaman Poma 1980a: 171.

2. Gutiérrez 1905: 491.

3. Díez 1964: 85/fol. 41r–41v, 92/fol. 45r, 106/fol. 52r.

4. Jesuíta Anónimo 1918: 188/no. 3.

5. Las Casas 1967: 237–238; Román y Zamora 1897: 226.

6. See Cobo 1979: 194–195; Díez 1964: 85/fol. 41v.

7. Cieza 1967: 96, 1959: 150.

8. Gutiérrez 1905: 492.

9. Cieza 1967: 96, 1959: 150; Gutiérrez 1905: 492.

10. Cieza 1967: 96, 1959: 150; Gutiérrez 1905: 491; Xerez 1985: 90.

11. Cieza 1967: 96, 1959: 150; Oviedo y Valdez 1959: 101; Xerez 1985: 90; Zárate 1968: 51.

12. Cieza 1967: 96, 1959: 150; Zárate 1968: 51.

13. Oviedo y Valdez 1959: 101.

14. Oviedo y Valdez 1959: 101.

15. Cieza 1967: 96, 1959: 150.

16. Gutiérrez 1905: 492.

17. Xerez 1985: 90.

18. Oviedo y Valdez 1959: 101; Xerez 1985: 90; Zárate 1968: 51.

19. Murúa 1964: 113/fol. 261v, 1946: 281; Polo 1916c: 193/sec. 8.

20. Cieza 1967: 96, 1959: 150; Gutiérrez 1905: 492; Pachacuti 1873: 104.

21. Las Casas 1967: 237.

22. Oviedo y Valdez 1959: 101; also see Las Casas 1967: 238; Román y Zamora 1897: 226.

23. Polo 1916c: 193.

24. Murúa 1964: 113/fol. 261v, 1946: 281.

25. Cieza 1967: 93.

26. Cieza 1967: 95–96, 1959: 150.

27. Pachacuti 1873: 104.

28. Ulloa 1885: 44–45/sec. 14.

29. Albornoz 1967: 20–21, 26–34.

30. Albornoz 1967: 35.

31. Cieza 1967: 97–98; for additional examples, see Murúa 1964: 113/fol. 261v, 1946: 281; Polo 1916c: 193/sec. 8.

32. See Díez 1964: 85/fol. 41r–41v, 92/fol. 45r, 106/fol. 52r; Jesuíta Anónimo 1918: 196; Murúa 1964: 113/fol. 261v, 1946: 281; Polo 1916c: 193/sec. 8.

33. Las Casas 1967: 237–238; Román y Zamora 1897: 226; for additional examples, see Albornoz 1967: 29, 30, 33.

34. Díez 1964: 85/fol. 41v; Oviedo y Valdez 1959: 101; Xerez 1985: 90; Zárate 1968: 51; also see Albornoz 1967: 26–30, 33, 34.

35. Albornoz 1967: 26–35.

36. Albornoz 1967: 25–27; Anónimo 1904: 227; Cieza 1967: 97, 1959: 151; Xerez 1985: 90.

37. Albornoz 1967: 26, 33.

38. Albornoz 1967: 26, 28, 29.

39. Albornoz 1967: 26, 33.

40. Albornoz 1967: 34.

41. Albornoz 1967: 26.

42. Ibid.

43. Ibid.

44. Albornoz 1967: 34.

45. Ibid.

46. Cieza 1967: 96, 1959: 150.

47. Zárate 1968: 51.
48. Ulloa 1885: 44–45/sec. 14.
49. Albornoz 1967: 20, 35.
50. Polo 1916c: 193/sec. 8; also see Murúa 1964: 113/fol. 261v, 1946: 281.
51. Pachacuti 1873: 104.
52. Polo 1916c: 193/sec. 8.
53. Murúa 1946: 281.
54. Calancha and Torres 1972: 155/sec. 4.
55. Zárate 1968: 51.
56. Cieza 1967: 95–96.
57. Cieza 1967: 97, 1959: 151.
58. Cieza 1967: 97–98, 1959: 151–152.
59. Cieza 1967: 215.
60. Gutiérrez 1905: 490–493.
61. Zárate 1968: 51.
62. Albornoz 1967: 35.
63. Murúa 1946: 280; Polo 1916c: 193/sec. 8.
64. Calancha and Torres 1972: 155/sec. 4.
65. Pachacuti 1873: 104.
66. Cieza 1967: 215.
67. DiMaio and DiMaio 1993: 236–241; Galloway 1999: 79, 80; Pollanen and Chiasson 1996; Ubelaker 1992: 1219, 1220.
68. Galloway 1999: 66–69.
69. Cobo 1979: 143.
70. Cobo 1979: 154.
71. Murúa 1962: 61.
72. Cabello 1920: 35.
73. Gutiérrez 1905: 438.
74. Avila 1991: 120/secs. 321–322, fnn. 619, 620.
75. Cieza 1985: 222.
76. Betanzos 1996: 87–88, 1987: 93; also see Sarmiento 1907: 105.
77. Betanzos 1996: 87, 89, 1987: 93, 95.
78. Sarmiento 1907: 105.
79. Alcayá 1914?: 156.
80. Betanzos 1996: 89–90, 1987: 95.
81. Betanzos 1996: 190, 1987: 208.
82. Betanzos 1996: 41, 1987: 45.
83. Garcilaso 1961: 321.
84. Cieza 1967: 155, 1959: 227–228.
85. Cobo 1979: 143.
86. Guaman Poma 1980a: 308.
87. Guaman Poma 1980a: 130–131, 168.

88. Cobo 1990: 187.

89. Betanzos 1996: 41, 1987: 45.

90. Avila 1991: 120/secs. 321–322, fnn. 619, 620.

91. Cobo 1979: 143, 154.

92. Murúa 1962: 61.

93. Cabello 1920: 35.

94. Avila 1991: 120/sec. 321.

95. Avila 1991: 120/sec. 322, fn. 619.

96. See Guaman Poma 1980a: 168–171.

97. See Byrd and Castner 2001; Catts and Haskell 1990; Smith 1986.

98. See Acosta 1880: 313; Montesinos 1920: 65; Polo 1916b: 92.

99. Betanzos 1996: 131–132, 1987: 141–142.

100. Pachacuti 1873: 100.

101. Betanzos 1996: 162, 1987: 177.

102. Pachacuti 1873: 104.

103. Cobo 1979: 161.

104. Murúa 1964: 99/fol. 252, 1946: 76; also see Acosta 1880: 313–314, 433; Ramos 1976: 72.

105. Pizarro 1921: 226.

106. Cieza 1985: 230.

107. Zárate 1968: 52; for additional examples, see Acosta 1880: 344; Anónimo 1897a: 93–94; Atienza 1931: 155; Bello Galloso 1897: 193; Cieza 1985: 222, 223, 262–264, 266–268, 309–310, 357–358, 1959: 110, 274–276, 308–310, 311–312; Herrera 1730: 92; Matienzo 1967: 9, 128, 129; Murúa 1946: 245; Oviedo y Valdez 1959: 101; Ramos 1976: 72; Toledo 1989: 414.

108. Acosta 1880: 313–314, 344, 433; Bello Galloso 1897: 193; Betanzos 1996: 162, 1987: 177; Cieza 1985: 263–264, 309, 357–358, 1959: 110, 310, 275–276; Cobo 1979: 161; Herrera 1730: 92; Matienzo 1967: 128; Murúa 1964: 99, 1946: 76; Pachacuti 1873: 100, 104; Pizarro 1921: 226; Polo 1916b: 92; Ramos 1976: 72; Toledo 1989: 414; Zárate 1968: 52.

109. Bello Galloso 1897: 193/sec. 14.

110. Cieza 1985: 223.

111. See Kertzer 1988: 25–27.

112. Betanzos 1996: 131–132.

113. Betanzos 1996: 131–132, 162, 1987: 141–142, 177; Cieza 1985: 264, 1959: 310; Pizarro 1921: 226.

114. Atienza 1931: 155; Cieza 1985: 222, 223, 263, 264, 267, 309, 357–358, 1959: 110, 275, 310, 311; Matienzo 1967: 9; Oviedo y Valdez 1959: 101.

115. Acosta 1880: 344; also see Cobo 1990: 112–113; Ramos 1976: 73.

116. Herrera 1730: 92; also see Murúa 1964: 120/fol. 267.

117. Calancha and Torres 1972: 155/sec. 4.

118. Duviols 1976: 36.

CHAPTER FOUR

1. For contemporary research on the relationship between mountain worship and social/political control, see Acuto 2004: 107–123, 166, 239–242; Beorchia 1985: 391; Ceruti 2004: 119; Gose 1986; Reinhard 2005, 1999a: 47, 1993: 48, 1992a: 110, 1985: 310, 314, 1983a: 62, 1983b: 55; Salomon 1991: 10; Schobinger 1998: 389, 390, 1991: 66, 67, 1986: 301; Topic, Topic, and Melly 2002: 328–332.

2. Compare Cobo 1990: 51–83 with Polo 1917: 3–42.

3. Compare Murúa 1946: 283 with Polo 1916c: 190/sec. 8.

4. Arriaga 1968: 24; Avila 1904: 388.

5. Valera 1968: 157; see also Hyland 1996: 4.

6. Garcilaso 1991: 171.

7. Means 1928: 300–301, 308–309.

8. See Arriaga 1968: 24.

9. Means 1928: 367, 497–499.

10. See Hyland 1996: 4–5, 14.

11. Acosta 1880: 308; Agustinos 1918: 35; Albornoz 1967: 20–21, 27–34; Avila 1991: 43/sec. 3, 44/sec. 6, 51–52/secs. 31–34, 54/sec. 38, 61/sec. 75, 78/sec. 146; Ayala 1976: 276; Cobo 1990: 54 [Ch 1:5], 57 [Ch 4:8], 58 [Ch 5:7, 5:9], 59 [Ch 6:9], 60 [Ch 7:7, 8:7], 61 [Ch 9:3], 64 [An 2:3], 65 [An 3:6], 66 [An 4:1, 4:6], 67 [An 6:3, 6:7], 70 [Co 1:3], 71 [Co 2:2], 72 [Co 3:9, 4:4, 4:7], 73 [Co 4:9, 4:10, 5:6, 5:10], 74 [Co 6:7], 75 [Co 6:9, 8:4], 76 [Co 9:5], 77 [Co 9:13], 78 [Cu 1:7], 79 [Cu 2:4, 3:2], 80 [Cu 5:5], 81 [Cu 7:4, 8:6, 8:11, 8:15], 82 [Cu 9:2, 9:3, 10:4, 11:4], 83 [Cu 13:3, 13:4, 14:4; Ch-Ex:3, Ch-Ex:4]; Garcilaso 1991: 170; Guaman Poma 1980a: 253; Jesuíta Anónimo: 1918: 183; Molina 1873: 4–5, 8–9, 17, 55, 57; Pachacuti 1873: 96; Polo 1917: 8, 10, 11, 13–14, 18, 20, 21, 23, 26–42; Ulloa 1885: 44–45/sec. 14.

12. For contemporary research on the relationship between mountains and oracles, see MacCormack 1991: 143, 144; Reinhard 1985: 310–311, 1983a: 61, 1983b: 45; Topic, Topic, and Melly 2002: 305, 308, 311–312, 313, 319, 322, 329–330, 331, 332.

13. For contemporary scholarship on mountains and the relationship between mountains/ancestors/*paqarikus* (places of origin), see Acuto 2004: 110, 118, 119, 121, 240–241; MacCormack 1991: 96, 144, 413; Reinhard 1985: 309, 1983a: 61, 1983b: 42, 54; Salomon 1991: 19; Topic, Topic, and Melly 2002: 308, 331.

14. Paz 1897: 152.

15. Ulloa 1885: 44–45.

16. Avila 1991: 67–68/secs. 99–104; Dávila 1881: 72.

17. Avila 1991: 93.

18. Avila 1991: 94/sec. 212.

19. Avila 1991: 71/sec. 116.

20. Avila 1991: 61/sec. 75, 272.

21. Avila 1991: 92/sec. 204.

22. Velasco 1978: 61–62.

23. Anónimo 1897b: 132.

24. Matienzo 1967: 129.

25. Cieza 1967: 97–98, 1959: 151–152.

26. Guaman Poma 1980a: 248.

27. Betanzos 1996: 231, 1987: 249.

28. See Guerra 1881: 85; Ayala 1976: 275.

29. See Gonçález 1952: 266.

30. Molina 1873: 4–5; also see Betanzos 1996: 7–8; Cobo 1990: 13.

31. Ulloa 1885: 40.

32. Albornoz 1967: 20, 32.

33. Paz 1897: 150.

34. Agustinos 1918: 21.

35. Betanzos 1987: 14b; also see MacCormack 1991: 96.

36. Cobo 1990: 13–14; Molina 1873: 5.

37. Molina 1873: 8–9; also see Albornoz 1967: 32; Cobo 1990: 14–15.

38. Avila 1991: 51–52/secs. 29–34.

39. Cobo 1990: 16; also see Molina 1873: 9–10.

40. Albornoz 1967: 32.

41. Cieza 1967: 95, 1959: 150; also see Cobo 1990: 74 [Co 6:7]; Fernández 1963: 83; Guaman Poma 1980a: 248, 253, 1978: 76; Hernández 1923: 61; Molina 1873: 17; Polo 1917: 31.

42. Sarmiento 1907: 44–45, 51–52.

43. Cieza 1967: 95.

44. Guaman Poma 1980a: 234–235.

45. Avila 1991: 51/secs. 31–34, 72/sec. 119, 93/secs. 208–209.

46. For contemporary research on the relationship between mountain worship and volcanic eruptions, see Reinhard 1998: 134.

47. Pachacuti 1873: 96.

48. Avila 1991: 68/sec. 103; also see 66/sec. 96.

49. Avila 1991: 67–68/sec. 101.

50. Avila 1991: 115/sec. 293.

51. Avila 1991: 61/sec. 75 (also see sec. 74), sec. 76.

52. Avila 1991: 59/sec. 72; 67/sec. 99; 68/sec. 102; 92/secs. 201–202, 204.

53. Demarest 1981: 40–41.

54. Avila 1991: 54/secs. 36, 38, 57/sec. 55, 59/sec. 72, 61/sec. 74.

55. For contemporary scholarship on the relationship between mountains and weather, see Acuto 2004: 118; MacCormack 1991: 144; Reinhard 1999a: 38, 1996: 74, 1993: 51, 1992a: 87, 91–92, 1985: 307, 314, 1983a: 61–62, 1983b: 40, 44–45, 54, 55; Reinhard and Ceruti 2000: 86; Salomon 1991: 15; Topic, Topic, and Melly 2002: 308, 311, 313, 323, 329, 330, 331–332.

56. Avila 1991: 54/secs. 36, 38; 57/sec. 55; 92/sec. 201.

57. Gonçález 1952: 321; also see Avila 1991: 57.

58. Avila 1991: 62/sec. 80; for another example, see Avila 1991: 66/sec. 98.

59. Dávila 1881: 72.

60. For contemporary scholarship on the relationship between mountains and water/rain, see Acuto 2004: 118; Barthel 1986; Gelles 2000; Gose 1986: 298, 301; Isbell 1980: 139, 143, 151; Reinhard 2005, 1999a: 44, 1998: 130, 1996: 66, 70, 1992a: 91, 101, 1985: 303–306, 308–309, 310, 313, 314, 1983a: 56, 59, 61, 62, 64, 1983b: 33–36, 38, 39, 40–42, 54, 55; Reinhard and Ceruti 2000: 86; Salomon 1991: 15; Schobinger 1998: 382, 390, 1991: 66, 1986: 301; Topic, Topic, and Melly 2002: 304, 312, 315, 321, 323, 329, 330–331, 332; Zuidema 1982: 432.
61. Avila 1991: 61–62/sec. 80.
62. Avila 1991: 68/sec. 102.
63. Dávila 1881: 72.
64. Avila 1991: 127/secs. 348–349, 350, 353.
65. Avila 1991: 115/secs. 295–296.
66. Avila 1991: 139/sec. 409–410.
67. Avila 1991: 140–141/secs. 422–424.
68. Avila 1991: 57/sec. 55.
69. Avila 1991: 125/secs. 342–345.
70. Avila 1991: 127/sec. 350.
71. Avila 1991: 72/sec. 119.
72. Avila 1991: 58/sec. 63.
73. Avila 1991: 93/sec. 209.
74. Avila 1991: 68/secs. 102, 104, 92/sec. 204.
75. Avila 1991: 127/sec. 350.
76. Avila 1991: 115/sec. 296.
77. Polo 1917: 3–42; Cobo 1990: 51, 54–83.
78. See Bauer and Dearborn 1995: 94; Zuidema 1990: 73, 1982: 439.
79. Cobo 1990: 54 [Ch 1:5]; Polo 1917: 4.
80. Cobo 1990: 82 [Cu 9:2]; Polo 1917: 40.
81. Molina 1873: 17–18.
82. Acosta 1880: 308.
83. Jesuíta Anónimo: 1918: 183.
84. Ayala 1976: 279.
85. Molina 1873: 8–9.
86. Albornoz 1967: 26–35.
87. Albornoz 1967: 20–21.
88. See Torres 1974: 89–90; also see Reinhard 1997.
89. Guaman Poma 1980a: 248.
90. Agustinos 1918: 35; Avila 1904: 388; Bello 1897: 173/sec. 16; Monzón 1881a: 172/sec. 14; Paz 1897: 150–152; Ulloa 1885: 44–45/sec. 14.
91. Cobo 1990: 67 [An 6:7]; Polo 1917: 23.
92. Cobo 1990: 70 [Co 1:3]; Polo 1917: 26.
93. Cobo 1990: 59 [Ch 6:9]; Polo 1917: 11; for additional examples, see Cobo 1990: 57 [Ch 4:8], 58 [Ch 5:9], 60–61 [Ch 8:7], 64 [An 2:3], 66 [An 4:1, 4:6], 71 [Co 2:2], 72 [4:4], 73 [Co 5:6, 5:10], 74 [Co 6:7], 75 [Co 6:9], 76 [Co 9:5], 78 [Cu 1:7],

79 [Cu 3:2], 80 [Cu 5:5], 81 [Cu 8:11], 82 [Cu 9:3], 83 [Cu 13:3]; and Polo 1917: 8, 10, 13–14, 18, 20, 21, 34–42.

94. Albornoz 1967: 29, 32, 33, 34.

95. Guaman Poma 1980a: 235, 238, 242, 246.

96. Cobo 1990: 64 [An 2:9]; Polo 1917: 19.

97. Cobo 1990: 61–62 [Ch 9:6]; Polo 1917: 15.

98. Cobo 1990: 75 [Co 8:3]; Polo 1917: 33; for additional examples, see Cobo 1990: 59 [Ch 6:8, 7:4, 7:5], 60 [Ch 8:7], 61 [Ch 8:13], 62 [Ch 9:11], 66 [An 4:3], 67 [An 5:9, 6:4], 69 [An 8:8, 8:10, 8:11, 9:4], 70 [Co 1:7], 72 [Co 4:6], 74 [Co 6:7], 76 [Co 8:5, 9:10, 9:11], 77 [Co 9:12], 78 [Cu 1:8, 1:10], 79 [Cu 1:14, 4:4], 80 [Cu 5:3], 81 [Cu 8:8]; and Polo 1917: 8, 11, 12, 14, 15, 21, 22, 24–26, 29, 33–39, 41.

99. Albornoz 1967: 32.

100. Albornoz 1967: 30, 31; for additional examples, see 27–35.

101. Arriaga 1968: 25.

102. See Cobo 1990: xxii.

103. Cobo 1990: 74 [Co 6:7]; also see Polo 1917: 31–32.

104. Sarmiento 1907: 51–52.

105. Agustinos 1918: 31.

106. Molina 1873: 43.

107. Ramos 1976: 103.

108. Albornoz 1967: 34.

109. Hernández 1923: 29.

110. Monzón 1881: 206–207.

111. Cobo 1990: 65 [An 3:4]; Polo 1917: 19–20.

112. Cobo 1990: 56 [Ch 4:5]; Polo 1917: 8.

113. Albornoz 1967: 33.

114. Fuente 1885: 91; Cieza 1967: 97–98, 1959: 151–152.

115. Velasco 1978: 61, 63–64.

116. Paz 1897: 151.

117. Cobo 1990: 83 [Cu 14:3]; Polo 1917: 41.

118. Velasco 1978: 63–64.

119. Martínez 1991: lámina LXXXV, p. 9.

120. Gonçález 1952: 30.

121. Arriaga 1968: 59; Ayala 1976: 283; Murúa 1964: 112, 1946: 282, 283; Polo 1916c: 189–190/secs. 4, 8; Ramos 1976: 68; Sarmiento 1907: 212.

122. Cobo 1990: 45, 116; Acosta 1880: 309.

123. Garcilaso 1991: 171.

124. Garcilaso 1991: 171–172.

125. Cobo 1990: 54–83; Polo 1917: 3–42.

126. Albornoz 1967: 20–21, 26–35.

127. For the Spanish system of measures, see Cobo 1990: xxii; also see Betanzos 1996: xix.

128. Arriaga 1968: 78–79.

129. Arriaga 1968: 82–83.
130. Arriaga 1968: 85–86.
131. Hernández 1923: 62; also see Silverblatt 1987: 99; Zuidema 1978: 142.
132. Martínez 1991: lámina LXXXV, p. 9.
133. Martínez 1991: 11.
134. Guaman Poma 1980a: 230–231.
135. Sarmiento 1907: 102.
136. Molina 1873: 35–36.
137. Polo 1917: 9.
138. Sarmiento 1907: 102.
139. Guaman Poma 1980a: 232–233.
140. Molina 1873: 38.
141. Cobo 1990: 74 [Co 6:7]; Polo 1917: 31–32.
142. Molina 1873: 38; also see Cobo 1990: 129–130.
143. Molina 1873: 41–42; also see Cobo 1990: 131–132.
144. Molina 1873: 43–44.
145. Cobo 1990: 79; Polo 1917: 36.
146. Pachacuti 1873: 80.
147. Cobo 1990: 132.
148. Cobo 1990: 61; Polo 1917: 15.
149. Fernández 1963: 83.
150. Cieza 1967: 95–96, 1959: 150–151.
151. Murúa 1946: 271–272, 1964: 110; Molina 1873: 54–55.
152. Jesuíta Anónimo 1944: 108–109.
153. Velasco 1978: 67.
154. Avila 1991: 75/secs. 138–139.
155. Avila 1991: 256.
156. Avila 1991: 122/sec. 329.
157. Avila 1991: 122; Arriaga 1968: 29.
158. Pachacuti 1873: 103–104.
159. Murúa 1946: 397–398; for a similar example, see Torres 1974: 95.
160. Oberem 1968: 82, 83; also see Silverblatt 1987: 17.
161. Agustinos 1918: 31.
162. Cobo 1990: 57 [Ch. 4:8]; Polo 1917: 8.
163. Cobo 1990: 60 [Ch 7:7]; Polo 1917: 12.
164. Cobo 1990: 70 [Co 1:3]; Polo 1917: 26; for additional examples, see Cobo 1990: 60–61 [Ch 8:7], 72 [Co 3:9]; and Polo 1917: 13–14, 28.
165. Molina 1873: 42, 43.
166. Cobo 1990: 67 [An 6:3].
167. Molina 1873: 55–57.
168. Noboa 1986: 248/fol. 117.
169. Hernández 1923: 62.
170. Velasco 1978: 61, 63.

171. Alcayá 1914?: 156.
172. See Reinhard 1983a: 62, 1983b: 57.
173. Avila 1991: 72/secs. 119–122.
174. Avila 1991: 74–75/secs. 135–138.
175. Hernández 1923: 62.
176. Cobo 1990: 59 [Ch 6:9]; Polo 1917: 11.
177. Cobo 1990: 60–61 [Ch 8:7]; Polo 1917: 13–14; for similar examples, see Cobo 1990: 83 [Cu 13:3]; Polo 1917: 41; Herrera 1730: 93.
178. Jesuíta Anónimo 1918: 183.
179. Guaman Poma 1980a: 238–239.
180. Guaman Poma 1980a: 240–241.
181. See Valcarcel 1978: VI, 475.
182. Guaman Poma 1980a: 242–243.
183. Guaman Poma 1980a: 244–245.
184. Guaman Poma 1980a: 246–247.
185. Cobo 1990: 66 [An 4:7]; Polo 1917: 21.
186. Ayala 1976: 279–280.
187. Agustinos 1918: 35.
188. Ulloa 1885: 40–41/sec. 1.
189. Avila 1991: 114/secs. 285–290.
190. Avila 1991: 114–115/sec. 291.
191. Betanzos 1996: 231–232, 1987: 249–250; also see Agustinos 1918: 23.
192. Guaman Poma 1980a: 269.
193. Avila 1991: 73/secs. 127–128, 129/sec. 358.
194. Guaman Poma 1980a: 271.
195. Polo 1916c: 194.
196. Murúa 1964: 100/fol. 252v.
197. Jesuíta Anónimo 1981: 190.

CHAPTER FIVE

1. Cobo 1990: 111.
2. Cobo 1990: 65 [An 3:6]; Polo 1917: 20.
3. Guaman Poma 1980a: 239; also see Molina 1873: 57.
4. Cieza 1967: 95–96, 1959: 150–151.
5. Pachacuti 1873: 104.
6. Pachacuti 1873: 95.
7. See Albornoz 1967: 35; Bello 1897: 189; Murúa 1964: 113, 1946: 281; Polo 1916c: 193/sec. 8.
8. Paz 1897: 150.
9. Ulloa 1885: 45.
10. Guaman Poma 1980a: 241.

11. Guaman Poma 1980a: 245.

12. Velasco 1978: 67.

13. Avila 1991: 43/sec. 3, 67/sec. 99; also see Dávila 1881: 72.

14. Cobo 1990: 64 [An 2:9]; Polo 1917: 19.

15. Cobo 1990: 72 [Co 4:4]; Polo 1917: 29.

16. Cobo 1990: 78 [Cu 1:7]; Polo 1917: 35; for additional examples, see Cobo 1990: 69 [An 8:11], 73 [Co 5:6], 76–77 [Co 9:11], 78 [Cu 1:10], 79 [Cu 4:4]; and Polo 1917: 24–25, 30, 34, 35–36, 37.

17. Herrera 1730: 93.

18. Cieza 1967: 97–98, 1959: 151–152.

19. Guaman Poma 1980a: 242, and text on p. 243; for additional examples, see Albornoz 1967: 26–35.

20. Cobo 1990: 57 [Ch 4:8]; Polo 1917: 8.

21. Cobo 1990: 65 [An 3:6]; Polo 1917: 2.

22. Cobo 1990: 72 [Co 3:9]; Polo 1917: 28.

23. Molina 1873: 54–55.

24. Albornoz 1967: 17, 35.

25. Martínez 1991: 9.

26. Murúa 1964: 105/fol. 256, 1946: 291; Polo 1916a: 37, 1873: 167.

27. Cobo 1990: 128, 147; Murúa 1964: 104/fol. 255v.

28. Acosta 1880: 341; Cobo 1990: 128, 129, 135, 140, 147–148.

29. Acosta 1880: 341; Cobo 1990: 113, 115, 135, 148; Murúa 1964: 104/fol. 255v, 105/fol. 256, 1946: 291; Polo 1916a: 37.

30. Cobo 1990: 113, 128, 147; Murúa 1964: 104/fol. 255v.

31. Cobo 1990: 129, 140; Murúa 1964: 105/fol. 256, 1946: 291; Polo 1916a: 37.

32. Acosta 1880: 341; Cobo 1990: 113; Murúa 1964: 105/fol. 256, 1946: 291; Polo 1916a: 37; also see Rowe 1946: 306.

33. Acosta 1880: 341; Cobo 1990: 113, 114; Murúa 1946: 288.

34. Arriaga 1968: 42.

35. Cobo 1990: 114, 128.

36. Acosta 1880: 341; Cobo 1990: 128.

37. Acosta 1880: 341; Cobo 1990: 114; Murúa 1946: 288.

38. Cobo 1990: 128.

39. Guaman Poma 1980b: 826.

40. Arriaga 1968: 42.

41. Cobo 1990: 65 [An 3:6]; Polo 1917: 20.

42. Cobo 1990: 66 [An 4:1]; Polo 1917: 20.

43. See Guaman Poma 1980c: 1040.

44. Molina 1873: 17–18.

45. Molina 1873: 38.

46. Cobo 1990: 129.

47. Molina 1873: 41–42.

48. Molina 1873: 43–44.

49. Cobo 1990: 132.
50. Paz 1897: 150.
51. Bello 1897: 189.
52. Monzón 1881: 188.
53. Ulloa 1885: 44.
54. Guaman Poma 1980a: 244.
55. Avila 1991: 96/secs. 220–221.
56. Dávila 1881: 71; for another example, see Torres 1974: 95.
57. Murúa 1964: 110–111, 1946: 271–272.
58. Murúa 1946: 397–398.
59. See Hernández 1923: 61–62; Noboa 1986: 248/fol. 117.
60. Matienzo 1967: 129.
61. Jesuíta Anónimo 1944: 108.
62. Monzón 1881: 206–207.
63. Noboa 1986: 247.
64. See Albornoz 1967: 26–35.
65. Cobo 1990: 60–61 [Ch 8:7]; Polo 1917: 13–14.
66. Molina 1873: 54–55; Albornoz 1967: 17, 35.
67. Martínez 1991: 9.
68. Acosta 1880: 341; Cobo 1990: 113, 115; Murúa 1964: 105/fol. 256, 1946: 291; Polo 1916a: 37.
69. Arriaga 1968: 43.
70. Matienzo 1967: 129.
71. Ulloa 1885: 44.
72. Monzón 1881: 188.
73. Monzón 1881: 206–207.
74. Guaman Poma 1980a: 241.
75. Guaman Poma 1980a: 243.
76. Guaman Poma 1980a: 246.
77. Jesuíta Anónimo 1944: 108.
78. Noboa 1986: 247.
79. Agustinos 1918: 26.
80. Avila 1991: 131/sec. 370, 153/sec. 483.
81. Avila 1991: 100/sec. 234.
82. Cobo 1990: 116–117; also see Acosta 1880: 340; Molina 1873: 54; Murúa 1964: 104/fol. 256, 106/fol. 257, 1946: 294; Polo 1916a: 39.
83. See Cobo 1990: 57 [Ch 4:8], 60–61 [Ch 8:7], 72 [Co 3:9]; Polo 1917: 8, 13–14, 28.
84. Cobo 69 [An 8:10]; Polo 1917: 24.
85. Cobo 1990: 70 [Co 1:7]; Polo 1917: 26.
86. Cobo 1990: 74 [Co 6:7]; Polo 1917: 31.
87. Cieza 1967: 95–96, 1959: 150–151.
88. Pachacuti 1873: 104.

89. Guaman Poma 1980a: 245.

90. Guaman Poma 1980a: 247.

91. Guaman Poma 1980a: 248.

92. Bello 1897: 189.

93. Dávila 1881: 71.

94. Ulloa 1885: 44–45.

95. Albornoz 1967: 20–21.

96. See Albornoz 1967: 26–35.

97. Matienzo 1967: 129.

98. Cieza 1967: 97–98, 1959: 151–152.

99. Noboa 1986: 247.

100. Jesuíta Anónimo 1944: 108.

101. Martínez 1991: lámina LXXXV, p. 9.

102. Agustinos 1918: 23.

103. Noboa 1986: 248.

104. Arriaga 1968: 43.

105. Acosta 1880: 343; Cobo 1990: 117; Murúa 1964: 106/fol. 257, 1946: 294; Polo 1916a: 39.

106. Arriaga 1968: 45.

107. See Blower 1995.

108. Gonçález 1952: 249.

109. Blower 1995: 111.

110. Cobo 1990: 73 [Co 4:10]; Polo 1917: 29.

111. Cobo 1990: 75–76 [Co 8:4]; Polo 1917: 33.

112. Cobo 1990: 69 [An 8:8]; Polo 1917: 24.

113. Cobo 1990: 75 [Co 6:9]; Polo 1917: 32.

114. Cobo 1990: 75 [Co 8:3]; Polo 1917: 33.

115. Molina 1873: 17.

116. Guaman Poma 1980a: 241.

117. Ibid.

118. Guaman Poma 1980a: 247.

119. Albornoz 1967: 26–35.

120. Avila 1991: 67/sec. 99, 68/sec. 101.

121. Avila 1991: 116/sec. 299.

122. Cobo 1990: 117; also see Acosta 1880: 341; Molina 1873: 54; Murúa 1964: 104/fol. 256, 1946: 291; Polo 1916a: 37, 1916b: 94–95.

123. Cobo 1990: 65 [An 3:6]; Polo 1917: 20.

124. Cobo 1990: 66 [An 4:1]; Polo 1917: 20.

125. Cobo 1990: 70 [Co 1:7]; Polo 1917: 26.

126. Cobo 1990: 75 [Co 6:9]; Polo 1917: 32.

127. Cobo 1990: 74 [Co 6:7]; Polo 1917: 31.

128. Bello 1897: 189.

129. Jesuíta Anónimo 1944: 108.

130. Agustinos 1918: 21; for another example, see Torres 1974: 95.
131. Arriaga 1968: 43.
132. Cobo 1990: 116.
133. Murúa 1964: 106, 1946: 294; Polo 1916a: 40/sec. 3.
134. Cobo 1990: 76 [Co 9:5]; Polo 1917: 34.
135. Molina 1873: 17.
136. See Matienzo 1967: 129.
137. Polo 1916c: 190/sec. 8; also see Acosta 1880: 309; Herrera 1730: 91.
138. Ayala 1976: 280.
139. Guaman Poma 1980a: 241.
140. Guaman Poma 1980a: 243.
141. Guaman Poma 1980a: 247.
142. Guaman Poma 1980a: 244.
143. Avila 1991: 67/sec. 99.
144. Avila 1991: 75/sec. 138.
145. Avila 1991: 149/sec. 471.
146. Arriaga 1968: 44.
147. Polo 1916c: 190/sec. 8.
148. Molina 1873: 17.
149. Arriaga 1968: 44; Murúa 1964: 106, 1946: 294; Polo 1916a: 39.
150. Cobo 1990: 116.
151. Guaman Poma 1980a: 247; also see 1980c: 1107.
152. Avila 1991: 64/sec. 91, 256.
153. Avila 1991: 146/sec. 454, 256.
154. Murúa 1964: 106, 1946: 294; Polo 1916a: 39; also see Arriaga 1968: 184.
155. Avila 1991: 67/sec. 99.
156. Guaman Poma 1980a: 221.
157. Molina 1873: 17.
158. Cobo 1990: 65 [An 3:6]; Polo 1917: 20.
159. See Molina 1873: 59.
160. Polo 1916c: 190/sec. 8.
161. Jesuíta Anónimo 1944: 109.
162. Ayala 1976: 280.
163. Guaman Poma 1980a: 241.
164. Guaman Poma 1980a: 240.
165. Guaman Poma 1980a: 243.
166. Guaman Poma 1980a: 247.
167. Avila 1991: 67/sec. 99, 68/sec. 101.
168. Avila 1991: 75/sec. 138.
169. Avila 1991: 153/sec. 483.
170. Arriaga 1968: 41–42.
171. Cobo 1990: 119.
172. Arriaga 1968: 41.

173. Cobo 1990: 115–116.
174. Molina 1873: 43.
175. Ulloa 1885: 44–45.
176. Ayala 1976: 279–280.
177. Agustinos 1918: 21.
178. Guaman Poma 1980a: 241; for another example, see Torres 1974: 95.
179. Acosta 1880: 340.
180. Arriaga 1968: 45.
181. Arriaga 1968: 45; Guaman Poma 1980a: 247.
182. Guaman Poma 1980a: 245.
183. Polo 1916c: 190/sec. 8; also see Acosta 1880: 309; Herrera 1730: 91; Murúa 1964: 112, 1946: 283.
184. Guaman Poma 1980a: 243.
185. Guaman Poma 1980a: 247.
186. Cieza 1967: 96–98.
187. Guaman Poma 1980a: 241.
188. Ibid.
189. Ayala 1976: 279.
190. Ulloa 1885: 44–45.
191. Cobo 1990: 65 [An 3:6]; Polo 1917: 20.
192. Cobo 1990: 77 [Co 9:13]; Polo 1917: 34.
193. See Jesuíta Anónimo 1918: 183/fn. 4.
194. Guaman Poma 1980a: 241.
195. Arriaga 1968: 45–46.
196. Reinhard 1997b.
197. Torres 1974: 95.
198. Polo 1916c: 190/secs. 8–9; also see Acosta 1880: 309; Herrera 1730: 91; Murúa 1964: 112, 1946: 283.
199. Ayala 1976: 283; Ramos 1976: 68.
200. Avila 1991: 70/secs. 110–111, 93/sec. 209; also see Guaman Poma 1980a: 241.
201. Agustinos 1918: 26–27.
202. Acosta 1880: 309; Albornoz 1967: 19; Arriaga 1968: 59, 166/sec. 7; Ayala 1976: 283; Cobo 1990: 45, 116; Garcilaso 1991: 171–172; Herrera 1730: 91; Murúa 1964: 112, 1946: 282, 283, 289; Polo 1916c: 189–190/secs. 4, 8, 9; Ramos 1976: 68; Sarmiento 1907: 212.
203. Cobo 1990: 117.
204. Cobo 1990: 117.
205. Cobo 1990: 51–83; Polo 1917: 3–42.
206. Acosta 1880: 343; Cobo 1990: 117; Murúa 1964: 106/fol. 257, 1946: 294; Polo 1916a: 39.
207. Cobo 1990: 51–83; Polo 1917: 3–42.

208. E.g., Cobo 1990: 57 [Ch 4:8], 60 [Ch 7:7]; Polo 1917: 8, 12.
209. E.g., Cobo 1990: 51–83; Polo 1917: 3–42.
210. E.g., Guaman Poma 1980a: 240–248.
211. Compare Guaman Poma 1980a: 240–248 and Jesuíta Anónimo 1944: 108–109.
212. See Ayala 1976: 279–280.
213. Ulloa 1885: 45.
214. Albornoz 1967: 17, 20, 35.
215. For the source of the translation, see Gonçáléz Holguín 1952: 79.
216. See Albornoz 1967: 35.
217. Albornoz 1967: 20–21.
218. Albornoz 1967: 26–35.
219. Agustinos 1918: 22–23.
220. Agustinos 1918: 35.
221. Cieza 1967: 96, 1959: 151.
222. Cobo 1990: 172–174, 1979: 236.
223. Cobo 1990: 267.
224. Cieza 1967: 98, 1959: 152.
225. Guaman Poma 1980a: 253.
226. Avila 1991: 96/sec. 220, 99/sec. 229.
227. Avila 1991: 115/sec. 297.
228. Avila 1991: 96/sec. 221.
229. Cobo 1990: 122–123.
230. Cobo 1990: 124–125.
231. Agustinos 1918: 31.
232. Jesuíta Anónimo 1944: 108.
233. Cobo 1990: 118.
234. Ulloa 1885: 44.
235. Jesuíta Anónimo 1944: 108.
236. Cobo 1990: 119.
237. Ayala 1976: 279, 280.
238. See Cobo 1990: 121.
239. Jesuíta Anónimo 1944: 108.
240. Cieza 1967: 96, 1959: 151.
241. See Cobo 1990: 121.
242. Jesuíta Anónimo 1944: 108.
243. Cieza 1967: 96, 1959: 151.
244. Polo 1916c: 191/sec. 12; also see Murúa 1946: 284.
245. Avila 1991: 75/secs. 138–139; for another example, see Torres 1974: 95.
246. Agustinos 1918: 21, 24.
247. See Cobo 1990: 121.
248. Polo 1916c: 191/sec. 12; also see Murúa 1946: 284.

249. Murúa 1964: 112; also see Polo 1916c: 190–191/sec. 10.
250. Molina 1873: 43–44.
251. Molina 1873: 41–42; for another example, see Torres 1974: 95.

CHAPTER SIX

1. Bello 1897: 179/sec. 14; Garcilaso 1991: 171; Monzón 1881b: 188/sec. 14; Polo 1916c: 189/sec. 1; Ramos 1976: 68; also see Salomon 1991: 6.
2. For contemporary research on the idea that mountains were important due to their extraordinary nature, see Kunstmann 1994; Reinhard 1993: 53; Reinhard and Ceruti 2000: 85–86; Salomon 1991: 6, 15.
3. Cobo 1990: 45.
4. Acosta 1880: 308; Albornoz 1967: 33; also see Herrera 1730: 91.
5. Garcilaso 1991: 171; also see Arriaga 1968: 23–24; Avedaño 1904: 380; Cobo 1990: 45; Polo 1916c: 191/sec. 11; Monzón 1881a: 172/sec. 14.
6. Cobo 1990: 72 [Co 4:7]; Polo 1917: 29.
7. Arriaga 1968: 24.
8. Ulloa 1885: 40.
9. Ulloa 1885: 44.
10. Cabeza 1885: 71.
11. Albornoz 1967: 29.
12. Albornoz 1967: 30.
13. Albornoz 1967: 33.
14. Dávila 1881: 71–72; also see Avila 1904: 388.
15. See Avila 1991: 72/sec. 119, 94/sec. 211.
16. See Ulloa 1885: 44/sec. 14.
17. For contemporary scholarship on the relationship between mountains and Andean mythology, see Reinhard 1985: 300, 306, 1983b: 27, 37; Salomon 1991: 6.
18. Paz 1897: 152; for additional examples, see Avila 1991: 67–68/secs. 99–104; Dávila 1881: 72; Ulloa 1885: 44–45.
19. Avila 1991: 93/secs. 208–209.
20. See Betanzos 1967: 11–13; Cobo 1990: 13; Guerra y Céspedes 1881: 85/sec. 14; Molina 1873: 4–5.
21. Ulloa 1885: 40.
22. Albornoz 1967: 20.
23. Albornoz 1967: 32.
24. Paz 1897: 150.
25. Agustinos 1918: 21.
26. Betanzos 1987: 14b; also see MacCormack 1991: 96.
27. Albornoz 1967: 32; Cobo 1990: 14–15; Molina 1873: 8–9.
28. Avila 1991: 51–52/secs. 29–34.

29. Albornoz 1967: 32.

30. Cobo 1990: 16; Molina 1873: 9–10.

31. Sarmiento 1907: 51–52.

32. Cobo 1990: 129–130; Molina 1873: 38.

33. Cieza 1967: 95–96, 1959: 150–151.

34. Molina 1873: 41–42; also see Cobo 1990: 131–132.

35. For contemporary research on the idea that mountains could be used as "stepping stones" to higher gods, see Beorchia 1985: 391; Reinhard 1993: 49, 1992a: 91, 1992b: 170, 1985: 311, 1983a: 62, 1983b: 47; Schobinger 1991: 67.

36. Cobo 1990: 57 [Ch 4:8]; Polo 1917: 8.

37. Cobo 1990: 60 [Ch 7:7]; Polo 1917: 12; for additional examples, see Cobo 1990: 60–61 [Ch 8:7], 70 [Co 1:3], 72 [Co 3:9]; Polo 1917: 13–14, 26, 28.

38. Molina 1873: 43.

39. Noboa 1986: 248/fol. 117.

40. Hernández 1923: 60–62.

41. For contemporary scholarship on the relationship between mountains and weather, see Acuto 2004: 118; Beorchia 1985: 390; MacCormack 1991: 144; Reinhard 1999a: 38, 47, 1996: 74, 1993: 51, 1992a: 87, 91–92, 101, 1985: 307, 314, 1983a: 61–62, 1983b: 40, 44–45, 54, 55; Reinhard and Ceruti 2000: 86; Salomon 1991: 15; Topic, Topic, and Melly 2002: 308, 311, 313, 323, 329, 330, 331–332.

42. Cobo 1990: 69 [An 8:10]; Polo 1917: 24.

43. Pachacuti 1873: 104.

44. Paz 1897: 150.

45. Avila 1991: 62/sec. 80; also see 54/secs. 36, 38, 57/sec. 55, 92/sec. 201; and Dávila 1881: 72.

46. Avila 1991: 125/secs. 342–345; also see 57/sec. 55.

47. Avila 1991: 127/sec. 350.

48. Avila 1991: 72/sec. 119; also see 94/sec. 211.

49. Avila 1991: 68/secs. 102, 104; also see 92/sec. 204, 127/sec. 350.

50. For contemporary research on the relationship between mountains and water/rain, see Acuto 2004: 118; Barthel 1986; Beorchia 1985: 396; Gelles 2000; Gose 1986: 298, 301; Isbell 1980: 139, 143, 151; Reinhard 2005, 1999a: 38, 44, 1998: 130, 1996: 66, 70, 76, 1992a: 87, 91, 101, 1985: 303–306, 308–309, 310, 313, 314, 1983a: 56, 59, 61, 62, 64, 1983b: 33–36, 38, 39, 40–42, 54, 55; Reinhard and Ceruti 2000: 86; Salomon 1991: 15; Schobinger 1998: 382, 390, 1991: 66, 1986: 301; Topic, Topic, and Melly 2002: 304, 312, 315, 321, 323, 329, 330–331, 332; Zuidema 1982: 432.

51. Murúa 1964: 110/fol. 260.

52. Albornoz 1967: 20.

53. Ulloa 1885: 40.

54. Ulloa 1885: 44/sec. 14.

55. Ramos 1976: 103.

56. Bibar 1966: 138.

57. Velasco 1978: 63–64.

58. Allen n.d.

59. Avila 1991: 61–62/sec. 80.

60. Avila 1991: 68/sec. 102; also see Dávila 1881: 72.

61. Avila 1991: 126/secs. 348–350, 353.

62. Avila 1991: 62–63/secs. 82–85, 88.

63. For another example of a myth in which a male mountain-deity unites with a female earth-goddess, see Avila 1991: 82–83/secs. 167–171.

64. Avila 1991: 139–143/secs. 408–440.

65. Salomon 1991: 15–16.

66. Salomon 1991: 15–16.

67. See Avila 1991: 138/sec. 407, 141/sec. 431, 142/secs. 433–434, 142/fn. 808.

68. For contemporary scholarship on the relationship between mountains and human health, see Gose 1986: 305; Isbell 1980: 151; Reinhard 1992a: 93, 95, 1985: 307, 1983a: 61, 1983b: 40, 45; Topic, Topic, and Melly 2002: 330.

69. Cobo 1990: 66 [An 4:6]; Polo 1917: 21.

70. Cobo 1990: 54 [Ch 1:5]; Polo 1917: 4.

71. Cobo 1990: 70 [Co 1:7]; Polo 1917: 26; for additional examples, see Cobo 1990: 59–60 [Ch 7:5]; 69 [An 8:8]; Polo 1917: 12, 24.

72. Cobo 1990: 67 [An 6:4]; Polo 1917: 22.

73. Arriaga 1968: 165/sec. 1.

74. Ayala 1976: 280.

75. Jesuíta Anónimo 1944: 108.

76. Arriaga 1968: 77.

77. Ayala 1976: 283.

78. Cobo 1990: 122.

79. Agustinos 1918: 21.

80. Murúa 1946: 398; for a similar example, see Torres 1974: 89–90, 95.

81. Ayala 1976: 282–283; Murúa 1964: 112; Polo 1916c: 190/sec. 8; Ramos 1976: 68.

82. Albornoz 1967: 19–20.

83. See Cobo 1990: 17.

84. Agustinos 1918: 22.

85. Polo 1916c: 198/sec. 5.

86. Avila 1991: 75–76/sec. 140, fn. 282.

87. For contemporary research on the relationship between mountains and the economy, see Reinhard 1993: 48, 1985: 315, 1983a: 62, 1983b: 56.

88. Herrera 1730: 93.

89. Cobo 1990: 60–61 [Ch 8:7]; Polo 1917: 13–14.

90. Cobo 1990: 83 [Cu 13:3]; Polo 1917: 41.

91. For contemporary research on the relationship between mountains and crop fertility, see Acuto 2004: 118; Bastien 1985: xix; Beorchia 1985: 388–389; Gose 1986: 298; Reinhard 1996: 66, 70, 1993: 51, 1992a: 95, 103, 1985: 314, 1983a: 61, 1983b:

39, 40, 43, 55; Reinhard and Ceruti 2000: 86; Salomon 1991: 15–16; Schobinger 1998: 382, 390, 1991: 66, 1986: 301; Topic, Topic, and Melly 2002: 304, 311.

92. Ayala 1976: 279–280.

93. Velasco 1978: 67.

94. Cobo 1990: 65 [An 3:6]; Polo 1917: 21.

95. Rowe 1946: 219, 239.

96. Paz 1897: 150.

97. Avila 1991: 72/sec. 120.

98. For contemporary scholarship on the relationship between mountains and animal fertility, see Bastien 1985: xix; Beorchia 1985: 388–389; Flores-Ochoa 1979; Gose 1986: 298, 300, 301, 302; Isbell 1980: 59, 151–163, 202–203; Reinhard 1999a: 44, 47, 1993: 51, 52, 1992a: 95, 103, 1985: 311, 313–314, 1983a: 61, 1983b: 39, 40, 43, 46, 55; Reinhard and Ceruti 2000: 86; Salomon 1991: 15–16; Topic, Topic, and Melly 2002: 304, 311.

99. Agustinos 1918: 22.

100. Avila 1991: 121/sec. 327, fn. 632.

101. Avila 1991: 122/sec. 329, fn. 641.

102. Monzón 1881: 206–207/sec. 14, fn. a.

103. See Cobo 1979: 208–222, 228–234; Rowe 1946: 265–268.

104. Cobo 1990: 17; Arriaga 1968: 165.

105. Rowe 1946: 268; Cobo 1979: 209.

106. Cobo 1990: 45; Murúa 1946: 284; Polo 1916c: 191/sec. 12.

107. For contemporary research on the relationship between mountains and minerals/mining, see Beorchia 1985: 396, 406–407; Gose 1986: 303–304, 308; Nash 1979; Reinhard 1993: 52, 1992a: 95, 1985: 311–312, 314, 1983b: 49, 54; Reinhard and Ceruti 2000: 86; Schobinger 1998: 388–389; Taussig 1980.

108. Cabeza 1885: 71/sec. 14.

109. Agustinos 1918: 26–27.

110. For contemporary scholarship on the relationship between mountains and travel/trade/roads, see Beorchia 1985: 405–406; Reinhard 1993: 51, 52; Reinhard and Ceruti 2000: 86; Schobinger 1998: 382, 384, 389, 391, 1991: 68, 1986: 300, 304.

111. Rowe 1946: 270–271.

112. Rowe 1946: 219, 239.

113. Acosta 1880: 309; Cobo 1990: 116; Herrera 1730: 91; Murúa 1964: 112, 1946: 283; Polo 1916c: 190/secs. 8, 9; Ramos 1976: 68.

114. Acosta 1880: 309; Albornoz 1967: 19; Arriaga 1968: 59, 166/sec. 7; Ayala 1976: 283; Cobo 1990: 45, 116; Garcilaso 1991: 171; Herrera 1730: 91; Murúa 1964: 112, 1946: 283; Polo 1916c: 190/sec. 8; Ramos 1976: 68; Sarmiento 1907: 212.

115. Anónimo 1897b: 132.

116. Ayala 1976: 282–283.

117. Polo 1916c: 191/sec. 10; Murúa 1964: 112.

118. Agustinos 1918: 22; Avila 1991: 122/sec. 329, fn. 641; Monzón 1881: 206–207.

119. For contemporary research on the idea that mountains were worshipped out of fear, see Gose 1986: 305; Reinhard 1992a: 87, 91, 1985: 307, 310, 311, 313, 314, 315, 1983a: 65, 66, 1983b: 40, 45, 46, 51–52, 54, 57.

120. Murúa 1964: 113/fol. 261v, 1946: 281, 398; Ulloa 1885: 45.

121. Molina 1873: 55.

122. Avila 1991: 43/sec. 3, 67/secs. 99–100.

123. For contemporary scholarship on the relationship between mountains and oracles, see MacCormack 1991: 143, 144; Reinhard 1985: 310–311, 1983a: 61, 1983b: 45; Topic, Topic, and Melly 2002: 305, 308, 311–312, 313, 319, 322, 329–330, 331, 332.

124. Matienzo 1967: 129.

125. Anónimo 1897b: 132.

126. Cieza 1967: 97–98, 1959: 151–152.

127. Cieza 1967: 95–96.

128. Guaman Poma 1980a: 234–235.

129. Betanzos 1996: 231–232, 1987: 249–250; for a slightly different version of the story, see Agustinos 1918: 23.

130. Velasco 1978: 61–62.

131. Avila 1991: 96–97/secs. 220–223.

132. Avila 1991: 99–100/sec. 232.

133. For contemporary research on the relationship between mountains and sight-lines, see Bauer and Dearborn 1995; Beorchia 1985: 391; Reinhard 1985: 311, 1983b: 47; Urton 1981: 196–197; Zuidema 1990: 70–71, 73–75, 1982: 431, 432, 435–438, 439–445.

134. See Mostny 1957: 114/no. 5.

135. Garcilaso 1991: 171.

136. Avila 1991: 72/secs. 119–120.

137. Avila 1991: 74–75/secs. 135–137.

138. Hernández 1923: 62.

139. Guaman Poma 1980a: 238–239.

140. Guaman Poma 1980a: 240–241.

141. For contemporary scholarship on the relationship between mountains and astronomical observations, see Reinhard 1993: 49, 1992a: 110; Urton 1981; Zuidema 1982: 438.

142. Cobo 1990: 59 [Ch 6:9]; Polo 1917: 11.

143. Cobo 1979: 103.

144. Cobo 1990: 70 [Co 1:6]; Polo 1917: 26.

145. Arriaga 1968: 79.

146. Cobo 1979: 104.

147. Oberem 1968: 82.

148. Oberem 1968: 83; also see Silverblatt 1987: 17.

149. Avila 1991: 114–115/secs. 285–296.

150. See Salomon 1991: 9.

151. Avila 1991: 139/secs. 408–410.

152. Avila 1991: 78/sec. 146.

153. Cobo 1990: 67 [An 6:7]; Polo 1917: 23.

154. Cobo 1990: 81 [Cu 8:6]; Polo 1917: 39.

155. For contemporary scholarship on the relationship between mountains and limits/boundaries, see Zuidema 1982: 439–445.

156. Hernández 1923: 62.

157. Cobo 1990: 83 [Cu 14:4]; Polo 1917: 41.

158. Guaman Poma 1980a: 240.

159. Guaman Poma 1980a: 242.

160. Guaman Poma 1980a: 244.

161. Guaman Poma 1980a: 246.

162. Guaman Poma 1980a: 248.

163. See Monzón 1881: 206.

164. Cobo 1990: 57 [Ch 4:8]; Polo 1917: 8.

165. Cobo 1990: 67 [An 6:7]; Polo 1917: 23.

166. Cobo 1990: 72 [Co 3:9]; Polo 1917: 28; for additional examples, see Cobo 1990: 73 [Co 4:10, 5:10], 77 [Co 9:13], 79 [Cu 2:4], 80 [Cu 5:5], 81 [Cu 8:15], 82 [Cu 9:3, 10:4, 11:4], 83 [Cu 13:4]; and 61 [Ch 8:13], 66 [An 4:7]; also see Polo 1917: 29, 30, 34, 36, 38, 40, 41; and 14, 21.

167. Albornoz 1967: 32.

168. Ulloa 1885: 40–41/sec. 1.

169. Avila 1991: 82/secs. 167–168.

170. Avila 1991: 71–72/secs. 115, 119; 74–75/secs. 135–136.

171. See Guaman Poma 1980a: 240, 242, 244, 246.

172. See Guaman Poma 1980a: 248.

173. See Monzón 1881: 206.

174. Avila 1991: 66/sec. 97; 93/secs. 205, 207.

175. Avila 1991: 94/sec. 211; Dávila 1881: 71, 72.

176. Avila 1991: 68/sec. 105, 94/sec. 210, 92/sec. 203, 93/secs. 208–209.

177. For contemporary research on the relationship between mountains and ethnic identity, see Reinhard 1985: 310, 1983b: 43; Salomon 1991: 19.

178. Hernández 1923: 62.

179. See Guaman Poma 1980a: 240, 242, 244, 246.

180. See Avila 1991: 71–72/secs. 115, 119; 74–75/secs. 135–136.

181. Jesuíta Anónimo 1944: 108–109.

182. Ulloa 1885: 40–41/sec. 1.

183. Cobo 1990: 71 [Co 2:2]; Polo 1917: 27.

184. Cobo 1990: 61–62 [Ch 9:6]; Polo 1917: 15.

185. Cobo 1990: 59 [Ch 7:4]; Polo 1917: 12.

186. Avila 1991: 114–116/secs. 285–300.

187. For contemporary scholarship on the relationship between mountains and warfare, see Reinhard 1985: 310, 1983b: 44–45.

188. Agustinos 1918: 35.

189. For contemporary research on how volcanoes affected the well-being of the empire, see Reinhard 1998: 134.

190. Murúa 1946: 397–398.

191. Cobo 1990: 59 [Ch 6:8]; Polo 1917: 11.

192. For contemporary scholarship on the relationship between mountains and the king's health, see Zuidema 1982: 432.

193. Cobo 1990: 54 [Ch 1:5]; Polo 1917: 4.

194. Cobo 1990: 69 [An 8:8]; Polo 1917: 24.

195. Cobo 1990: 122.

196. Ayala 1976: 283.

197. Molina 1873: 55.

198. Cobo 1990: 67 [An 6:4]; Polo 1917: 22.

199. For contemporary research on the relationship between mountains and social/political control, see Acuto 2004: 107–123, 166, 239–242; Beorchia 1985: 391; Ceruti 2004: 119; Gose 1986; Reinhard 2005, 1999a: 47, 1993: 48, 1992a: 110, 1985: 310, 314, 1983a: 62, 1983b: 55; Salomon 1991: 10; Schobinger 1998: 389, 390, 1991: 66, 67, 1986: 301; Topic, Topic, and Melly 2002: 328–332.

200. Giddens 1979: 195; also see Hodder 1986: 67.

201. Cobo 1979: 105–106; also see Garcilaso 1961: 43–45.

202. Avila 1991: 82/secs. 166–168.

203. Cobo 1979: 103.

204. Cobo 1979: 104.

205. Avila 1991: 114–115/secs. 285–296.

206. Bello 1897: 173–174/sec. 16.

207. Alcayá 1914?: 156.

208. Molina 1873: 43–44.

209. For contemporary research on the worship of high mountains from lower hills, see Reinhard 1985: 312, 315, 1983a: 62, 1983b: 51, 57.

210. Hernández 1923: 61–62.

211. Dávila 1881: 71.

212. Guaman Poma 1980a: 240–241, 248.

213. Avila 1991: 96/sec. 220, 115/sec. 297.

214. Avila 1991: 72/sec. 119.

215. Cobo 1990: 57 [Ch 4:8]; Polo 1917: 8.

216. Cobo 1990: 60–61 [Ch 8:7]; Polo 1917: 13–14.

217. Cobo 1990: 66 [An 4:1]; Polo 1917: 20.

218. Cobo 1990: 75 [Co 6:9]; Polo 1917: 32.

219. Cobo 1990: 73 [Co 4:10]; Polo 1917: 29.

220. Reinhard 1985: 311; also see Garcilaso 1961.

221. Hernández 1923: 61–62.

222. Noboa 1986: 248/fol. 117.

223. Velasco 1978: 61/sec. 3.

224. Velasco 1978: 63/sec. 6.

225. Cobo 1979: 103.
226. See Avila 1991: 43/sec. 4 and fn. 21, 70/sec. 112.
227. Avila 1991: 43/secs. 3–4, 66/secs. 96–97.
228. Avila 1991: 70/sec. 113, 77/sec. 141, 79–80/secs. 155–156 and fn. 312.
229. Avila 1991: 68/secs. 102–105, 92–93/secs. 203–208.
230. Avila 1991: 71/sec. 115, 75/sec. 138, 80/sec. 156 and fn. 312.
231. See Duviols 1976: 33–34.
232. Albornoz 1967: 20–21.
233. Albornoz 1967: 21; for additional examples, see Albornoz 1967: 26–35.
234. See Guaman Poma 1980a: 240–248, 253.
235. Hernández 1923: 60–62; also see Duviols 1976: 30; Silverblatt 1987: 94–95; Zuidema 1982: 429, 1977: 143.
236. Oberem 1968: 82.
237. Oberem 1968: 83; also see Silverblatt 1987: 17.

CHAPTER SEVEN

1. NMNH 2003.
2. See Cobo 1990: 51–83; Polo 1917: 3–42.
3. Cobo 1990: 69 [An 8:8]; Polo 1917: 24; also see Cobo 1990: 59 [Ch 7:4]; Polo 1917: 12.
4. Medina 1958: 55; Reinhard 1985: 314; also see Beorchia 1985: 393–396; Ceruti 2003: 117–118.
5. Schobinger 1986: 303, 1982: 77, 1966: 13, 207/fn. 8; Reinhard 1999a: 38, 1985: 314; Reinhard and Ceruti 2000: 75; also see Beorchia 1985: 393–395; Ceruti 2003: 116.
6. Agustinos 1918: 39.
7. See Mostny 1957: 114/no. 5.
8. See Arriaga 1968: 28–30.
9. See Polo 1916c: 192/sec. 14; Cobo 1990: 45.
10. See Reinhard 1998: 134.
11. See Bourget 1997: 55, 58–59.
12. See Cobo 1990: 169.
13. For a description of the alignment between funerary towers and peaks in northern Chile, see Aldunate and Castro 1981.
14. See McEwan 1996; Duviols 1976: 24–25.
15. Cobo 1990: 129, 266.
16. See Guaman Poma 1980a: 76–77, 81, 87, 90–91, 93, 94.
17. See Guaman Poma 1980a: 66–68, 76–77, 79, 81–83, 85, 87–89, 91, 93, 94, 96.
18. Cobo 1990: 129, 140.
19. See Guaman Poma 1980a: 67–69, 76–92, 94–95.

20. Betanzos 1996: 46–47, 1987: 51b.

21. See Guaman Poma 1980a: 66–69, 76–95.

CHAPTER EIGHT

1. Rowe 1946: 205/Map 4, 207–208.

2. See Rowe 1946: Map 3 between pp. 184 and 185, 205/Map 4, 206–208.

3. Larrain 1987: 232–234, Map 1.

4. See Acuto 2004: 107–123, 241; Beorchia 1985: 391; Bray et al. 2005: 85, 97–98; Ceruti 2003: 166–167; Duviols 1976: 29–30; Farrington 1998: 55; MacCormack 1991: 201–202; McEwan and Silva 1989: 180–182; McEwan and Van de Guchte 1992: 362, 366, 368, 370–371; Reinhard 2005, 1999a: 42, 47; Reinhard and Ceruti 2000: 85; Schobinger 1998: 390, 1986: 302, 304; Silverblatt 1987: 94–100; Zuidema 1982: 429, 1978: 141–143.

5. See Acuto 2004: 107–123, 166, 239–242; Beorchia 1985: 391; Ceruti 2004: 119; Gose 1986; Reinhard 2005, 1999a: 47, 1993: 48, 1992a: 110, 1985: 310, 314, 1983a: 62, 1983b: 55; Salomon 1991: 10; Schobinger 1998: 389, 390, 1991: 66, 67, 1986: 301; Topic, Topic, and Melly 2002: 328–332.

6. Cobo 1990: 54–83; Polo 1917: 3–42.

7. Albornoz 1967: 20–21, 26–35.

8. Hernández 1923: 60–62.

9. Randall 1990: 4.

10. See Ceruti 2003; Reinhard 2005, 1999a; Reinhard and Ceruti 2000.

11. See Schobinger 2001, 1995; Schobinger, Ampuero, and Guercio 1985.

12. See Beorchia 1985: 67–70; Bray et al. 2005: 88–89; Ceruti 2001; Millán 1966: 81–84; Pérez n.d.; Schobinger 1995: 33, 1982: 76; Martínez 1966: 85.

13. See Cabeza 1986; Cabeza, Kunstmann, and Krahl 1988; Figueroa 1958; Horne and Quevedo 1984; Horne, Quevedo, and Gryfe 1982; López and Cabeza 1983; Medina 1958; Mostny 1957; Reyes 1958; Servicio Informativo 1954.

14. See Beorchia 1985: 77–84; Checura 1985, 1977; Medvinsky, Peronard and Sanhueza 1979.

15. Mostny 1957.

16. Checura 1985, 1977.

17. Stahl 2001: 22.

18. Bowman 1918; Martínez 1966: 98.

19. Hrdlička 1911: 6; A. Rowe 1995–1996; Uhle 1903: 84–96, Plates 18–19.

20. Examples include pieces from **El Plomo** (Beorchia 1985: 180; Dransart 1995: 49; Mostny 1957: 46–54), **Llullaillaco** (Begley 1999: 48–49; Blank 1999: 60–61; Noble 1999: A-1, A-19; Reinhard 1999a: 38, 43–44, 46, 52–53; Reinhard and Ceruti 2000: 26, 58, 60, 61, 71, 72, 73, 75–77, 94, 98–101, 110–113, Fotos 21, 23, 24, 36, 37, 38; Sawyer 1999: A-1, A-10), **Aconcagua** (Bárcena 1989: 62, lámina II; Beorchia 1985: 20; Dransart 1995: 49; Schobinger 1995: 11–12, 17; Schobinger, Am-

puero, and Guercio 1985), **Ampato** (National Geographic 1997; Reinhard 1998: 130, 1997: 42, 1996: 66, 73, 76–77), **Pichu Pichu** (Beorchia 1985: 164; Dransart 1995: 47; Linares 1966: 23–25; Reinhard 1998: 128, 130–131; Schobinger 1982: 82), and **El Misti** (Associated Press 1998; Reuters 1998).

21. Examples include pieces from **Copiapó** (Dransart 1995: 48; Reinhard 1992a: 88–90, 1992b: 157, 160–163, 171), **Doña Ana** (Beorchia 1985: 76; Dransart 1995: 47), **Gallán** (Beorchia 1985: 93; Dransart 1995: 37–41, 48, 50–53; Martínez 1966: 86–90), **Huarancante** (Reinhard 1997), **Inca Huasi** (Gutiérrez 1991), **Licancabur** (Beorchia 1985: 111), **Llullaillaco** (Reinhard and Ceruti 2000: 26, 56–59, 92–93, 95–96, Fotos 20, 39), **Mercedario** (Beorchia 1985: 129; Dransart 1995: 49), **Mismi** (Beorchia 1985: 135; Dransart 1995: 47), **Pili** (Beorchia 1985: 171; Dransart 1995: 42–44, 47, 53–55), **Taapaca** (Beorchia 1985: 212; Dransart 1995: 47), and **Tórtolas** (Beorchia 1985: 241; Dransart 1995: 48).

22. Examples include pieces from **Esmeralda** (Checura 1985: 39 40), **Puntiudos** (Beorchia 1985: 187; Dransart 1995: 48), and **Quimal** (Beorchia 1985: 204).

23. Examples include pieces from **Lake Titi Qaqa** (Reinhard 1992a: 101, 103, 109), **Pachacamac** (Benson 1991: 592), **La Plata Island** (Dorsey 1901: 255, Plates XL–XLI; McEwan and Silva 1989: 169, 174–175), and **Túcume** (Heyerdahl, Sandweiss, and Narváez 1995: 103, 107–110).

24. Nova 1996: 16/57; Reinhard 1999a: 44, 1992b: 160–161, 1985: 314.

25. Reinhard 1998: 130–131.

26. Reinhard 1999a: 38, 1985: 314; Schobinger 1986: 303, 1982: 77, 1966: 13.

27. Reinhard 1985: 314.

EPILOGUE

1. Reinhard and Ceruti 2000: 50, 144/Fig. 19a.
2. Reinhard and Ceruti 2000: 53.
3. Reinhard and Ceruti 2000: 72.
4. Reinhard 1999a: 47.
5. Reinhard and Ceruti 2000: 59.
6. Reinhard and Ceruti 2000: 60.
7. Reinhard and Ceruti 2000: 115.
8. Reinhard and Ceruti 2000: 115.
9. Reinhard 1999a: 44.

GLOSSARY OF ANDEAN
NAMES AND TERMS

The following words have a Quechua origin, unless otherwise noted. In spelling them, I have used a phonemic alphabet.

ají (word of Taino origin): capsicum or chile pepper (Betanzos 1996: 315; Cobo 1990: 261; MacCormack 1991: 457; Silverblatt 1987: 227).

Anti Suyu: the northeastern quarter of the Inka Empire (Betanzos 1996: 305; Cobo 1990: xii/Map 1; Hyslop 1990: 241; Rowe 1946: 262).

apachita: a large pile of stones located at the top of a pass or where a road reaches its highest point. As *apachitas* were considered sacred, offerings were left at them (Gonçález 1952: 30; Guaman Poma 1980c: 1076; Rowe 1946: 297; for a different definition, see Cobo 1990: 261).

apu panaka: an imperial official in charge of picking girls to become *aqllas,* or "chosen women" (Cobo 1990: 261; Rowe 1946: 269).

aqlla-kuna: the "chosen women"; virgin girls who served the imperial gods and state (Cobo 1990: 261; Gonçález 1952: 15; Rowe 1946: 269; Silverblatt 1987: 227).

aqsu: a long wrap-around dress worn by Inka women (Gonçález 1952: 17; Guaman Poma 1980c: 1076; A. Rowe 1996: 12).

Atawalpa: the last Inka king. He was captured by the Spanish in 1532 and executed the following year (Betanzos 1996: 203–275; Cobo 1979: 163–171; Rowe 1946: 208–209).

Awqay Pata: the main plaza in the center of Cuzco. Its name translates as "square of celebration" (Hyslop 1990: 37; MacCormack 1991: 458; Rowe 1946: 298).

ayllu: an Andean kin group, the members of which were believed to have a common ancestor. An *ayllu* controlled its own land (MacCormack 1991: 457; Olsen 1994: 386; Silverblatt 1987: 227).

ayni: balanced reciprocity (Gonçález 1952: 40; Silverblatt 1987: 227).

chakra: a plot of land or field that was cultivated (Cobo 1990: 262; Gonçález 1952: 91; Guaman Poma 1980c: 1078).

chaski: a runner who carried messages from the Inka to officials in the provinces. The *chaskis* operated as part of a relay system and were stationed about 1 km apart (Betanzos 1996: 316; Cobo 1979: 264; Gonçález 1952: 98).

chicha (word of Panamanian origin?): beer made from maize (Cobo 1990: 262; MacCormack 1991: 457; Silverblatt 1987: 227).

Chinchay Suyu: the northwestern quarter of the Inka Empire (Cobo 1990: xii/Map 1; Gonçález 1952: 111; Hyslop 1990: 241; Rowe 1946: 262).

chumpi: a belt worn by Inka women (Gonçález 1952: 121; Guaman Poma 1980c: 1080; A. Rowe 1996: 23).

ch'uñu: freeze-dried potatoes (Cobo 1990: 262; Gonçález 1952: 121; Guaman Poma 1980c: 1081).

ch'uspa: a bag used by the Inkas, principally men (Gonçález 1952: 125; Guaman Poma 1980c: 1081; A. Rowe 1996: 30).

coca (kuka): a plant, *Erythroxylon coca,* whose leaves are chewed with lime to release a mild narcotic (Betanzos 1996: 316; Cobo 1990: 262–263; Guaman Poma 1980c: 1085).

Cuzco: the capital of the Inka Empire. Located in the highlands of southern Peru, at an altitude of about 3,400 m, it was considered sacred (Cobo 1979: 185; Hyslop 1990: 29; Rowe 1946: 262, 296).

Illapa: the Inka god of thunder and lightning (Guaman Poma 1980c: 1082; Rowe 1946: 294–295; Silverblatt 1987: 228).

Inti: the Sun, which was the patron god of the Inka Empire (Cobo 1990: 264; Gonçález 1952: 369; Guaman Poma 1980c: 1082; Rowe 1946: 294).

Inti Raymi: an important festival of the Sun that took place in June and involved elaborate sacrifices (Cobo 1990: 142–143; Guaman Poma 1980a: 220–221, 1980c: 1082; Rowe 1946: 310/no. 7).

kamayuq: a craftsman, professional, or official who worked for the state and who was exempt from the labor tax (Betanzos 1996: 315; Cobo 1979: 263; Rowe 1946: 268).

khipu: a mnemonic device consisting of knotted strings and used to record numeric information (Cobo 1979: 267; Guaman Poma 1980c: 1086; Silverblatt 1987: 229).

Kunti Suyu: the southwestern quarter of the Inka Empire (Betanzos 1996: 305; Cobo 1990: xii/Map 1; Hyslop 1990: 241; Rowe 1946: 262).

kuraka: a provincial leader (Gonçález 1952: 55; Guaman Poma 1980c: 1085; Silverblatt 1987: 228).

llama: a domesticated camelid of the Andes. It was sacrificed as part of important religious rites (Betanzos 1996: 317; Cobo 1990: 264; Gonçález 1952: 208).

llawt'u: a braided headband worn by Inka men (Gonçález 1952: 212; Guaman Poma 1980c: 1087–88; A. Rowe 1996: 27).

lliklla: a shawl worn by Inka women (Gonçález 1952: 213; Guaman Poma 1980c: 1088; A. Rowe 1996: 16).

mallki: an ancestral mummy (Arriaga 1968: 27–28, 76; Silverblatt 1987: 229; Urton 1999: 10, 72).

Mama Killa: Mother Moon, a significant Inka Goddess believed to be the sister and wife of the Sun (Gonçález 1952: 308; Rowe 1946: 295; Silverblatt 1987: 229).

mama-kuna: the cloistered women whose lives were dedicated to the service of the Inka gods and state. They trained the *aqlla-kuna,* the chosen girls (Cobo 1990: 264; Rowe 1946: 269; Silverblatt 1987: 229).

Mama Qucha: Mother Sea, an Inka goddess who was important as the ultimate source of all terrestrial water (Cobo 1990: 33–34; Guaman Poma 1980c: 1088; Rowe 1946: 295; Silverblatt 1987: 229).

Mama Uqllu: the "Pure Mother," a mythical founder of the royal lineage of the Inkas. She was the sister and wife of Manqu Qhapaq (Cobo 1979: 104; Rowe 1946: 316–318; Urton 1999: 46–47).

Manku Qhapaq: the mythical founder of the Inka royal dynasty. He was considered the son of the Sun (Cobo 1979: 103–107; Rowe 1946: 316–318; Urton 1999: 45–51).

maskha paycha: a red fringe the Inka king wore on his forehead that served as a symbol of office (Cobo 1979: 266; Guaman Poma 1980c: 1089; Rowe 1946: 258).

mit'a: a labor tax that most Inka subjects owed to the state; corvée labor. *Mit'a* service, which rotated, provided soldiers, workers who built imperial roads and buildings, servants for nobles, and tillers of government fields (Cobo 1979: 266; Olsen 1994: 391–392; Silverblatt 1987: 229).

mitmaq-kuna: settlers moved by the Inkas either from a part of the empire that had long been pacified to a newly conquered region, or vice versa. The purpose of this shuffling of populations was to break up rebellious peoples and to spread Inka culture (Betanzos 1996: 318; Cobo 1979: 266; Olsen 1994: 392).

mullu: Spondylus shell, a common offering for the *waqas* (Avila 1991: 269; Gonçález 1952: 249; Guaman Poma 1980c: 1090).

ñapa: a sacred white llama that the Inkas used in special rituals (Cobo 1990: 265; Rowe 1946: 309).

Pacha Kamaq: in some Andean myths, the Creator of the universe; also the name of an important temple located on the north coast of Peru and dedicated to the Creator (Cobo 1990: 12; Gonçález 1952: 270; Guaman Poma 1980c: 1091).

Pacha Kuti: name given to the ninth Inka king; it literally means "cataclysm." He is characterized as a great conqueror who transformed a minor state into an empire (Betanzos 1996: 318; Cobo 1979: 133–141; Guaman Poma 1980a: 88–89; Rowe 1946: 203–207).

Pacha Mama: Mother Earth, an important Andean goddess associated with fertility and agriculture (Cobo 1990: 34; Rowe 1946: 295; Silverblatt 1987: 229).

paqariku: the place of origin of an ethnic group. Such places—which included caves, mountains, springs, lakes, and so on—were considered sacred and were worshipped (Arriaga 1968: 24; Guaman Poma 1980a: 66, 1980c: 1092; Urton 1990: 19; also see Cobo 1990: 13).

Parya Qaqa: a high mountain and important *waqa* located in the northwestern quarter of the Inka Empire (Avila 1991: 269; Guaman Poma 1980a: 240–241, 248; Urton 1999: 63–64).

pukará: an Inka fortress, often situated on top of a hill (Gonçález 1952: 292; Guaman Poma 1980c: 1093; Hyslop 1990: 333).

qhapaq hucha: a child or *aqlla* sacrificed by the Inkas in a special ceremony (Betanzos 1996: 316; Guaman Poma 1980c: 1096; Silverblatt 1987: 227; Urton 1999: 14).

Qhapaq Raymi: the most solemn Inka festival. It was held around the December solstice and included the initiation of boys from the royal lineages (Betanzos 1996: 319; Cobo 1990: 126–134; Guaman Poma 1980a: 232–233; Rowe 1946: 308–309/no. 1).

Qhuru Puna: a high mountain and significant *waqa* located in the southwestern quarter of the Inka Empire (Cieza 1959: 151–152; Guaman Poma 1980a: 246–248; Rowe 1946: 296).

q'ipi: knapsack (Cobo 1990: 266; Gonçález 1952: 305).

quinua (kinuwa):   an important highland grain, *Chenopodium quinoa* (Betanzos 1996: 319; Gonçález 1952: 309; Olsen 1994: 27; Rowe 1946: 210).

Qulla Suyu: the southeastern quarter of the Inka Empire (Cobo 1990: xii/Map 1; Hyslop 1990: 241; Rowe 1946: 262).

qullqa: a silo where produce was kept or a storehouse for goods collected as tribute (Cobo 1979: 264; Guaman Poma 1980c: 1095; Hyslop 1990: 333).

qumpi: the finest quality cloth, which was woven for the Inka aristocracy (Cobo 1990: 263; Gonçález 1952: 67; Guaman Poma 1980c: 1095; A. Rowe 1996: 9–10).

qunupa: a small figurine worshipped at the household level. It often had the form of, and was thought to be responsible for the fertility of, a particular plant or animal (Arriaga 1968: 28–30, 178; MacCormack 1991: 458; Silverblatt 1987: 228).

Quri Kancha: the most sacred Inka temple, which was located in Cuzco and which housed the images of the Creator, Sun, Moon, and Thunder. Its name means "golden enclosure," and it is often referred to as the Temple of the Sun (Betanzos 1996: 316; Cobo 1990: 263; Hyslop 1990: 44–47; Urton 1999: 10–13).

quwi: the common guinea pig. An important domesticated animal in the Andes, it was often used as a sacrifice (Cobo 1990: 263; Guaman Poma 1980c: 1095; Rowe 1946: 219; Silverblatt 1987: 228).

sara: corn (Gonçález 1952: 79; Guaman Poma 1980c: 1099; Rowe 1946: 210).

siq'e: a ceremonial line connecting various *waqas* or sacred shrines (Cobo 1990: 262; Gonçález 1952: 81; Hyslop 1990: 334; MacCormack 1991: 457).

taki: a ceremonial song and/or dance (Cobo 1990: 266; Gonçález 1952: 338; Guaman Poma 1980c: 1101; Molina 1873: 18).

Tawantin Suyu: the Inka Empire as a whole. Its name translates as "Land of the Four Quarters" (Cobo 1990: xii/Map 1; MacCormack 1991: 459; Rowe 1946: 262).

Thupa Yapanki: the tenth Inka king. He is credited with having conquered many lands and with having consolidated the largest empire in prehistoric America (Betanzos 1996: 122–127, 140–162; Cobo 1979: 142–151; Guaman Poma 1980a: 90–91; Rowe 1946: 207–208).

tikti: a thick residue of maize beer, used as an offering (Avila 1991: 256).

Titi Qaqa (Titicaca): an enormous lake situated on the altiplano of Peru and Bolivia, at an altitude of about 3,800 m. The Titi Qaqa basin was incorporated into the Inka Empire by Pacha Kuti (Cobo 1979: 140; Olsen 1994: 331–333; Rowe 1946: 205/Map 4, 206).

tupu: a large metal pin used by Inka women to fasten their dresses (Gonçález 1952: 347; Guaman Poma 1980c: 1102; A. Rowe 1996: 22).

ujut'a: a sandal worn by Inka men and women (Gonçález 1952: 359; Guaman Poma 1980c: 1102; A. Rowe 1996: 31).

unku: a knee-length sleeveless tunic worn by Inka men (Cobo 1990: 266; Gonçález 1952: 355; A. Rowe 1996: 24–25).

usnu: a ritual/administrative complex situated in the center of an Inka settlement and consisting of a large platform and a drain with a stone basin (Guaman Poma 1980b: 370–371, 1980c: 1103; Hyslop 1990: 334; MacCormack 1991: 459).

Wallullu: in Huarochirí mythology, a high volcano and significant *waqa* that is defeated by Parya Qaqa (Avila 1991: 267; Guaman Poma 1980a: 241, 248; Urton 1999: 63–64).

Wana Kawri: one of the most sacred *waqas* in the Inka Empire. Wana Kawri—whose name refers both to a hill near Cuzco and to a stone situated on top of the hill—was offered human sacrifices (Cobo 1990: 74; Guaman Poma 1980a: 238–239; Rowe 1946: 296; Urton 1999: 49–50).

wanqa: a sacred stone worshipped as a *waqa* (Arriaga 1968: 30; Ayala 1976: 279–280; Heyerdahl, Sandweiss, and Narváez 1995: 102; Rostworowski 1983: 62–64).

waqa: an Andean idol or deity; any person, place, or object thought to have sacred power and thus venerated. In the Inka Empire, *waqas* included mountains, lakes, stones, temples, mummies, images, and so on (Betanzos 1996: 316–317; Cobo 1990: 263; Gonçález 1952: 165; Guaman Poma 1980a: 234–237, 1980c: 1104).

wara: a breech-cloth worn by Inka men (Gonçález 1952: 182; Guaman Poma 1980c: 1105; A. Rowe 1996: 27).

warak'a: a sling used by Inka men (Betanzos 1996: 317; Gonçález 1952: 182; Guaman Poma 1980c: 1105).

wasi: a house (Betanzos 1996: 317; Gonçález 1952: 169; Guaman Poma 1980c: 1105).

Waskar: the twelfth Inka king. He fought a long civil war against his half-brother Atawalpa (Betanzos 1996: 189–268; Cobo 1979: 163–171; Guaman Poma 1980a: 94–97; Rowe 1946: 208–209).

Wayna Qhapaq: the eleventh Inka king. During his reign, the empire reached its greatest extent (Betanzos 1996: 163–185; Cobo 1979: 152–162; Guaman Poma 1980a: 92–94; Rowe 1946: 208).

Willka Nuta: a high mountain and important *waqa* that was located in the southeastern quarter of the Inka Empire (Cieza 1959: 151; Guaman Poma 1980a: 244–245, 248; Rowe 1946: 296).

Wira Qucha: the Inka creator god, a major figure in the imperial pantheon (Cobo 1990: 267; Gonçález 1952: 353; Guaman Poma 1980c: 1107; Rowe 1946: 293–294).

yana-kuna: the servants or retainers of a lord. They were exempt from the *mit'a* labor tax (Betanzos 1996: 104; Cobo 1979: 268; MacCormack 1991: 459).

yawar sankhu: a sacred food consisting of ground corn mixed with the blood of sacrificed llamas (Guaman Poma 1980c: 1107; MacCormack 1991: 459; Molina 1873: 27; Rowe 1946: 309).

REFERENCE LIST

ETHNOHISTORIC SOURCES

Acosta, José de, 1962 [1590]. *Historia natural y moral de las Indias*. Mexico City: Fondo de Cultura Económica.

———, 1880 [1590]. *The Natural and Moral History of the Indies*. Edited by Clements Markham. London: Hakluyt Society.

Agustinos, 1918 [1557]. "Relación de la religión y ritos del Perú hecha por los primeros Agustinos que alli pasaron para la conversión de los naturales." *Colección de libros y documentos referentes a la historia del Perú*, tomo XI: 3–56. Edited by Horacio Urteaga. Lima, Peru: Sanmartí y Cía.

Albornoz, Cristóbal de, 1967 [1583?]. "Instrucción para descubrir todas las guacas del Pirú y sus camayos y haziendas." Reprinted in Pierre Duviols, "Un inédit de Cristóbal de Albornoz," *Journal de la Société des Américanistes* 56(1): 17–39. Paris: Musée de l'Homme.

Alcayá, Diego Felipe de, 1914? [late 16th cent.?]. "Relación del padre Felipe de Alcayá, cura de Mataca." *Bolivia—Paraguay*, anexos, tomo I, "Epoca colonial": 144–173. Published by Ricardo Mujía. La Paz, Bolivia: Editora "El Tiempo."

Anónimo, 1897a [1573]. "La cibdad de Sant Francisco del Quito." *Relaciones geográficas de Indias*, tomo III: 60–101. Madrid: Ministerio de Fomento.

Anónimo, 1897b [late 16th cent.]. "Relación en suma de la doctrina e beneficio de Pimampiro y de las cosas notables que en ella hay, de la cuál es beneficiado el P. Antonio Borja." *Relaciones geográficas de Indias*, tomo III: 128–136. Madrid: Ministerio de Fomento.

Anónimo, 1904 [17th cent.?]. "Parecer acerca de la perpetuidad y buen gobierno de los indios del Perú, y aviso de lo que deben hacer los encomenderos para salvarse." *La imprenta en Lima*, tomo I: 222–231. Edited by José Toribio Medina. Santiago, Chile: Impreso en casa del autor.

Arriaga, José de, 1968 [1621]. *The Extirpation of Idolatry in Peru*. Translated and edited by L. Clark Keating. Lexington: University of Kentucky Press.

———, 1920 [1621]. *Extirpación de la idolatría del Perú*. Lima, Peru: Sanmartí y Cia.

Atienza, Lope de, 1931 [1572]. "Compendio historial del estado de los indios del

Perú." *La religión del imperio de los Incas.* Edited by Jacinto Jijón y Caamaño. Quito, Ecuador: Escuela Tipográfica Salesiana.

Avedaño, Hernando de, 1904 [1617]. "Relación de las idolatrias de los indios." *La imprenta en Lima,* tomo I: 380–383. Edited by José Toribio Medina. Santiago, Chile: Impreso en casa del autor.

Avila, Francisco de, 1904. "Relación que yo, el doctor Francisco de Avila, presbí-tero, cura y beneficiado de la ciudad de Huánuco, hice por mandado del señor Arzobispo de Los Reyes acerca de los pueblos de Indios de este arzobispado donde se ha descubierto la idolatría y hallado gran cantidad de ídolos, que los dichos Indios adoraban y tenían por sus dioses." *La imprenta en Lima (1584–1824),* vol. 1: 386–389. Edited by José Toribio Medina. Santiago, Chile: Impreso y gra-bado en casa del autor.

———, 1966 [1598]. *Dioses y hombres de Huarochirí.* Translated by José María Ar-guedas. Lima, Peru: Museo Nacional de Historia y el Instituto de Estudios Peruanos.

———, 1991 [1598]. *The Huarochirí Manuscript.* Translated by Frank Salomon and George Urioste. Austin: University of Texas Press.

Ayala, Fabian de, 1974–1976 [1614]. "Errores, ritos, supersticiones y ceremonias de los yndios de la prouincia de Chinchaycocha y otras del Pirú." Reprinted in Pierre Duviols, "Une petite chronique retrouvée," *Journal de la Société des Améri-canistes* 63: 275–286. Paris: Musée de l'Homme.

Bello Galloso, Antonio, 1897 [1582]. "Relación que enbio a mandar su magestad se hiziese desta ciudad de Cuenca y de toda su provincia." *Relaciones geográficas de Indias,* tomo III: 155–196. Madrid: Ministerio de Fomento.

Betanzos, Juan de, 1968 [1557]. "Suma y narración de los Incas." *Biblioteca peruana,* primera serie, tomo III: 197–296. Lima, Peru: Editores Técnicos Asociados.

———, 1987 [1557]. *Suma y narración de los Incas.* Edited by María del Carmen Mar-tín R. Madrid: Ediciones Atlas.

———, 1996 [1557]. *Narrative of the Incas.* Translated and edited by Roland Hamilton and Dana Buchanan. Austin: University of Texas Press.

Bibar, Jerónimo de, 1966 [1558]. *Crónica y relación copiosa y verdadera de los reynos de Chile.* Santiago, Chile: Fondo Histórico y Bibliográfico "José Toribio Medina."

Cabello de Balboa, Miguel, 1920 [1586]. *Historia del Perú bajo la dominación de los Incas.* Colección de libros y documentos referentes a la historia del Perú, serie 2, tomo II. Lima, Peru: Sanmartí y Cia.

Cabeza de Vaca, Diego, 1885 [1586]. "Descripción y relación de la ciudad de La Paz." *Relaciones geográficas de Indias,* tomo II: 65–80. Madrid: Ministerio de Fomento.

Calancha, Antonio de la, 1931 [1638]. Fragment of the "Corónica moralizada del orden de San Agustín en el Perú, con sucesos egemplares en esta monarquía." Reprinted in Philip Means, trans. and ed., *Ancient Civilizations of the Andes,* 60–63. New York: Charles Scribner's Sons.

Calancha, Antonio de la, and Bernardo de Torres, 1972 [1657]. *Crónicas agustianas del Perú,* vol. I. Biblioteca "missionalia hispánica," tomo XVII. Edited by Manuel

Merino. Madrid: Consejo Superior de Investigaciones Científicas, Instituto "Enrique Florez."

Carabajal, Pedro de, 1881 [1586]. "Descripción fecha de la provincia de Vilcas Guaman. . . ." *Relaciones geográficas de Indias,* tomo I: 145–168. Madrid: Ministerio de Fomento.

———, 1965 [1586]. "Descripción fecha de la provincia de Vilcas Guaman." *Relaciones geográficas de Indias—Perú.* Biblioteca de autores españoles, tomo 183: 205–219. Edited by Marcos Jiménez de la Espada. Madrid: Ediciones Atlas.

Cieza de León, Pedro de, 1959 [1553]. *The Incas of Pedro de Cieza de León.* Translated by Harriet de Onis; edited by Victor Wolfgang von Hagen. Norman: University of Oklahoma Press.

———, 1967 [1553]. *El señorío de los Incas.* La crónica del Perú, segunda parte. Lima, Peru: Instituto de Estudios Peruanos.

———, 1985 [1553]. *La crónica del Perú,* primera parte. Madrid: Historia 16.

Cobo, Bernabé, 1979 [1653]. *History of the Inca Empire.* Translated and edited by Roland Hamilton. Austin: University of Texas Press.

———, 1990 [1653]. *Inca Religion and Customs.* Translated and edited by Roland Hamilton. Austin: University of Texas Press.

Dávila Brizeño, Diego, 1881 [1586]. "Descripsión y relación de la provincia de los Yauyos. . . ." *Relaciones geográficas de Indias,* tomo I: 61–78. Madrid: Ministerio de Fomento.

Díez de San Miguel, Garcí, 1964 [1567]. *Visita hecha a la provincia de Chucuito por Garcí Díez de San Miguel en el año 1567.* Documentos regionales para la etnología y etnohistoria andinas, tomo 1. Transcribed by Waldemar Espinoza S. Lima, Peru: Casa de la Cultura del Perú.

Fernández, Diego "El Palentino," 1963 [1571]. "Historia del Perú," segunda parte. *Crónicas del Perú,* vol. II: 1–131. Biblioteca de autores españoles, tomo 165. Madrid: Ediciones Atlas.

Fornee, Niculoso de, 1885 [1586]. "Descripción de la tierra del corregimiento de Abancay. . . ." *Relaciones geográficas de Indias,* tomo II: 199–221. Madrid: Ministerio de Fomento.

Fuente, Rodrigo de la, 1885 [1572]. "Relación del cerro de Potosí y su descubrimiento." *Relaciones geográficas de Indias,* tomo II: 88–96. Madrid: Ministerio de Fomento.

García, Gregorio, 1981 [1607]. *Origen de los indios del nuevo mundo.* Biblioteca americana. Mexico City: Fondo de Cultura Económica.

Garcilaso de la Vega, "el Inca," 1945 [1609]. *Commentarios reales de los Incas.* Buenos Aires, Argentina: Editorial A. Rosenblatt.

———, 1961 [1609]. *The Incas.* Translated by María Jolas; edited by Alain Gheerbrant. New York: Discus/Avon Books.

———, 1991 [1609]. "Dioses y huacas." Fragment of the "Commentarios reales de los Incas." Reprinted in César Toro Montalvo, *Mitos y leyendas del Perú—Sierra,* tomo II: 170–173. Lima, Peru: A.F.A. Editores Importadores, S.A.

Gonçález Holguín, Diego, 1952 [1608]. *Vocabvlario de la lengva general de todo el Perv llamada lengua Qqichua o del Inca.* Edited by Raúl Porras. Lima, Peru: Instituto de Historia, Universidad Nacional Mayor de San Marcos.

Guaman Poma de Ayala, Felipe, 1978 [1615]. *Letter to a King.* Translated and edited by Christopher Dilke. London: George, Allen & Unwin.

——, 1980a [1615]. *El primer nueva corónica y buen gobierno,* tomo 1: 1–340. Colección América nuestra, número 31. Transcribed and translated by Jorge Urioste. Mexico City: Siglo Veintiuno Editores, S.A.

——, 1980b [1615]. *El primer nueva corónica y buen gobierno,* tomo 2: 341–850. Colección América nuestra, número 31. Transcribed and translated by Jorge Urioste. Mexico City: Siglo Veintiuno Editores, S.A.

——, 1980c [1615]. *El primer nueva corónica y buen gobierno,* tomo 3: 851–1175. Colección América nuestra, número 31. Transcribed and translated by Jorge Urioste. Mexico City: Siglo Veintiuno Editores, S.A.

Guerra y Céspedes, Francisco de la, 1881 [1582]. "La descripción que se hizo en la provincia de Xauxa por la instrución de S.M. que a la dicha provincia se invio de molde." *Relaciones geográficas de Indias,* tomo I: 79–95. Madrid: Ministerio de Fomento.

Gutiérrez de Santa Clara, Pedro, 1905 [1548]. *Historia de las guerras civiles del Perú y de otros sucesos de las Indias.* Colección de libros y documentos referentes a la historia de América, tomo IV. Madrid: Librería General de Victoriano Suárez.

Hacas Poma, Hernando, 1981 [1656]. "Apéndice I: Testimonio." Reprinted in Lorenzo Huertas Vallejos, *La religión en una sociedad rural andina (siglo XVII),* 104–120. Ayacucho, Peru: Universidad Nacional San Cristóbal de Huamanga.

Hernández Príncipe, Rodrigo, 1923 [1622]. "Mitología andina: idolatrías de Recuay, 1622." *Inca* 1: 25–78. Lima, Peru.

Herrera, Antonio de, 1730 [1610]. *Descripción de las Indias occidentales.* Madrid: Nícolas Rodríguez Franco.

Jesuíta Anónimo, 1918 [1613]. "Misión de las provincias de los Huachos y Yauyos." Reprinted in Carlos Romero, "Idolatrias de los indios Huachos y Yauyos," *Revista histórica* 6: 180–197. Lima: Instituto Histórico del Perú.

Jesuíta Anónimo, 1944 [1600]. *Historia general de la compañía de Jesús en la provincia del Perú,* tomo II. Edited by F. Mateos. Madrid: Consejo Superior de Investigaciones Científicas, Instituto Gonzalo Fernández de Oviedo.

"Justicia 413," 1988 [1558–1570]. In *Conflicts Over Coca Fields in Sixteenth-Century Perú,* 83–291. Studies in Latin American Ethnohistory and Archaeology, volume IV. Edited by María Rostworowski de Diez C. Ann Arbor: Museum of Anthropology, University of Michigan.

Las Casas, Bartolomé de, 1967 [1550]. *Apologética historia sumaria.* Mexico City: Instituto de Investigaciones Históricas, Universidad Nacional Autónoma de México.

Martínez Compañón y Bujanda, Baltazar Jaime, 1991 [1766]. "Huaca sita en el cerro nombrado Tantalluc de la provincia de Caxamarca que se descubrió y excavó el año pasado de 1765," lámina LXXXV: 9. *Trujillo del Perú a fines del siglo XVIII,* tomo IX. Madrid: Agencia Española de Cooperación Internacional.

Matienzo, Juan de, 1967 [1567]. *Gobierno del Perú.* Travaux de l'Institut Français d'Études Andines, tome XI. Paris: Institut Français d'Études Andines.

Mercado de Peñalosa, Pedro de, 1885 [1586]. "Relación de la provincia de los Pacajes." *Relaciones geográficas de Indias,* tomo II: 51–64. Madrid: Ministerio de Fomento.

Molina (of Cuzco), Cristóbal de, 1873 [1575?]. "The Fables and Rites of the Yncas." *Narratives of the Rites and Laws of the Yncas,* 3–64. Translated and edited by Clements Markham. New York: Burt Franklin.

———, 1943 [1575?]. *Relación de las fábulas y ritos de los Incas.* Los pequeños grandes libros de historia americana, serie I, tomo IV. Edited by Francisco A. Loayza. Lima, Peru: D. Miranda.

Montesinos, Fernando de, 1920 [1644]. *Memorias antiguas historiales del Perú,* series 2, no. 48. Translated and edited by Philip Means. London: Hakluyt Society.

Monzón, Luis de, 1881a [1586]. "Discripción de la tierra del repartimiento de Atun-sora, encomendado en Hernando Palomino, jurisdición de la ciudad de Guamanga." *Relaciones geográficas de Indias,* tomo I: 169–178. Madrid: Ministerio de Fomento.

———, 1881b [1586]. "Discripción de la tierra del repartimiento de San Francisco de Atunrucana y Laramati, encomendado en Don Pedro de Córdova, jurisdición de la ciudad de Guamanga." *Relaciones geográficas de Indias,* tomo I: 179–196. Madrid: Ministerio de Fomento.

———, 1881c [1586]. "Descripción de la tierra del repartimiento de los Rucanas Antamarcas de la corona real, jurisdición de la ciudad de Guamanga." *Relaciones geográficas de Indias,* tomo I: 197–216. Madrid: Ministerio de Fomento.

Murúa, Martín de, 1946 [1590]. *Historia del origen y genealogía real de los reyes Incas del Perú.* Edited by Constantino Bayle. Madrid: Consejo Superior de Investigaciones Científicas, Instituto Santo Toribio de Mogrovejo.

———, 1962 [1611]. *Historia general del Perú: Origen y descendencia de los Incas.* Bibliotheca americana vetus, vol. I. Edited by M. Ballesteros-Gaibrois. Madrid: Instituto Gonzalo Fernández de Oviedo.

———, 1964 [1590]. *Historia general del Perú.* Bibliotheca americana vetus, vol. II. Madrid: Instituto Gonzalo Fernández de Oviedo.

Noboa, Bernardo de, 1986 [1658]. "Denuncia que hace don Juan Tocas, principal y fiscal de la dicha visita, contra Hernando Hacas Cristobal, Poma Libiac, y muchos indios del pueblo de San Pedro de Hacas." In *Cultura andina y represión: Procesos y visitas de idolatrías y hechicerías; Cajatambo, siglo XVII,* 135–262. Edited by Pierre Duviols. Cuzco, Peru: Centro de Estudios Rurales Andinos "Bartolomé de Las Casas."

Oberem, Udo, 1968. Fragments of testimony from Don Sancho Hacho in 1585 and from Doña Francisca Sinasigchi in 1580. Reprinted in "Amerikanistische Angaben aus Dokumenten des 16. Jahrhunderts," 82–83. *Tribus* 17: 81–92. Stuttgart, Germany: Museum für Länder und Völkerkunde.

Oliva, Anello, 1895 [1598]. *Historia del Perú y varones insignes en santidad de la compañía de Jesús.* Lima, Peru: Juan Pazos V. and Luis Varela O.

Oviedo y Valdez, Gonzalo Fernández de, 1959 [1535–1557]. *Historia general y natural de las Indias.* Biblioteca de autores españoles, tomo 121. Edited by Juan P. de Tudela B. Madrid: Ediciones Atlas.

Pachacuti Yamqui, Joan de Santa Cruz, 1873 [1613]. "An Account of the Antiquities of Peru." In *Narratives of the Rites and Laws of the Yncas,* 67–120. Translated and edited by Clements Markham. New York: Burt Franklin.

Paz Maldonado, Fray Juan de, 1897 [late 16th cent.?]. "Relación del pueblo de Sant-Andres Xunxi para el muy ilustre señor licenciado Francisco de Auncibay. . . ." *Relaciones geográficas de Indias,* tomo III: 149–154. Madrid: Ministerio de Fomento.

Pizarro, Pedro, 1921 [1571]. *Relation of the Discovery and Conquest of the Kingdoms of Peru,* volume I. Translated by Philip Means. New York: Cortes Society.

Polo de Ondegardo, Juan, 1873 [1567]. "Of the Lineage of the Yncas, and How They Extended Their Conquests." In *Narratives of the Rites and Laws of the Yncas,* 151–171. Translated and edited by Clements Markham. New York: Burt Franklin.

———, 1916a [1554]. "Los errores y supersticiones de los indios, sacadas del tratado y averigación que hizo el licenciado Polo." *Colección de libros y documentos referentes a la historia del Perú,* serie I, tomo III: 1–43. Edited by Horacio Urteaga and Carlos Romero. Lima, Peru: Sanmartí y Cía.

———, 1916b [1571]. "Relación de los fundamentos acerca del notable daño que resulta de no guardar a los indios sus fueros." *Colección de libros y documentos refe-rentes a la historia del Perú,* serie I, tomo III: 45–188. Edited by Horacio Urteaga and Carlos Romero. Lima, Peru: Sanmartí y Cía.

———, 1916c [1567]. "Instrución contra las ceremonias y ritos que usan los indios conforme al tiempo de su infidelidad." *Colección de libros y documentos referentes a la historia del Perú,* serie I, tomo III: 189–203. Edited by Horacio Urteaga and Carlos Romero. Lima, Peru: Sanmartí y Cía.

———, 1917 [1571]. "Relación de los adoratorios de los indios en los cuatro cami-nos que salian del Cuzco." *Colección de libros y documentos referentes a la historia del Perú,* tomo IV: 3–43. Edited by Horacio Urteaga. Lima, Peru: Sanmartí y Cía.

Ramos Gavilán, Alonso, 1976 [1621]. *Historia de nuestra señora de Copacabana.* La Paz, Bolivia: Publicaciones Culturales.

Rocha, Diego Andrés de, 1891 [1681]. *Tratado único y singular del origen de los indios del Perú, Méjico, Sante Fe y Chile.* Colección de libros raros ó curiosos que tratan de América, tomo III. Madrid: Tomás Minuesa.

Román y Zamora, Jerónimo, 1897 [1575]. *Repúblicas de Indias: Idolatrías y gobierno en México y Perú antes de la conquista.* Colección de libros raros ó curiosos que tratan de América, tomo XIV. Madrid: Tomás Minuesa.

Ruiz de Navamuel, Alvaro, 1904 [1570s?]. "Sobre la manera que tenían de adorar a sus dioses y ídolos y lo que les ofrecían." *La imprenta en Lima,* tomo I: 181–182. Edited by José Toribio Medina. Santiago, Chile: Impreso en casa del autor.

San Pedro, Juan de, 1992 [1560]. *La persecución del demonio: Crónica de los primeros agustinos en el norte del Perú.* Colección nuestra América, tomo 1. Transcribed by Eric Deeds. Málaga, Spain: Editorial Algazara.

Santillán, Hernando de, 1968 [1563]. "Relación por el licenciado Hernando de Santillán." *Biblioteca peruana,* serie 1, tomo III: 375–463. Lima, Peru: Editores Técnicos Asociados.

Sarmiento de Gamboa, Pedro, 1907 [1572]. *History of the Incas,* series 2, no. 22. Translated and edited by Clements Markham. Cambridge: Hakluyt Society.

———, 1942 [1572]. *Historia de los Incas.* Buenos Aires: Emece Editores.

Toledo, Francisco de, 1904 [1573]. "Carta al Rey." *La imprenta en Lima,* tomo I: 177–178. Edited by José Toribio Medina. Santiago, Chile: Impreso en casa del autor.

———, 1989 [1580]. "Instrucción y ordenanzas de los corregidores de naturales." In *Disposiciones gubernativas para el virreinato del Perú, 1575–1580,* 409–449. Sevilla, Spain: Escuela de Estudios Hispano-Americanos.

Torres, Bernardo de, 1974 [1657]. *Crónica Agustina de Bernardo de Torres,* vol. 1. Crónicas del Perú. Transcribed by Ignacio Prado P. Lima, Peru: Universidad Nacional Mayor de San Marcos.

Ulloa Mogollón, Juan de, 1885 [1586]. "Relación de la provincia de los Collaguas para la discrepción de las yndias que su magestad manda hacer." *Relaciones geográficas de Indias,* tomo II: 38–50. Madrid: Ministerio de Fomento.

Valera, Blas, 1968 [1590]. "Relación de las costumbres antiguas de los naturales del Pirú." *Crónicas peruanas de interés indígena.* Biblioteca de autores españoles, tomo 209: 151–189. Edited by Francisco Esteve B. Madrid: Ediciones Atlas.

Velasco, Juan de, 1978 [1789]. *Historia del reino de Quito en la América meridional,* tomo I, parte I. Quito, Ecuador: Talleres Gráficas.

Xerez, Francisco de, 1985 [1534]. *Verdadera relación de la conquista del Perú.* Madrid: Edición de Concepción Bravo.

Zárate, Agustín de, 1968 [1556]. *The Discovery and Conquest of Peru.* Translated by John Cohen. Baltimore: Penguin Books.

CONTEMPORARY SOURCES

Acuto, Félix, 2004. "Landscapes of Ideology and Inequality: Experiencing Inka Domination." Unpublished Ph.D. dissertation. Department of Anthropology, Binghamton University, Binghamton, NY.

Aldunate, C., and V. Castro, 1981. "Las chullpa de Toconoce y su relación con el poblamiento altiplánico en el Loa superior período tardío." Unpublished master's thesis. Universidad de Chile, Santiago.

Associated Press, 1998. "Peruvian Mountain Yields Six Mummies." *Post-Standard* (Syracuse, NY), Friday, October 2: A-1.

Bárcena, Roberto, 1989. "Pigmentos en el ritual funerario de la momia del cerro

Aconcagua (provincia de Mendoza, República Argentina)." *Xama* 2: 61–116. Mendoza, Argentina: Unidad de Antropología, Centro Regional de Investigaciones Científicas y Tecnológicas.

Barthel, Thomas, 1986. "El agua y el festival de primavera entre los atacameños." *Allpanchis* 28: 147–184. Cuzco, Peru: Instituto de Pastoral Andina.

Bastien, Joseph, 1985. *Mountain of the Condor: Metaphor and Ritual in an Andean Ayllu.* Prospect Heights, IL: Waveland Press.

Bauer, Brian, and David Dearborn, 1995. *Astronomy and Empire in the Ancient Andes: The Cultural Origins of Inca Sky Watching.* Austin: University of Texas Press.

Begley, Sharon, 1999. "Children of the Ice." *Newsweek,* April 19, 48–49.

Benson, Elizabeth, 1991. "Seven Human Figurines." In *Circa 1492: Art in the Age of Exploration,* 590–592. Edited by Jay Levenson. Washington, DC: National Gallery of Art.

Beorchia N., Antonio, 1985. *El enigma del los santuarios indígenas de alta montaña.* San Juan, Argentina: Centro de Investigaciones Arqueológicas de Alta Montaña.

Biggar, John, 1999. *The Andes: A Guide for Climbers.* Castle Douglas, Scotland: BigR Publishing (Andes).

Bingham, Hiram, 1979. *Machu Picchu: A Citadel of the Incas.* New York: Hacker Art Books.

Blank, Jonah, 1999. "Tiny Sacrifices at 22,000 Feet: Archaeologists Find Mummified Incan Children on an Andean Peak." *U.S. News & World Report* 126(15): 60–61.

Blower, David, 1995. "The Quest for Mullu: Concepts, Trade, and the Archaeological Distribution of Spondylus in the Andes." Unpublished master's thesis. Department of Anthropology, Trent University, Peterborough, Ontario.

Bourget, Steve, 1997. "Las excavaciones en la plaza 3A de la Huaca de la Luna." In *Investigaciones en la Huaca de la Luna 1995: Proyecto arqueológico Huacas del Sol y de la Luna,* 51–59. Edited by S. Uceda, E. Mujica and R. Morales. Trujillo, Peru: Facultad de Ciencias Sociales, Universidad Nacional de La Libertad.

Bowman, Eric, 1918. "Una momia de Salinas Grandes (Puna de Jujuy)." *Anales de la Sociedad Científica Argentina* 85: 94–102. Buenos Aires.

Bray, Tamara, 2003. "Inka Pottery As Culinary Equipment: Food, Feasting, and Gender in Imperial State Design." *Latin American Antiquity* 14(1): 3–28.

Bray, Tamara, Leah Minc, Constanza Ceruti, et al., 2005. "A Compositional Analysis of Pottery Vessels Associated With the Inca Ritual of Capacocha." *Journal of Anthropological Archaeology* 24(1): 82–100.

Byrd, Jason, and James Castner, eds., 2001. *Forensic Entomology: The Utility of Arthropods in Legal Investigations.* Boca Raton, FL: CRC Press.

Cabeza M., Angel, 1986. "El santuario de altura inca cerro El Plomo." Unpublished thesis for the degree of licenciate in archaeology and anthropology. Departamento de Antropología, Universidad de Chile, Santiago.

Cabeza M., Angel, Sergio Kunstmann Z., and Luis Krahl T., 1988. "Santuario de altura inca—cerro El Plomo, nuevos descubrimientos, conservación inicial de las ruinas, y síntesis interpretativa." Unpublished paper. Santiago, Chile.

"Caleta Molle: 2015–7000," 1950s. Map at scale of 1:50,000. Santiago, Chile: Instituto Geográfico Militar.

Cartmell, Larry, 1994. Unpublished letter addressed to Thomas Besom and dated April 11. Department of Anatomical and Clinical Pathology, Valley View Regional Hospital, Ada, OK.

Cartmell, Larry, Arthur Aufderheide, Angela Springfield, et al., 1991. "The Frequency and Antiquity of Prehistoric Coca-Leaf-Chewing Practices in Northern Chile: Radioimmunoassay of a Cocaine Metabolite in Human-Mummy Hair." *Latin American Antiquity* 2(3): 260–268.

Catts, Paul, and Neal Haskell, eds., 1990. *Entomology and Death: A Procedural Guide.* Clemson, SC: Joyce's Print Shop.

Ceruti, Constanza, 2001. "La *capacocha* del nevado de Chañi: Una aproximación preliminar desde la arqueología." *Chungará: Revista de antropología chilena* 33(2): 279–282. Arica, Chile: Universidad de Tarapacá.

———, 2003. *Llullaillaco: Sacrificios y ofrendas en un santuario inca de alta montaña.* Salta, Argentina: Instituto de Investigaciones de Alta Montaña, Universidad Católica de Salta.

———, 2004. "Human Bodies as Objects of Dedication at Inca Mountain Shrines (North-west Argentina)." *World Archaeology* 36(1): 103–122.

Checura J., Jorge, 1977. "Funebria incaica en el cerro Esmeralda (Iquique, I Región)." *Estudios atacameños* 5: 125–141. San Pedro de Atacama, Chile: Museo de Arqueología, Universidad del Norte.

———, 1985. *Museo Regional de Iquique: Hallazgo arqueológico en el cerro Esmeralda—1976.* Iquique, Chile: Corporación Municipal de Desarrollo Social.

Conway, William, 1901. *The Bolivian Andes: A Record of Climbing and Exploration in the Cordillera Real in the Years 1898 and 1900.* New York: Harper & Brothers.

D'Altroy, Terence, 1992. *Provincial Power in the Inka Empire.* Washington, DC: Smithsonian Institution Press.

Demarest, Arthur, 1981. *Viracocha: The Nature and Antiquity of the Andean High God.* Peabody Museum Monographs 6. Cambridge, MA: Peabody Museum of Archaeology and Ethnology, Harvard University.

DiMaio, Dominick, and Vincent DiMaio, 1993. *Forensic Pathology.* Boca Raton, FL: crc Press.

Donnan, Christopher, 1992. *Ceramics of Ancient Peru.* Los Angeles, CA: Fowler Museum of Cultural History, University of California.

Dorsey, George, 1901. *Archaeological Investigations on the Island of La Plata, Ecuador.* Publication 56, Anthropological Series 11(5). Chicago: Field Columbian Museum.

Dransart, Penny, 1995. *Elemental Meanings: Symbolic Expression in Inka Miniature Figurines.* Research Paper 40. London: University of London, Institute of Latin American Studies.

Duviols, Pierre, 1976. "La capacocha: Mecanismo y función del sacrificio humano, su proyección geométrica, su papel en la política integracionista y en la economía redistributiva del Tawantinsuyu." *Allpanchis* 9: 11–57. Cuzco, Peru: Instituto de Pastoral Andina.

————, 1980. "Periodización y política: La historia del Perú según Guaman Poma de Ayala." *Bulletin de l'Institut Français d'Études Andines* 9: 1–18. Lima, Peru.

Farrington, Ian, 1998. "The Concept of Cuzco." *Tawantinsuyu: An International Journal of Inka Studies* 5: 53–59. Gundaroo, Australia: Brolga Press.

Figueroa G., Gonzalo, 1958. "Cerámica de los sitios arqueológicos 'Piedra Numerada' y 'cerro El Plomo.'" *Arqueología chilena,* publicación número 4: 73–83. Santiago: Universidad de Chile, Centro de Estudios Antropológicos.

Flores-Ochoa, Jorge, 1979. *Pastoralists of the Andes: The Alpaca Herders of Paratía.* Translated by Ralph Bolton. Philadelphia: Institute for the Study of Human Issues.

Galloway, Alison, 1999. "Fracture Patterns and Skeletal Morphology: Introduction and the Skull." In *Broken Bones: Anthropological Analysis of Blunt Force Trauma,* 63–80. Edited by Alison Galloway. Springfield, IL: Charles C. Thomas.

Gelles, Paul, 2000. *Water and Power in Highland Peru: The Cultural Politics of Irrigation and Development.* New Brunswick, NJ: Rutgers University Press.

Giddens, Anthony, 1979. *Central Problems in Social Theory: Action, Structure and Contradiction in Social Analysis.* Berkeley and Los Angeles: University of California Press.

Gose, Peter, 1986. "Sacrifice and the Commodity Form in the Andes." *Man* 21(2): 296–310. Journal of the Royal Anthropological Institute of Great Britain and Ireland, London.

Gutiérrez, Felipe, 1991. "Tras la pista de un santuario inca a 6700 metros de altitud." *La Nación,* diciembre 1, sección 3, 8.

Haskel, Guillermo, 1999. "Inca Child Mummy Found on Frozen Argentine Mountain." ABC *News/Reuters,* March 3. http://abcnews.go.com/wire/World/Reuters19990303_1515. html

Heyerdahl, Thor, Daniel Sandweiss, and Alfredo Narváez, 1995. *Pyramids of Túcume: The Quest for Peru's Forgotten City.* London: Thames and Hudson.

Hodder, Ian, 1986. *Reading the Past: Current Approaches to Interpretation in Archaeology.* Cambridge: Cambridge University Press.

Horizon, 1997. "Frozen in Heaven." *Horizon/BBC.* London. http://www.bbc.co.uk/horizon/96–7/frozen.html

Horne, Patrick, and Silvia Quevedo K., 1984. "The Prince of El Plomo: A Paleopathological Study." *Bulletin of the New York Academy of Medicine* 60(9): 925–931.

Horne, Patrick, Silvia Quevedo K., and Arthur Gryfe, 1982. "The Prince of El Plomo." *Paleopathology Newsletter* 40(7): 7–10. Detroit, MI: Paleopathology Association.

Hrdlička, Aleš, 1911. "Some Results of Recent Anthropological Exploration in Peru." *Smithsonian Miscellaneous Collections* 56(16): 1–16.

Hyland, Sabine, 1996. "The Imprisonment of Blas Valera: Heresy and Inca History in Sixteenth Century Peru." Paper presented at the Northeast Conference on Andean Archaeology and Ethnohistory, University of Pennsylvania, Philadelphia, and submitted to the *Colonial Latin American Historical Review.*

Hyslop, John, 1984. *The Inka Road System.* Orlando, FL: Academic Press.

————, 1990. *Inka Settlement Planning.* Austin: University of Texas Press.

Isbell, Billie Jean, 1980. *To Defend Ourselves: Ecology and Ritual in an Andean Village.* Latin American Monographs no. 47. Austin: Institute of Latin American Studies, University of Texas.

Kauffman D., Federico, 1980. *Manual de arqueología peruana.* Lima, Peru: Ediciones Peisa.

Kertzer, David, 1988. *Ritual, Politics and Power.* New Haven, CT: Yale University Press.

Kunstmann Z., Sergio, 1994. Personal communication, Santiago, Chile. Kunstmann is a well-known Chilean climber who has discovered Inka artifacts on numerous peaks, including Cerro El Plomo.

Kurtz, Donald, 1978. "The Legitimation of the Aztec State." In *The Early State,* 169–189. Edited by Henri Claessen and Peter Skalník. New Babylon Studies in the Social Sciences 32. The Hague, Netherlands: Mouton Publishers.

Larrain B., Horacio, 1987. "Apéndice No. 1—Grupos indígenas en Chile: Ecología y evolución de su población 1535–1980." In *Etnogeografía,* 229–241. Geografía de Chile, tomo XVI. Santiago, Chile: Instituto Geográfico Militar.

Linares M., Eloy, 1966. "Restos arqueológicos en el nevado Pichu Pichu (Arequipa, Perú)." *Anales de arqueología y etnología,* tomo XXI: 7–47. Mendoza, Argentina: Universidad Nacional de Cuyo.

López A., Hilda, and Ángel Cabeza M., 1983. "La momia de 'El Plomo' (Chile): Un sensacional hallazgo." *GeoMundo* 7(5): 465–476. Santiago, Chile.

MacCormack, Sabine, 1991. *Religion in the Andes: Vision and Imagination in Early Colonial Peru.* Princeton, NJ: Princeton University Press.

Martínez S., Josefa de, 1966. "Apéndice 1: Descripción sumaria del niño naturalmente momificado del cerro Chañi." *Anales de arqueología y etnología,* tomo XXI: 85–99. Mendoza, Argentina: Facultad de Filosofía y Letras, Universidad Nacional de Cuyo.

McEwan, Colin, 1996. Personal communication at the 15th Annual Conference of Andean Archaeology and Ethnohistory held at the University of Pennsylvania Museum, Philadelphia. McEwan is currently at the British Museum of Mankind in London.

McEwan, Colin, and María Isabel Silva, 1989. "¿Qué fueron a hacer los Incas en la costa central del Ecuador?" In *Relaciones interculturales en el área ecuatorial del Pacífico durante la época precolombina,* 163–185. Edited by J. Bouchard and M. Guinea. BAR International Series 503. Oxford: British Archaeological Reports.

McEwan, Colin, and Maarten Van de Guchte, 1992. "Ancestral Time and Sacred Space in Inca State Ritual." In *The Ancient Americas: Art From Sacred Landscapes,* 358–371. Edited by Richard Townsend. Chicago: Art Institute of Chicago.

Means, Philip, 1928. *Biblioteca andina,* part 1. Transactions of the Connecticut Academy of Arts and Sciences, vol. 29: 271–525. New Haven: Connecticut Academy of Arts and Sciences.

Medina R., Alberto, 1958. "Hallazgos arqueológicos en el 'cerro El Plomo.'" *Arqueología chilena,* publicación número 4: 43–63. Santiago, Chile: Universidad de Chile, Centro de Estudios Antropológicos.

Medvinsky L., Dina, Kai Peronard T., and Julio Sanhueza T., 1979. *Fajas y trenzados: Textiles incaicos del cerro Esmeralda (Iquique—I Región).* Documento de trabajo número 5. Iquique, Chile: Centro Isluga de Investigaciones Andinas, Universidad del Norte.

Menzel, Dorothy, 1976. *Pottery Style and Society in Ancient Peru: Art As a Mirror of History in the Ica Valley, 1350–1570.* Berkeley: University of California Press.

Millán de Palavecino, María, 1966. "Descripción de material arqueológico proveniente de yacimientos de alta montaña en el área de la puna." *Anales de arqueología y etnología,* tomo XXI: 81–100. Mendoza, Argentina: Universidad Nacional de Cuyo.

Moseley, Michael, 1992. *The Incas and Their Ancestors.* London: Thames and Hudson.

Mostny, Grete, 1957. "La momia del cerro el Plomo." *Boletín del Museo Nacional de Historia Natural* 27(1): 1–119. Santiago, Chile.

Mountain Institute, 1996. "The Ice Maiden of Mt. Ampato." Franklin, WV: Mountain Institute. http://www.mountain.org/zicemaiden.html

Nash, June, 1979. *We Eat the Mines and the Mines Eat Us: Dependency and Exploitation in Bolivian Tin Mines.* New York: Columbia University Press.

National Geographic Society, 1997. "Andes." Washington, DC. http://nationalgeographic.com/features/97/andes/expedition.html

National Museum of Natural History (NMNH), 2003. *Forces of Change: Global Links, El Niño's Powerful Reach.* Ongoing exhibit. Washington, DC: Smithsonian Institution.

Noble W., John, 1999. "Entirely Preserved Inca Mummies Found." *New York Times,* Wednesday, April 7: A-1, A-19.

Nova, 1996. "Ice Mummies of the Inca." *Nova/PBS Online Adventure.* Boston, MA: WGBH Educational Foundation. http://www.pbs.org/wgbh/pages/nova/peru/table.html

Olsen B., Karen, 1994. *Ancient South America.* Cambridge World Archaeology. Cambridge: Cambridge University Press.

Pérez, Norma, n.d. Information sheet on the conservation of archaeological materials at the Museo Etnográfico. Facultad de Filosofía y Letras, Universidad de Buenos Aires, Argentina.

Pollanen, Michael, and David Chiasson, 1996. "Fracture of the Hyoid Bone in Strangulation: Comparison of Fractured and Unfractured Hyoids from Victims of Strangulation." *Journal of Forensic Sciences* 41(1): 110–113. Philadelphia, PA: American Society for Testing and Materials.

Randall, Robert, 1990. "The Mythstory of Kuri Qoyllur: Sex, *Seqes,* and Sacrifice in Inka Agricultural Festivals." *Journal of Latin American Lore* 16(1): 3–45. UCLA Latin American Center.

Reinhard, Johan, 1983a. "High Altitude Archaeology and Andean Mountain Gods." *American Alpine Journal* 25: 54–67. New York: American Alpine Club.

———, 1983b. "Las montañas sagradas: Un estudio etnoarqueológico de ruinas en las altas cumbres andinas." *Cuadernos de historia* 3: 27–62. Santiago: Departamento de Ciencias Históricas, Universidad de Chile.

———, 1985. "Sacred Mountains: An Ethno-Archaeological Study of High Andean Ruins." *Mountain Research and Development* 5(4): 299–317. Boulder, CO: International Mountain Society.

———, 1992a. "Sacred Peaks of the Andes." *National Geographic* 181(3): 84–111.

———, 1992b. "An Archaeological Investigation of Inca Ceremonial Platforms on Volcano Copiapó, Central Chile." In *Ancient America: Contributions to New World Archaeology,* 145–172. Edited by Nicholas Saunders. Oxbow Monograph 24. Oxford, England: Oxbow Books.

———, 1993. "Llullaillaco: An Investigation of the World's Highest Archaeological Site." *Latin American Indian Literatures Journal* 9(1): 31–65. Beaver Falls, PA: Department of Foreign Languages, Geneva College.

———, 1996. "Peru's Ice Maidens: Unwrapping the Secrets." *National Geographic* 189(6): 62–81.

———, 1997. Personal communication at a public lecture on April 17 at Binghamton University, NY. Reinhard is currently a Senior Research Fellow at the Mountain Institute in Franklin, WV, and an Explorer-in-Residence at National Geographic in Washington, DC.

———, 1998. "Research Update: New Inca Mummies." *National Geographic* 194(1): 128–135.

———, 1999a. "Children of Inca Sacrifice Found Frozen in Time." *National Geographic* 196(5): 36–55.

———, 1999b. Unpublished letter addressed to Thomas Besom and dated January 4.

———, 1999c. "Inca Mummies." Public lecture delivered on November 10 in the Gilbert Grosvenor Auditorium. Washington, DC: National Geographic Society.

———, 2005. *The Ice Maiden: Inca Mummies, Mountain Gods, and Sacred Sites in the Andes.* Washington, DC: National Geographic Society.

Reinhard, Johan, and Contanza Ceruti, 2000. *Investigaciones arqueológicas en el Volcán Llullaillaco: Complejo ceremonial incaico de alta montaña.* Salta, Argentina: Ediciones Universidad Católica de Salta.

Reuters, 1998. "Frozen Mummies of Sacrificed Incas Found in Peru." *Reuters/Latin American News,* Wednesday, September 30. http://www.reuters.com/news/

Reyes C., Francisco, 1958. "Informe sobre construcciones el la cumbre del 'cerro

El Plomo' y sus alrededores." *Arqueología chilena,* publicación número 4: 64–72. Santiago, Chile: Universidad de Chile, Centro de Estudios Antropológicos.

Rostworowski de Diez C., María, 1983. *Estructuras andinas del poder: Ideología religiosa y política.* Historia Andina/10. Lima, Peru: Instituto de Estudios Peruanos.

————, 1988. "Prologue." In *Conflicts Over Coca Fields in Sixteenth-Century Peru,* 53–67. Edited by María Rostworowski de Diez C. Studies in Latin American Ethnohistory and Archaeology, vol. IV. Ann Arbor, MI: Museum of Anthropology, University of Michigan.

Rowe, Ann, 1995–1996. "Inca Weaving and Costume." *Textile Museum Journal* 34–35: 5–53. Washington, DC: Textile Museum.

Rowe, John, 1946. "Inca Culture at the Time of the Spanish Conquest." In *Handbook of South American Indians,* bulletin 143, vol. 2: 183–330. Edited by Julian Steward. Washington, DC: Smithsonian Institution.

Salomon, Frank, 1991. "Introductory Essay." In *The Huarochirí Manuscript,* 1–38. Austin: University of Texas Press.

Sawyer, Kathy, 1999. "Frozen Mummies of Incas Unearthed." *Washington Post,* April 7, A-1, A-10.

Schobinger, Juan,, ed., 1966. *La "momia" del cerro el Toro.* Mendoza, Argentina: Taller Gráfico y Editorial Fasanella.

————, 1982. "La 'momia' del cerro el Toro y sus relaciones con otros sitios arqueológicos de la cordillera del los Andes." In *Estudios de arqueología sudamericana,* 75–95. Buenos Aires, Argentina: Ediciones Castañedas.

————, 1986. "La red de santuarios de alta montaña en el Contisuyo y el Collasuyo: Evaluación general, problemas interpretativos." In *El imperio inka: Actualización y perspectivas por registros arqueológicos y etnohistóricos, 297–317.* Comechingonia, número especial. Bogotá, Colombia: Universidad de los Andes.

————, 1991. "Sacrifices of the High Andes." *Natural History* 100(4): 62–69.

————, 1995. *Aconcagua: Un enterratorio incaico a 5.300 metros de altura.* Mendoza, Argentina: Inca Editorial.

————, 1998. "Arqueología de alta montaña: Santuarios incaicos en los andes centro-meridionales." *Beiträge zur Allgemeinen und Vergleichenden Archäologie,* band 18: 363–399. Mainz, Germany: Philipp von Zabern.

————, ed., 2001. *El santuario incaico del cerro Aconcagua.* Mendoza, Argentina: Editorial de la Universidad Nacional de Cuyo.

Schobinger, Juan, Mónica Ampuero, and Eduardo Guercio, 1985. "Descripción de las estatuillas que conforman el ajuar acompañante del fardo funerario hallado en el cerro Aconcagua (provincia de Mendoza)." *Relaciones de la Sociedad Argentina de Antropología,* tomo XVI: 175–190. Buenos Aires.

Servicio Informativo de los E.E.U.U. (USIS), 1954. *La momia y la expedición al cerro El Plomo.* Santiago, Chile: Empresa Editora Zig-Zag.

Silva G., Osvaldo, 1978. "Consideraciones acerca del período inca en la cuenca de Santiago (Chile central)." *Boletín del Museo Arqueológico de La Serena* 16: 211–243. La Serena, Chile.

Silverblatt, Irene, 1987. *Moon, Sun, and Witches*. Princeton, NJ: Princeton University Press.

Smith, Kenneth, 1986. *A Manual of Forensic Entomology*. Ithaca, NY: Cornell University Press.

Stahl, Ann, 2001. *Making History in Banda: Anthropological Visions of Africa's Past*. Cambridge: Cambridge University Press.

Taussig, Michael, 1980. *The Devil and Commodity Fetishism in South America*. Chapel Hill, NC: University of North Carolina Press.

Topic, John, Theresa Topic, and Alfredo Melly C., 2002. "Catequil: The Archaeology, Ethnohistory, and Ethnography of a Major Provincial Huaca." In *Andean Archaeology*, vol. 1: *Variations in Sociopolitical Organization*, 303–336. Edited by William Isbell and Helaine Silverman. New York: Kluwer Academic/Plenum Publishers.

Ubelaker, Douglas, 1992. "Hyoid Fracture and Strangulation." *Journal of Forensic Sciences* 37(5): 1216–1222. Philadelphia: American Society for Testing and Materials.

Uhle, Max, 1903. *Pachacamac: Report of the William Pepper Peruvian Expedition of 1896*. Philadelphia: Department of Archaeology, University of Pennsylvania.

Urton, Gary, 1981. *At the Crossroads of the Earth and the Sky*. Austin: University of Texas Press.

———, 1990. *The History of a Myth: Pacariqtambo and the Origin of the Inkas*. Austin: University of Texas Press.

———, 1999. *Inca Myths*. The Legendary Past. Austin: University of Texas Press; published in cooperation with the British Museum Press.

Valcarcel, Luis, 1978. *Historia del Perú antiguo*. Lima, Peru: Editorial Juan Mejía Baca.

Velasco de Tord, Emma, 1978. "La k'apakocha: Sacrificios humanos en el incario." In *Etnohistoria y antropología andina*, primera jornada, 193–199. Compiled by Marcia Koth de Paredes and Amalia Castelli. Lima, Peru: Museo Nacional de Historia.

Zuidema, Tom, 1977–1978. "Shaft Tombs and the Inca Empire." *Journal of the Steward Anthropological Society* 9(1–2): 133–179. Champaign-Urbana, IL.

———, 1982. "Bureaucracy and Systematic Knowledge in Andean Civilization." In *The Inca and Aztec States, 1400–1800*, 419–458. Edited by George Collier, Renato Rosaldo, and John Wirth. New York: Academic Press.

———, 1990. *Inca Civilization in Cuzco*. Translated by Jean-Jacques Decoster. Austin: University of Texas Press.

INDEX

ETHNOHISTORIC AUTHORS

Acosta, José de, 15, 16, 62, 74, 78, 80, 117
Agustinos, 74, 126
Albornoz, Cristóbal de, 8, 11, 13, 17, 22,
    46, 47, 48, 69, 70, 74, 76, 77, 80, 95,
    99, 101, 103, 112, 113, 118, 121, 125, 136,
    144, 159, 160
Arriaga, José de, 13, 16, 65, 76, 78, 80, 81,
    96, 99, 101, 102, 106, 125, 133
Avila, Francisco de (Huarochirí manu-
    script), 17, 22, 53, 54, 62, 65, 68, 72,
    74, 85, 88, 98, 101, 118, 127, 132, 138,
    141, 142, 144, 159
Ayala, Fabian de, 74, 78, 91, 104, 105, 106,
    108, 115, 125, 126, 130
Bello Galloso, Antonio, 58, 74, 98, 101,
    104, 141
Betanzos, Juan de, 30, 38, 50, 51, 53, 55, 57,
    58, 69, 92, 132
Bibar, Jerónimo de, 121
Cabello de Balboa, Miguel, 50, 54
Calancha, Antonio de la, 13, 28, 38
Calancha, Antonio de la, and Bernardo
    de Torres, 47, 62
Cieza de León, Pedro de, 14–16, 18, 19,
    22, 38, 46, 47, 48, 50, 51, 57, 58, 69, 70,
    71, 77, 83, 94, 95, 100, 108, 113, 131, 158
Cobo, Bernabé, 15–16, 18, 19, 21, 22, 28,
    29, 33, 36, 49, 51, 52, 54, 57, 62, 64, 73,
    74, 76, 77, 78, 80, 82, 83, 87, 88, 91,
    94, 95, 96, 98, 99, 100, 102, 103, 104,
    105, 108, 109, 111, 114, 115, 117, 118,
    120, 125, 126, 127, 128, 133, 134, 135,
    136, 138, 139, 140, 141, 144, 148, 152,
    158, 159
Dávila Brizeño, Diego, 65, 72, 98, 101,
    118
Garcilaso de la Vega, 4, 16, 19, 21, 25, 28,
    51, 65, 79, 80, 117, 132, 143, 158, 159
Gonçález Holguín, Diego, 78, 80, 102
Guaman Poma de Ayala, Felipe, 16, 18,
    22, 24, 40, 52, 71, 74, 75, 94, 95, 96,
    98, 100, 101, 102, 104, 105, 106, 108,
    131, 132, 133, 135, 136, 145, 159, 160
Hacas Poma, Hernando, 14
Hernández Príncipe, Rodrigo, 8, 11, 13,
    22, 25, 30, 33, 36, 37, 38, 77, 80, 81, 88,
    120, 132, 133, 135, 142, 145, 155, 158, 160
"Justicia 413," 13, 32, 39
Las Casas, Bartolomé de, 16, 44, 46
Martínez Compañón, Baltazar, 78, 81, 95,
    99, 147
Molina (of Cuzco), Cristóbal de, 16, 28,
    30, 69, 74, 77, 82, 84, 87, 95, 96, 98,
    99, 102, 104, 105, 106, 116, 120, 131,
    140, 141
Murúa, Martín de, 32, 36, 37, 38, 46, 47,
    50, 54, 64, 78, 84, 85, 93, 98, 116, 121,
    125, 128, 130, 131, 139
Noboa, Bernardo de, 88, 99, 100, 120
Oberem, Udo, 86, 134

Pachacuti Yamqui, Joan de, 46, 47, 57, 72, 83, 85, 94, 120
Polo de Ondegardo, Juan, 15–16, 18, 22, 28, 33, 36, 37, 46, 47, 64, 73, 74, 76, 77, 78, 80, 82, 83, 87, 88, 91, 93, 94, 95, 96, 99, 100, 102, 103, 104, 105, 108, 109, 111, 115, 116, 120, 125, 126, 127, 128, 130, 135, 136, 138, 139, 140, 148, 158
Ramos Gavilán, Alonso, 28, 62, 77, 78, 121, 125
Sarmiento de Gamboa, Pedro, 16, 51, 70, 78, 119
Ulloa Mogollón, Juan de, 37, 46, 65, 69, 74, 91, 94, 98, 99, 101, 106, 108, 115, 118, 121, 131, 137, 153
Valera, Blas, 25, 28, 65, 158, 159
Zárate, Agustín de, 47, 48, 57

CONTEMPORARY SCHOLARS

Ceruti, Constanza, 161
Demarest, Arthur, 72
Kurtz, Donald, 8
Randall, Robert, 19, 160
Reinhard, Johan, 9, 11, 143, 144, 161
Rowe, John, 157
Salomon, Frank, 17, 134
Schobinger, Juan, 161
Silverblatt, Irene, 16, 25
Uhle, Max, 162
Urton, Gary, 20
Zuidema, Tom, 20

ETHNIC GROUPS IN THE INKA EMPIRE

Aymara, 84, 99, 100, 101, 104, 105, 115, 125, 138, 159
Cañari, 5, 69, 74, 75, 85, 94, 119, 127, 136, 149, 159
Cavana, 46, 69, 91, 119, 121, 137, 138, 153
Chanca, 4, 51
Chauca Ricma, 88, 133, 137
Checa, 85, 88, 127, 133
Chimu, 5
Chiriguano, 50, 51, 88, 141
Collagua, 8, 46, 69, 91, 98, 118, 119, 137, 138, 153
Colli, 73, 121, 137
Concha, 88, 133, 137
Huacho, 74, 89, 93
Huanca, 102, 108, 109, 118
Lupaca, 4
Poma Canche, 94, 101
Pormocae, 121
Quiteño, 5
Rucana, 77, 98, 99, 127
Sora, 50, 51, 52, 98
Yauyo, 74, 89, 93, 100, 101, 102, 108, 113, 118, 142
Yunca, 85, 88, 105, 106, 115, 122, 126, 127, 131, 137, 140, 144
Yunguyo, 77, 121

IMPERIAL GODS

Illapa (Thunder-lightning), 25, 30, 35, 37, 38, 46, 47, 82, 87, 88, 96, 106, 120, 143
Inti (Sun), 2, 16, 25, 30, 35, 38, 39, 40, 46, 50, 54, 55, 62, 70, 72, 77, 82, 83, 87, 88, 89, 96, 97, 98, 99, 100, 106, 111, 119, 120, 133, 140, 142, 143, 144, 145, 149, 155, 159, 165
Mama Killa (Moon), 30, 35, 82, 83, 87, 88, 100, 106, 120
Mama Qucha (Sea), 35, 102, 111, 148
Pacha Mama (Earth), 35
Wira Qucha (Creator), 30, 32, 35, 38, 46, 62, 69, 82, 83, 87, 88, 96, 100, 106, 111, 119, 120, 143

MYTHICAL BEINGS

Ayar Uchu, 70, 76, 83
Collquiri, 73, 122, 123, 134
Maca Uisa, 72, 73, 92, 100, 103, 132, 134,
    139, 141
Mama Uqllu, 70, 140
Manku Qhapaq, 70, 76, 133, 134, 140,
    141, 144
Paria Carco, 68, 72, 73, 137
Parya Qaqa, 17, 67, 68, 72, 73, 74, 85, 88,
    89, 90, 92, 93, 98, 100, 101, 102, 103,
    104, 105, 106, 108, 109, 113, 114, 115,
    118, 120, 121, 122, 123, 126, 127, 132,
    133, 135, 136, 137, 138, 142, 144, 152, 160

PEOPLE

Atawalpa, 57, 69, 92, 101, 132
Pacha Kuti, 4, 28, 50, 51, 53, 55, 57, 85,
    98, 139
Pizarro, 7, 57
Poma Caque, 37
Tanta Carhua, 11, 12, 33, 35, 37, 38, 39, 81,
    88, 99, 120, 133, 138, 142, 143, 145, 147,
    155, 160
Thupa Yapanki, 5, 6, 36, 46, 49, 50, 51, 57,
    71, 75, 85, 92, 132, 134, 139, 154, 157
Waskar, 92, 101, 132
Wayna Qhapaq, 6, 15, 19, 38, 48, 50, 51,
    57, 59, 77, 87

PLACES

Aconcagua (oracle), 36, 47
Anti Suyu (NE quarter), 31, 74, 75, 76,
    77, 85, 88, 90, 100, 102, 103, 104, 106,
    108, 120, 125, 135, 136, 137
Awqay Pata (main plaza), 25, 30
Chinchay Suyu (NW quarter), 31, 40, 41,

42, 74, 76, 77, 87, 89, 90, 94, 100, 102,
    104, 105, 106, 108, 126, 133, 135, 136,
    142, 160
Cuzco (capital and surrounding region),
    4, 8, 13, 15, 25, 28, 30, 32, 33, 35, 37, 39,
    40, 43, 46, 48, 50, 64, 70, 73, 74, 76,
    77, 82, 83, 87, 88, 89, 91, 94, 95, 96, 98,
    99, 100, 102, 103, 104, 105, 108, 111,
    112, 118, 119, 120, 125, 126, 128, 133,
    134, 135, 136, 138, 139, 141, 143, 148, 153,
    155, 159, 160
Kunti Suyu (SW quarter), 6, 31, 46, 69,
    74, 91, 93, 101, 103, 104, 106, 108, 112,
    113, 131, 135, 136
Pacha Kamaq, 35, 36, 77
Qulla Suyu (SE quarter), 2, 6, 31, 40, 42,
    74, 76, 87, 90, 93, 94, 95, 100, 101, 102,
    103, 104, 108, 118, 135, 136
Quri Kancha (main temple), 30, 39, 46, 73
Titi Qaqa (Lake), 1, 2, 3, 4, 8, 28, 33, 35,
    47, 50, 77, 121, 133, 140

SACRED MOUNTAINS

Aconcagua (Argentine peak), 11, 161
Ashuay, 77, 78, 88, 121, 122, 144, 150
Ausan Cata, 74, 101, 113
Chachani, 9, 161
Chañi, 11, 161
Chimborazo, 8, 65, 69, 77, 94, 98, 118,
    119, 120, 127
Chuscha, 10, 161
Collaguata, 46, 69, 91, 94, 98, 99, 118, 119,
    121, 137
Cotopaxi, 68, 132
Esmeralda, 11, 161, 162
Gualcagualca (Hualca Hualca), 46, 69, 91,
    94, 98, 99, 118, 119, 121, 137
Hambato (Ampato), 8, 9, 74, 101, 113,
    144, 161
Huaca Yñan, 69, 74, 119, 149

Llullaillaco, 11, 161
Mantocalla, 37, 77, 94, 95, 96, 103, 105, 108, 127, 148
Mollotoro, 75
Pachatusun, 46, 47, 48, 94, 95, 101, 120, 159
Pichu Pichu, 9, 10, 161
Pitu Ciray, 74, 75, 90, 95, 100, 101, 103, 104, 106, 108, 113, 135, 136
(El) Plomo, 11, 161, 162
Potosí, 77
Putina (El Misti), 8, 9, 74, 85, 101, 113, 136, 144, 159, 161
Qhuru Puna, 36, 46, 47, 69, 74, 75, 77, 91, 93, 95, 100, 101, 103, 104, 106, 108, 113, 131, 135, 136, 144
Quehuar, 10, 161
Raco, 104, 105, 106, 108, 115, 125, 127
Sara Sara, 9, 69, 74, 75, 101, 112, 113, 119, 144, 161
Saua Ciray, 74, 75, 90, 95, 100, 101, 103, 104, 106, 108, 113, 135, 136
Sucanca, 89, 99, 126, 143
Tantalluc, 78, 81, 101
(El) Toro, 10, 161
Tungurahua, 65, 118
Wallullu, 67, 68, 72, 73, 74, 95, 101, 103, 104, 108, 109, 118, 122, 123, 131, 136, 137, 144
Wana Kawri (mountain and *wanqa*), 30, 35, 36, 46, 47, 70, 71, 75, 76, 82, 83, 89, 91, 94, 97, 98, 100, 102, 104, 105, 113, 115, 119, 131, 132, 133, 134, 136, 140, 141, 148, 159, 160
Willka Nuta, 36, 74, 90, 98, 101, 104, 108, 135, 136

SOCIAL POSITIONS

apu panaka (imperial official), 1, 29
aqlla-kuna ("chosen women"), 2, 29, 35, 39, 40, 42, 155, 162, 163, 164

cacique (headman), 86, 145
corregidor (Spanish official), 15
kamayuq (craftsman, imperial official), 2, 31, 32, 34, 83, 112, 128
kuraka (local lord), 28, 30, 39, 40, 50, 51, 57, 58, 62, 63, 134, 145, 155
mama-kuna ("Mothers"), 2, 29, 30, 38, 113
mitmaq-kuna (settlers), 38, 112, 144, 155
qhapaq hucha (sacrificial victim), 25–43, 94–95
runa (sacrificial victim), 44–49, 94–95
warrior (sacrificial victim), 49–55

YEARLY FESTIVALS

Inti Raymi, 30, 36, 105
Qhapaq Raymi, 36, 82, 83, 87, 138
Wara Chicuy, 82, 83, 97, 98, 116, 119, 120, 141

TERMS

agriculture, 36, 37, 38, 47, 113, 121, 126, 127, 148, 150
ají (peppers), 3, 35
apachitas (piles of stones), 64, 78, 79, 80, 109, 125, 130, 140, 151
aqsus (dresses), 42, 61, 162, 164
bags. See *ch'uspas*
bathing (ritual), 3, 114
beer residue. See *tikti*
belts. See *chumpis*
boundaries (territorial and social), 24, 32, 39, 117, 134, 135–137, 138, 152, 153, 159, 160
burials, 38, 39, 40, 46, 54, 55, 57, 59, 87, 146, 153
Catholic Church, 13, 17
censuses (Colonial). See *visitas*
chakras (fields), 36
chicha (corn beer as an offering), 2, 3, 30,

31, 35, 43, 45, 46, 48, 50, 51, 55, 56, 57,
59, 83, 84, 85, 87, 106, 107, 114, 116,
122, 150, 165
chumpis (belts), 57, 162, 164
ch'uspas (bags), 82
clothing. See *aqsus, chumpis, llawt'us,
llikllas,* and *unkus*
coca (as an offering), 23, 31, 34, 35, 42, 43,
55, 56, 59, 62, 85, 104–105, 109, 110,
126, 131, 147, 151, 160, 161, 162, 165
confession (ritual), 3, 114
corn (as an offering), 23, 30, 31, 37, 43, 49,
89, 102, 105–107, 109, 112, 124, 127,
147, 148, 150, 151, 160
corn beer. See *chicha*
cranial deformation, 91, 121, 137, 138,
153
dancing (ritual), 3, 45, 50, 54, 56, 57, 73,
83, 84, 85, 89, 93, 114, 115, 128, 134
divination, 36, 62, 71, 132, 152
drinking (ritual), 3, 30, 35, 37, 43, 46, 50,
55, 56, 57, 58, 59, 83, 84, 93, 106, 114,
116, 128, 165
economic production (offerings for), 117,
126–128
face painting (ritual), 3, 38, 84, 114, 115,
149
fasting (ritual), 3, 35, 46, 87, 106, 114, 115
feasting (ritual), 23, 30, 43, 59
feathers (as offerings), 23, 31, 42, 107–108,
109, 110, 147, 151, 160
fertility, (animals), 85, 127, 130, 151;
(humans), 38, 43, 126, 148, 150, 163;
(plants), 36, 54, 55, 91, 92, 123, 144,
148, 150, 159
fields. See *chakras*
food (as an offering), 42, 46, 49, 53, 57,
58, 59, 92, 93, 108, 127, 147, 158, 160.
See *yawar sankhu*
fringe (royal). See *maskha paycha*
guinea pigs. See *quwis*
headbands. See *llawt'us*
health (offerings for), 32, 36, 38, 47, 48,

62, 117, 124–126, 128, 130, 139, 140,
148, 150, 165
herding, 2, 70, 112, 113, 114, 119, 127, 144,
145, 150, 160
houses. See *wasis*
Huarochirí manuscript. See Avila
(Ethnohistoric authors)
irrigation, 37, 47, 118, 121, 122, 123, 124,
126
khipus (knotted strings), 2, 31, 32
knapsacks. See *q'ipis*
knotted strings. See *khipus*
labor tax. See *mit'a*
llamas (as offerings), 11, 23, 30, 31, 32, 42,
47, 81, 82, 83, 84, 85, 87, 88, 89, 92,
96–99, 105, 110, 120, 127, 131, 132, 143,
147, 151, 156, 159, 160
llawt'us (headbands), 40, 42, 49
llikllas (shawls), 1, 42, 162, 164
maskha paycha (royal fringe), 6, 153
material correlates, 12, 22, 23, 24, 40–43,
48–49, 50, 54–55, 58–59, 62, 63, 146–
156, 160, 162
metal (as an offering), 32, 46, 49, 59, 100–
102, 158, 160
meteorological phenomenon, 72, 73,
120–121, 150
mit'a (labor tax), 44, 128, 129, 130
mountain-gods. See *waqas* (mountains)
mullu (Spondylus shell), 2, 31, 42, 43, 49,
102–103, 110, 111, 148, 150, 156, 160,
162, 163, 164
music (ritual), 45, 114, 115
myths (Andean), 17, 28, 30, 65, 67, 68, 69,
70, 72, 73, 76, 82, 92, 100, 101, 103,
104, 106, 114, 117, 118–119, 120, 121,
122, 123, 132, 133, 134, 136, 137, 139,
140, 141, 144, 149, 159
necropampa (sacrifice), 44, 55–59, 62, 158,
159
ñapa (sacred llama), 153
oracles, 36, 47, 65, 68, 69, 70, 71, 92, 101,
117, 131–132, 152, 159

origin places. See *paqarikus*

paqarikus (origin places), 65, 69, 70, 91, 119, 136, 137, 153

pins. See *tupus*

peppers. See *ají*

plagiarism (by ethnohistoric authors), 15, 25, 28, 64

power (use of mountains to reinforce), 140–145

prayer, 32, 38, 82, 84, 96, 114, 115, 130, 166

pukarás (fortresses), 155

q'ipis (knapsacks), 32

Quechua (language), 17, 24, 79

quinua (highland grain), 123

qumpi (fine cloth), 103, 128

qunupas (sacred figurines), 151, 152, 163

quwis (guinea pigs as offerings), 9, 23, 32, 42, 84, 99–100, 127, 128, 131, 147, 160

shawls. See *llikllas*

shell. See *mullu*

sight-lines. See *siq'es*

singing (ritual), 3, 35, 45, 56, 57, 83, 84, 114, 115

siq'es (sight-lines), 39, 73, 74, 76, 77, 87, 108, 117, 132–135, 136, 137, 141, 142, 143, 146, 147, 149, 150, 151, 152, 155, 159, 160

slings. See *warak'as*

social hierarchy, 14, 58, 141, 142, 156

songs (sacred). See *takis*

specialized production, 38, 128, 148, 151, 160

springs (water sources), 32, 33, 37, 111, 123, 148

statuettes (anthropomorphic; as offerings), 2, 31, 42, 43, 81, 95, 100, 101, 102, 103, 143, 147, 148, 161, 163, 165;

(zoomorphic; as offerings), 31, 42, 61, 77, 81, 89, 99, 100, 101, 143, 147, 148, 160, 161

stones (sacred). See *wanqas*

substitute sacrifice, 23, 44, 62–63, 148, 158, 159, 163

takis (sacred songs), 82

textiles (as offerings), 103–104. See also *qumpi*

tikti (beer residue), 49, 85, 105, 106

torture (of captives), 55, 158

trade, 129, 130, 151

travel (offerings for), 129–130

trophy heads, 52, 55

tunics. See *unkus*

tupus (pins), 32, 42, 81, 83, 101, 162, 163, 164

unkus (tunics), 40, 41, 42, 83, 153, 154, 161, 162, 165

vara (unit of measure), 81

visitas (Colonial censuses), 13

wanqas (sacred stones), 43, 46, 74, 75, 76, 77, 82, 83, 84, 87, 91, 95, 99, 100, 101, 103, 104, 111, 119, 125, 146

waqas (mountains), 2, 3, 9, 65, 68, 69, 70, 72, 73, 74, 75, 76, 80, 81, 87, 89, 90, 95, 102, 103, 104, 105, 106, 108, 109, 110, 111, 112, 113, 114, 116, 119, 122, 125, 127, 132, 133, 135, 144, 148, 151, 160, 162, 165

warak'as (slings), 82

wasis (houses), 2, 29

water (offerings for), 37, 38, 43, 47, 49, 92, 102, 111, 117, 118, 121–124, 126, 144, 148, 150, 159, 160, 165

yawar sankhu (sacred food), 105

Lightning Source UK Ltd.
Milton Keynes UK
UKHW040149041122
411621UK00001B/8